BRITISH WOMEN WRITERS AND THE ASIATIC SOCIETY OF BENGAL, 1785–1835

To my son, Jordan Paul Freeman

British Women Writers and the Asiatic Society of Bengal, 1785–1835
Re-Orienting Anglo-India

KATHRYN S. FREEMAN
University of Miami, USA

LONDON AND NEW YORK

First published 2014 by Ashgate Publishing

Published 2016 by Routledge
2 Park Square, Milton Park, Abingdon, Oxon OX14 4RN
711 Third Avenue, New York, NY 10017, USA

Routledge is an imprint of the Taylor & Francis Group, an informa business

Copyright © Kathryn S. Freeman 2014

Kathryn S. Freeman has asserted her right under the Copyright, Designs and Patents Act, 1988, to be identified as the author of this work.

All rights reserved. No part of this book may be reprinted or reproduced or utilised in any form or by any electronic, mechanical, or other means, now known or hereafter invented, including photocopying and recording, or in any information storage or retrieval system, without permission in writing from the publishers.

Notice:
Product or corporate names may be trademarks or registered trademarks, and are used only for identification and explanation without intent to infringe.

British Library Cataloguing in Publication Data
A catalogue record for this book is available from the British Library

The Library of Congress has cataloged the printed edition as follows:
Freeman, Kathryn S., 1958–
  Women writers and the Asiatic Society of Bengal, 1785–1835 : re-orienting Anglo-India / by Kathryn S. Freeman.
    pages cm
  Includes bibliographical references and index.
  ISBN 978-1-4724-3088-5 (hardcover : alk. paper)
  1. English literature—Women authors—History and criticism. 2. English literature—18th century—History and criticism. 3. English literature—19th century—History and criticism. 4. Authorship—Sex differences—History—18th century. 5. Authorship—Sex differences—History—19th century. 6. Asiatic Society of Bengal. 7. Orientalism in literature. 8. India—In literature. I. Title.
  PR448.W65F74 2014
  820.9'928709033—dc23
                                                                                    2014001011

ISBN: 9781472430885 (hbk)

Contents

Acknowledgements vii

Introduction: British Women Writers and Late Enlightenment Anglo-India: The Paradoxical Binary of Vedic Nondualism and the Western Sublime 1

1 The Asiatic Society of Bengal: "Beyond the stretch of labouring thought sublime" 21

2 "Out of that narrow and contracted path": Creativity and Authority in Elizabeth Hamilton's *Translations of the Letters of a Hindoo Rajah* 45

3 Confronting Sacrifice, Resisting the Sentimental: Phebe Gibbes, Sidney Owenson, and the Anglo-Indian Novel 63

4 Female Authorship in the Anglo-Indian Meta-Drama of Mariana Starke's *The Sword of Peace* (1788) and *The Widow of Malabar* (1791) 95

Epilogue: Lost and Found in Translation: Re-Orienting British Revolutionary Literature through Women Writers in Early Anglo-India 119

Bibliography 133
Index 145

Acknowledgements

I am indebted to many people and institutions for the generosity and expertise they contributed to this book: to the East India Office at the British Library for allowing me access to the original manuscripts of the Asiatic Society of Bengal; to the University of Miami English Department for its support throughout the evolution of the book and to the College of Arts and Sciences for funding my study of Sanskrit at the outset of the project, for sabbatical leave time, and for assisting me with the costs of production; to the graduate students in my seminars on Orientalism and Anglo-Indian literature whose incisive questions and observations helped me crystallize several salient points about the book's argument; to the University of Colorado at Boulder's Special Collections Department, instrumental in providing manuscripts of the Anglo-Indian poems of British women not available elsewhere, and in particular to Jessica Damian who, as curator and transcriber, was extremely gracious in gathering these poems housed in Boulder's Romantic Women Poets Archive. I would like to thank *European Romantic Review* and *The Wordsworth Circle* for publishing my articles on Phebe Gibbes and Sidney Owenson, respectively, and for permission to reuse them in Chapter 3 of this book. To Ashgate and especially Ann Donahue I am grateful for the opportunity to publish this book and for the meticulous guidance throughout the process.

From the earliest phase of my research, my deep gratitude goes to Gurumayi Chidvilasananda for her teachings on nondualism, to the SYDA Foundation for graciously opening their library of Vedic texts to me, and to Professor Stephen A. Fredman of the University of Notre Dame for providing an early foundation in my study of the Asiatic Society of Bengal. For teaching me—and teaching me to teach myself—Sanskrit, I thank Professor Edwin Bryant of Rutgers University.

To the Mithila artist, Shalinee Kumari, I offer special thanks for granting me permission to use her painting, "Radiant yet Submissive," on the cover. It was a fascinating journey through cyberspace to discover this painting and its place in the rich folk tradition of Mithila artists. The process, from finding a photograph of the painting online to making contact with the artist, would have been impossible without the help of two people to whom I am most grateful: Melissa Bernabei of Gallery Wendi Norris in San Francisco and David Szanton of the Ethnic Arts Foundation at Berkeley. Because the painting reflects so poignantly this book's focus on Vedic nondualism, I wish to share David Szanton's description of the painting vis-à-vis the Mithila tradition:

> Ardhanarishvara is the ancient Hindu figure representing the fundamental non-dualistic unity, interdependence, and complementarity of male and female—in the gods, in humans, and ultimately throughout nature. Here Shalinee is using it to represent, critically, the problematic complementarity and interdependence of the Indian woman. She is both powerful and radiant (*shakti*), though into a

dark and difficult world. Yet she must also be submissive to the males in her life represented as the snakes (*naga*) that control her sexually (wrapped around the lower half of her body), socially and politically (many headed from above), and requiring offerings (the flowers). And when asked about the snake head protruding from the woman's forehead Shalinee responded, "and they have captured our minds."

And always, I thank my family: my sisters, Jane, Linda, and Elizabeth, for their unconditional love and encouragement, and Jory, for patience with my divided attention.

Introduction
British Women Writers and Late Enlightenment Anglo-India: The Paradoxical Binary of Vedic Nondualism and the Western Sublime

In her 1993 novel, *The Holder of the World*, Bharati Mukherjee has her protagonist, Hannah, describe her journey from colonial America to India as her "translation" (104). This usage, unusual to a modern ear, is a trope that reverberates with considerable irony in precolonial, Anglo-Indian texts by British women authors to describe themselves or their female protagonists. Their usage, now obsolete, is the primary meaning of *translation*: "to bear, convey, or remove from one person, place or condition to another; to transfer, transport."[1] The irony of their usage is the result of its dissonance with its extant meaning, "to turn from one language into another": these women writers were not only keenly aware of, but often at odds with, the renderings of the Asiatic Society of Bengal, known as the Orientalists, whose Sanskrit translations were England's introduction to India's Vedic philosophy and literature.[2]

---

[1] This meaning, along with several others, has been lost since the early nineteenth century. The *OED* traces the evolution in the eighteenth century:
> To turn from one language into another; "to change into another language retaining the sense" (J.); to render; also, to express in other words, to paraphrase. (The chief current sense.)... 1776 JOHNSON 11 Apr., in *Boswell*, Poetry. cannot be translated; and, therefore, it is the poets that preserve languages. b. *absol*. To practise translation; to make a version from one language or form of words into another; also *intr*. for *pass*., of a language, speech, or writing: To bear or admit of translation.... 1690 LOCKE *Hum. Und.* III. iv. §9 This is to translate, and not to define, when we change two words of the same signification one for another.... 1812 SOUTHEY *Omniana* II. 30 Claudian throughout would translate better than any of the ancients. 1827 *Lett.* (1856) IV. 64 The Welsh, I suspect, is not a language which translates well. 1831 MACAULAY *Ess. Johnson* (1887) 194 Sometimes Johnson translated aloud. Among the examples of late eighteenth-century uses are the following: "1794 J. HUTTON *Philos. Light*, etc. 47 Heat is translated among bodies in a certain manner, and electricity in another. 1865 *Pall Mall G*. 11 Apr. 4 A discussion has arisen on the question whether the Charterhouse School ought or ought not to be translated into the country."

[2] Orientalism is capitalized throughout this book to distinguish this specific historical phenomenon from a general western interest in the east as used, for instance, by Said. The term "Anglo-Indian" has different meanings historically, referring both to British living in India as well as the subcaste created through the intermarriage of British EIC employees

The premise of this book is that the texts of these women authors, in spite of their many differences, share an epistemological engagement with India that is often dissonant with the Orientalists' Vedic renderings and sociopolitical relationship to India. Some of these women lived in England and were introduced to India through the publications of the Asiatic Society while others experienced India first-hand, yet they are connected through various forms of intersubjectivity in their representations of India. That these women authors play on the multiple meanings of *translation* when writing about Anglo-India points to their fundamental commonality—for all the differences among them—involving the impulse to link personal, sociopolitical, and epistemological crises in subjectivity with their relationship to Orientalism. Simultaneously engaging and distancing, their usage connotes the paradox of an authorial identity at once subject and object: their being "translated" suggests that they undergo an implicitly distorting metamorphosis through publication, transforming them as creators of texts into texts themselves. Another ironic use of *translation*, "[t]o carry or convey to heaven without death," echoes through descriptions of *sati*, the Indian ritual of widows' immolation; as will be seen throughout the book, *sati* is one of the most ubiquitous and complex instances of their sociopolitical identification with India.[3]

The common impulse of these women writers to challenge the borders between subject and object distinguishes them not only from the Orientalists, but also from the late-Enlightenment epistemology informing literature by those male contemporaries canonized retrospectively as poets of "High Romanticism," the label connoting a poetics founded on the male persona's failed quest for a transcendent state (Bloom 6).[4] Yet another lost meaning of *translation*, then, "to remove the dead body or remains of a saint..., a hero or great man, from one place to another," suggests an even more subversive irony in its use by these women: it not only connects them to the widows performing *sati* but suggests their interrogating the assumed link between masculine heroism and virtue that is the foundation of both the sentimental tradition and the poetic tradition of Romanticism.

In spite of the passage of over 30 years since pioneering studies and editions of newly recovered texts by British women, including those writing on Anglo-India, began urging scholars to read these texts against the grain of Romanticism, its ideology continues to inform texts by women. That the inception of postcolonialism coincided with the recovery of noncanonical texts complicates this recent history. Because the two paradigms of Romanticism and Orientalism have held on tenaciously in spite of efforts to redefine the participation of noncanonical literature in its historical context, before addressing the relationship

---

and indigenous Indian women. In this book the context will make clear which meaning is relevant, as it is used for both meanings.

[3] As discussed later in this introduction, for example, Phebe Gibbes's character Sophia describes the widows preparing for their "translation" to heaven.

[4] The Romanticism label was coined in the mid-nineteenth century and continued through the twentieth century, as the following section details.

between women writers and Anglo-India, I turn first to those earlier caveats about Romanticism followed by a brief history of postcolonialism as a theoretical approach that has lacked precision to describe the precolonial Anglo-India of these writers.

Challenging the Romantic Canon: 1981–1995

The backlash against canonical Romanticism began with the scholarship of Marilyn Butler, Jerome McGann, and others in the early 1980s, Butler's 1981 *Romantics, Rebels and Reactionaries* challenging the notion of a single "Romantic Revolution" (184), and McGann's 1983 *Romantic Ideology* exposing the "forms of thought" that "begin to enter our consciousness via the critique developed out of certain past forms of feeling" (13). As these scholars laid bare the ideological readings of literature of the period and laid out the complications that would dismantle a single "Romanticism," studies of gender and genre proliferated through the mid-1990s, a movement that paralleled the recovery of long dormant, "noncanonical" texts.

With Mary Poovey's 1984 *The Proper Lady and Female Writer* came new attention to known women writers of the period, such as Mary Wollstonecraft, Mary Shelley, and Jane Austen, whose "stereotypical images of the female self" Poovey reappraised as "sources of strength" (xi). Stuart Curran's publication of Charlotte Smith's poetry and such studies as his 1989 "The I Altered" brought attention to the influence of women's poetry on the canonical poets, demanding a shift away from the old rubric of "English Romantic poetry as a poetry of vision" to "the cult of sensibility [that was] largely a female creation" (189, 195).[5] Reevaluating the voices of such poets as Mary Tighe, Anna Barbauld, and Mary Robinson, not only in the context of their male contemporaries but as defining a movement in its own right, these studies gave rise to fresh reconsideration of historical periodization created by these newly discovered texts.[6]

The new focus on female authorship has thus made incontrovertible the previous limitations in identifying the late eighteenth into the nineteenth centuries as an era whose very label of Romanticism had assumed a central male subjectivity, objectified the female, and excluded women writers; the challenge to the old rubric has materialized through curricula, anthologies, and scholarly discussion of the period's women writers. Catherine Gallagher's 1994 *Nobody's Story* distilled this challenge in a question that scholarship has continued addressing into the twenty-first century: "How can we explain the continuities, as well as the historical

---

[5] According to Curran, "If women tended to see differently from men, it was axiomatic in the eighteenth century that they felt differently too. A singular phenomenon, suddenly appearing in mid-century and not only coinciding with the rise of women poets but also its very hallmark, was the cult of sensibility" (195).

[6] See, for example, Miriam Wallace's *Enlightening Romanticism, Romancing the Enlightenment*.

ruptures, in the rhetoric of female authorship?" (xx).[7] As the scholarly conversation has unfolded, the reevaluation of the eighteenth into the nineteenth century has become more clearly pivotal not only for women writers but because of them.

A year after *Nobody's Story* was published, Isobel Armstrong described the epistemological underpinnings behind this evolving reconception of late Enlightenment women writers who, she wrote, critiqued the male philosophical traditions that led to a "demeaning discourse of feminine experience" and remade those traditions (15). Armstrong helped complicate the traditional gender binaries informing discussion of women writers in her claim that women used "affective discourse" to turn "the customary 'feminine' forms and languages" to "*analytical* account and used them to *think* with" (15). The paradox inherent in women using sensibility as rigorous intellectual engagement is a useful means of turning our attention away from the dualism that has dominated scholarly discussion itself. Underlying the binaries embedded in such social categories as male transcendence and female domesticity is a more problematic and hence more elusive binary nevertheless fundamental to the late Enlightenment in which the masculine is associated with dualism, the female with nondualism.[8]

This gendered distinction between dual and nondual tendencies has been central to French feminism, also beginning in the late twentieth century. Luce Irigaray, writing specifically on eastern nondualism and sexual difference, is "rightly suspicious of theories and experiences of oneness/nonduality [that] equate to sameness," but as Jean Marie Byrne points out, there is a difference between "the theory of nonduality" that "emerges out of duality" and "the realization of nonduality" in which the subject-object divide collapses" (68). I would suggest that, for the writers of late Enlightenment Anglo-India, there is a fundamental concern regarding the relationship between these two classes of nonduality with a consequent range of representations, from the nonduality that holds binaries in tension to the Vedic paradox of subjectivity that is simultaneously innate and transcendent.

In her 1988 essay, "On Romanticism and Feminism," Ann Mellor engaged with Irigaray and other French feminists such as Julia Kristeva as a means to show the philosophical foundation of the contrasting male and female poetics

---

[7] Although there is no consensus on a term that would be inclusive of the noncanonical—as may be best for the present—a more recent label, "the long eighteenth century," is one result of a common agreement that the period can no longer be described by a single "Romanticism." The history of how the canonical male writers came to define the period as Romantic can be found in many recent anthologies, such as those of Wu, Paula Feldman, Mellor and Matlak, and that of Backscheider and Ingrassia. Breen and Noble's handbook on Romanticism provides a useful discussion of the evolution of the field (135–48).

[8] The humorist Robert Benchley, writing in *Vanity Fair*, articulated the paradoxical binary of dualism and nondualism when he wryly noted, "There may be said to be two classes of people in the world; those who constantly divide the people of the world into two classes, and those who do not" (February 1920).

of the Romantic period. Describing a "fluid" female subjectivity of "permeable ego boundaries" that runs counter to the masculine construction of "an often violent antagonism between self and other," Mellor identified the "dualism inherent in Western thought" by way of French feminist theory's "attempt to call into question, even deny, the validity of the binary mode of thinking that has characterized philosophical discourse since the ancient Greeks" (*Romanticism and Feminism* 5).[9] This paradoxical dual/nondual binary is at the heart of women's representations of a spectrum of Anglo-Indian concerns, from the epistemological to the sociopolitical. That the collective call to reevaluate the Romantic ideology coincided not only with the recovery of Anglo-Indian texts by British women but with the advent of postcolonialism is discussed in the following sections; the effect of this historical convergence of postcolonialism and the recovery of noncanonical texts is that British women's Anglo-Indian texts became shunted into the framework of postcolonialism, leaving little room to allow their voices distinction from the imperialist hegemony that postcolonialist approaches have attributed to Orientalism and its literary influences.

The Limits of Postcolonial Approaches to Precolonial Anglo-India

Although the dissonance created by the paradoxical binary that opposes nondual and dual subjectivities is not confined to gender categories, as I discuss at greater length in the epilogue, it underlies a general pattern of female responses to Anglo-India during the late Enlightenment involving the common attraction among British women writers to Indian epistemology.[10] In order to address the dissonance between the Orientalists and women writers regarding Vedic nondualism, this book focuses on the ways these women writers engage with Orientalism in its historically specific usage: the systematic Sanskrit study, translation, and original verse of the scholars known as the Asiatic Society of Bengal, or the Orientalists,

---

[9] Mellor articulates a caveat important for this book as well: from the point of view of Anglo-American scholarship, the French feminist project "is both more theoretical and more radical ... and calls for no less than the deconstruction of all existing systems and institutions of cultural authority" having thus been criticized for "lacking a pragmatic political program"; Mellor answers by suggesting that "such Anglo-American political practices ... take place only within existing ... institutions and render those institutions ever more powerful by enabling them to coopt [sic] resistance" (6). Mellor's disclaimer of over 30 years ago, that the essays in her collection do not "settle the debate" can be extended to the twenty-first century. In spite of the French/Anglo-American binary often made, see such important voices as Catherine Belsey's 1985 discussion of "constructing the subject" as foundational in discussing female subjectivity.

[10] Blake's mythos revolves around this dissonance between Enlightenment dualism and a nondual poetic consciousness that predated his awareness of eastern philosophy, as my book, *Blake's Nostos*, addresses. In the epilogue, I explore Blake's female characters, Oothoon and Ololon, along with Coleridge's and Shelley's representations of the link between female subjectivity and nondualism.

under the director William Jones, and ending in 1835 with Thomas Macaulay's reversal of the Orientalist promotion of eastern languages.

With the advent of postcolonialism, marked by the publication of Said's *Orientalism* (1978), the members of the Asiatic Society were cast in the role of single-minded cultural imperialists, all but eclipsing the humanistic paradigm of the 1950s through the 1980s which saw Orientalism as a celebration of India's cultural legacy. Said claimed the goal of the Asiatic Society was to "gather in, to rope off, to domesticate the Orient and thereby turn it into a province of European learning" (*Orientalism* 78), a position he maintained in his 1993 *Culture and Imperialism* (153). A shift in the postcolonialist paradigm came a decade later with Homi Bhabha's assertion of the ambivalence of colonial discourse, whose authority Bhabha characterizes as "stricken by an indeterminacy" in which "mimicry emerges as the representation of a difference that is itself a process of disavowal"; this notion of a "double articulation" gave rise to a more nuanced approach to discussing Anglo-India and the Orientalists in particular (86).

Postcolonialist studies that followed Bhabha's exposure of the doubleness of colonial discourse have explored the intersection of political turbulence with the discovery and systematizing of the Sanskrit language and literature by the Asiatic Society.[11] This emphasis on Orientalist ambivalence has pointed to the problematic position of the Asiatic Society as scholars and East India Company employees whose intellectual relationship to rendering and transmitting the language and philosophy of ancient India was compromised by their participation in the East India Company and, later, the British government.[12] Bhabha's complication of postcolonialism's engagement with sexuality and gender is also important in addressing the ways eastern epistemology challenges western notions of masculinity. As Bhabha writes, "Questions of race and cultural difference overlay issues of sexuality and gender and overdetermine the social alliances of class and democratic socialism" (251). Jeffrey Cass, acknowledging the important work that Bhabha's claim has generated regarding colonial identity and "alternative" sexualities, contrasts Said's Orientalism, "for sexual deviance also underwrites

---

[11] See, for example, Viswanathan, Hoerner, and Rocher. In more recent challenges to the reductivism of earlier postcolonial approaches, Lalita Pandit has emphasized Said's own "distinction between those who did not have a direct colonial investment—such as the Germans, Italians, Dutch, and Swedish—and those who did" (115); Urs App notes the problematic issue that "only Islam—which had the least potential of loosening or dissolving the biblical framework because it made itself use of it—plays a role in Said's argument" (440).

[12] See Newman for a useful history of the British government's relationship to the EIC. Though Orientalism can be divided into phases, they are not a rigid sequence of events. Colebrooke, who succeeded Jones as director of the Asiatic Society, had worked along with Jones during the early period, yet he subsequently disparaged the early Orientalist project as "a repository of nonsense" (qtd. in Kopf *Orientalism*, 28). Adisasmito-Smith ("Forging Bonds") provides a detailed discussion of the relationship between changes in the colonial period and the two translations of the *Gita* by Charles Wilkins and Edwin Arnold a century later; he includes the transatlantic perspective of the Transcendentalists' influence on Arnold.

the stereotypical expectations evoked by the 'Oriental Other'" (108). Such a notion can be applied to the way women writers transform the othering of female sexuality from the perspective of the western tradition.[13]

Orientalism, Romanticism, and the Dualism of the Sublime

The contradictory pulls of the Orientalists differ from a spectrum of responses to Anglo-India in texts by women writers, thereby challenging critical claims that these women passively echoed the Asiatic Society's representations of India and its cultural heritage.[14] Most notable about this distinction is that the women's texts seldom replicate the Orientalists' ubiquitous references to the sublime, a vehicle for conveying their political and epistemological uncertainty. The repeated use of the term "sublime" in Orientalist descriptions of Sanskrit texts reveals the paradox behind this double view. The concept of the sublime had gained increasing significance in the masculinist aesthetic philosophy of the period through an already wide range of competing definitions and representations, including those of Hume and Burke in the eighteenth century and Wordsworth and Kant in the nineteenth century.

Sanskrit has no comparable term for the sublime, whose Latin etymology, "under the limen," orients the subject relative to what Blake called the "bounding line—the threshold between the self and dissolution of selfhood.[15] According to Frances Ferguson, even Burke, who "connects the sublime with death in order to attest to the genuineness of sublime emotions," adds a "safety net—the condition that danger and pain must not 'press too nearly'" and which "threatens to render the sublime into something of a shell game" (46). Thus, for the Burkean sublime, maintaining this separation and therefore the identity of the subject is all-important.[16] A significant element of the terror experienced by the British

---

[13] Noted by Lonsdale as forward in its "awareness of the genuine oriental scholarship which was beginning to appear through such scholars as Sir William Jones" (xxv), William Beckford's *Vathek*, though outside the parameters of this book, provides a compelling example of what Cass calls "arch-Orientalist texts" that make "'deviant' sexual practice visible and conventional readings of homoerotic representations quaint and perhaps even homophobic" (109). See also McClintock for another study of the relationship between colonialism and sexuality.

[14] See Chapter 3 of this book for the specific example of the way discussions of Owenson's *The Missionary* have been most distorted by this assumption; I contest the pattern of readings by Rajan, Leask, and Wright that contend the novel duplicates "orientalist clichés that align the East with the passive, emotional, and feminine, and the West with the active, rational, and masculine" (Wright 38).

[15] *A Descriptive Catalogue* XV (Erdman, 550). All further references to this edition are in the text. See the epilogue to this book for a fuller discussion of Blake's nondualism.

[16] Sara Suleri, noting that Burke's description of India as remote and obscure made it "the age's moral example of the sublime," points to the paradox of Burke turning the sublime on its head by cataloguing the uncategorizable, in which Burke creates the rhetorical effect of India embodying "colonial terror" (28).

discovery of ancient Indian philosophy is the threat the Sanskrit texts posed to the heart of Enlightenment epistemology: the twin principles of the primacy of the individual's separate and autonomous ego on the one hand and the separation of a single God from the phenomenal world on the other.[17]

As the Orientalists applied the term to Indian texts, the sublime suggests that, more than being used as an honorific, it was a means to place these texts under a particular rubric within the western aesthetic tradition.[18] Yet even as the Orientalists evoke the sublime, they express the awareness that the Sanskrit texts elude the sublime. When Hastings introduces Charles Wilkins's translation of the *Gita*, for instance, he warns that there are passages "elevated to a track of sublimity into which our habits of judgement will find it difficult to pursue them" (Wilkins, *Bhagavat-Geeta* 7). While Jones calls the Hindu epics "magnificent and sublime in the highest degree" (Marshall 259), he depicts Narayana as "beyond the stretch of laboring thought sublime" (Jones, *Poems* 204). Both Hastings's and Jones's descriptions of the texts suggest that what makes them "sublime" is the inability to "pursue them" with "laboring thought."

While the association between masculinity and duality is inherent in deism's paternalistic metaphor of God the Father's separation from his Creation, however, the male Orientalists' use of gender should be distinguished from that of British imperialists. Franklin emphasizes the important caveat, for instance, that Jones, who avoids the "predatory sexuality or the 'robust hypermasculinity' of the colonizer" should be distinguished from Burke, whose "sentimental idealization of women ... results in his obsessive emphasis on the Company's victimization of Indian women of 'quality'";[19] Franklin traces Jones's "understanding of traditional constructions of womanhood in India" to "his interest in the concepts of *prakriti* (created nature seen as the female principle) and *s'akti* wherein, as he explains in the Argument, 'the female divinity ... represents the active power of the male' in a union of immanent goddess and transcendent god." ("Accessing India" 58–9).[20]

---

[17] See Isobel Armstrong's detailed discussion of the gendered implications of the Burkean sublime.

[18] Suleri focuses on Burke's use of the rhetoric of the sublime in his speech about India as part of Hastings's impeachment trial, suggesting that "Burke's conflation of India as a conceptual possibility with the operation of the sublime works less to defamiliarize that idea than to render it canny through the very depictions of its difficulty.... [T]he Indian sublime becomes indistinguishable from the intimacy of colonial terror" (28).

[19] Sertoli's interpretation of Burke's sublime "delight" is especially interesting in light of Suleri's reading of "colonial terror." Such delight, Sertoli writes, is not "the relief that subjects feel when they discover themselves at a distance from the object that, threatening them with death, terrorizes them [but rather] it is the thrill felt as they draw near to it; in other words, as they masochistically approach death" (123–4).

[20] Just as the Orientalists' representations of gender are not always equivalent to those of the imperialists, so too are there striking exceptions among male poets in their depictions of India. See the epilogue for a fuller discussion of these exceptions among male writers whose renderings of the east and of nondualism contrast the otherness they depict in hegemonic representations. Blake's anti-Enlightenment texts and designs urge

India gave new and troubling meaning to the aesthetic category of the sublime, Sanskrit texts challenging the Enlightenment mind accustomed to reading philosophical, aesthetic, and theological texts through the discursive faculties, which seemed to offer no guidance in a realm outside the parameters of western logic. As it emerged through the late eighteenth-century British reading of Sanskrit texts, the Indian "sublime" stands apart from the spectrum of European versions of the sublime in its perceived nondualism which the Orientalists superimpose onto their Enlightenment dualism. The effect is one of profound ambivalence, revealed in the simultaneous attraction to and repulsion from the state they are calling sublime. By seeming to dissolve the separation between subject and object, the Indian texts connoted sublimity while they challenged the fundamental condition of the sublime: the necessity of the subject's safe distance from the object of terror embodying the sublime.

The Orientalists' dualistic renderings of *advaita* as sublime point to their kinship with the ambivalence underlying the "High Romantic" poets' quest for sublime transcendence. To illustrate the dualistic resistance among male Romantic poets to their own moments of nondual vision, I now trace a textual dialogue among William Wordsworth, Percy, and Mary Shelley. Wordsworth weaves ambivalence into the fabric of *Lines Composed a Few Miles above Tintern Abbey* (1798) while Percy Shelley subsequently heightens rather than resolves this ambivalence in *Alastor* (1815); the trajectory is complete with Mary Shelley's *Frankenstein* (1816) exposing the epistemological anxiety underlying the Romantic ideology, whose self-aggrandizement insists on a boundary between self and other even as it records visionary moments that dissolve such boundaries.

A prototype for the genre that would come to be known as the Romantic Ode, with its irregular stanzas and fluctuating moods, Wordsworth's *Tintern Abbey* depicts a persona foundering through waves of anxiety and an overwhelming visionary power that is ultimately repressed by the piety he projects onto his sister, Dorothy, whose presence has been suppressed until the poem's last stanza. After an opening paragraph that describes the poet's return to the unified beauty of nature and projects a sense of solitariness onto an imagined hermit that makes Dorothy's emergence at the end of the poem yet more surprising, the poet expresses gratitude for a boyhood that has imprinted the "beauteous forms" of nature on his memory. He moves through levels of consciousness through which he experiences these forms, from the visceral to "aspect more sublime"; underscoring his ambivalence, he affirms this deepest level of consciousness through litotes—"Nor less, I trust, / To [these beauteous forms] I may have owed another gift" (ll. 35–7). The following lines culminate in a prophetic moment of nondualism rare in Wordsworth's poetry:

England to overcome its habits of separation and fear by learning from the "philosophy of the east," a nondual "human divine." For Blake, the imagery of the eastern texts echoes through his own mythos, providing for him a means of linking east and west through the nondual, human divine he held to be the origin of the Judeo-Christian tradition lost in the Enlightenment.

> ... the breath of this corporeal frame
> And even the motion of our human blood
> Almost suspended, we are laid asleep
> In body, and become a living soul:
> While with an eye made quiet by the power
> Of harmony, and the deep power of joy,
> We see into the life of things. (ll. 42–8)

Wordsworth is masterful at holding in check the rhapsodic climax to this process of sublimation with multiple qualifications, as suggested by the litotes followed immediately by the weaker "I trust" (l. 35). A brief stanza of doubt that swings back to apostrophizing the Wye follows this stanza, intensifying the ambivalence: "If this / Be but a vain belief, yet oh how oft ... / have I turned to thee" (ll. 49–50, 55). Wordsworth here all but cancels the visionary experience of the preceding stanza, suggesting a desperation in passively turning over power to nature as embodied by the Wye.

He returns to a yet more explicit moment of nondualism in the penultimate stanza of "Tintern Abbey," rhapsodizing about the sublime moment in which the phenomenal world and the mind are interpenetrated with the same "motion and spirit":

> ... I have felt
> A presence that disturbs me with the joy
> Of elevated thoughts; a sense sublime
> Of something far more deeply interfused,
> Whose dwelling is the light of setting suns,
> And the found ocean and the living air,
> And the blue sky, and in the mind of man:
> A motion and a spirit, that impels
> All thinking things, all objects of all thought,
> And rolls through all things. (ll. 93–102)

The caesura at line 102 that ends this pantheistic climax is the divide between nondualism and dualism: the line continues, "Therefore am I still / A lover of the meadows and the woods," the discursive "therefore" abruptly shifting the subject to his mental power of that landscape with which he was one just a moment before. The final stanza both wipes away the prophetic moment of nondualism and portrays William as avuncular to Dorothy, actually only a year younger than he but whom he portrays as a voiceless repository for his "exhortations"; that he wishes her to remain like his former self speaks to the relationship in William's poetics between his repression of female energy and his resistance to nondualism.

Percy Shelley's *Alastor* complicates the poet's subjectivity, bifurcating it between the narrator, a nature poet akin to the Wordsworth of "Tintern Abbey," and the nameless Poet whose loss of grounding in nature is the story the narrator tells. Whether this poet is tormented by his own imagination or by an "evil genius" is a choice of interpretation Shelley gives the reader in his preface to the poem through two paragraphs of divergent descriptions.[21] The first paragraph celebrates the Poet, who "thirsts for intercourse with an intelligence similar to itself .... He seeks in vain for a prototype of his conception. Blasted by his disappointment, he descends to an untimely grave" in contrast to the second paragraph, a didactic warning against the "Poet's self-centred seclusion ... avenged by the furies of an irresistible passion pursuing him to speedy ruin."[22] The use of litotes in the second paragraph's didactic claim that the poem "is not barren of instruction" holds the key to Shelley's fear at the heart of the poem: namely, that the doubleness of its message indeed makes it barren of the instruction the Wordsworthian side of his poetics would relate.

Shelley's Wordsworthian narrator thus appears uncertain about the merits of a poetic subjectivity that erases the boundary between self and phenomena; this double vision reaches a crisis for both narrator and Poet when the Poet reaches the climactic end of his journey past the Caucasus, the geological divide between Europe and Asia. As the Poet moves further and further east, the narrator's own anxiety becomes as significant as the Poet's, for he uses the binary of life and death to describe it: "Nature's dearest haunt..., / Her cradle, and his sepulchre" (429–30).[23] That the narrator describes and then redescribes this final resting place in two separate stanzas expands this double view of the scene, reflecting the narrator's ambivalence about poetic subjectivity. In the first verse paragraph, the narrator personifies the scene as one of innocent gentleness, "as gamesome infants' eyes, / With gentle meanings, and most innocent wiles" (441–2). The second verse paragraph announces the shift in subjectivity abruptly, in the first half of the beginning line: "Hither the Poet came" (469). After the caesura, the landscape is redescribed, filtered through the Poet's narcissism: "His eyes beheld / Their own wan light through the reflected lines / Of his thin hair" (469–71). The double vision—new life in Nature's "cradle" and the premature aging, reflected in the Poet's thin hair, leading to his "sepulchre"—remains unresolved by the end of the stanza.

The identity of the tormenter that has lured the Poet on remains a double vision of a projected epipsyche and an external force: "two eyes, / two starry eyes, hung in the gloom of thought, /And seemed with their serene and azure smiles / To beckon him" (489–91). That Percy Shelley divides his poetic persona thus intricately, bifurcating a bifurcated subject through a split between narrator and Poet and a poet

---

[21] *Alastor* is Greek for "evil genius," the title given by Shelley's friend, Thomas Love Peacock; see Reiman and Fraistat for the textual history of the poem (71–2).

[22] Shelley (73). All further references to the poem are in the text, with parenthetical numbers indicating line numbers.

[23] See Reiman and Fraistat's detailed note on the geography of the Poet's journey (80n8). For Shelley's transformation of this landscape following his exposure to the Orientalists' Sanskrit translations, see the discussion of *Prometheus Unbound* in the epilogue. Shelley's 1816 poems such as "Hymn to Intellectual Beauty" have been discussed as influenced by Jones's hymns based on the Vedic texts. See Drew, Leask's *British Romantic Writers*, Pachori, and Rajan's *Under Western Eyes* for more on Shelley's influence by the Orientalists.

internally divided, becomes yet more compelling when Mary Shelley reconceives it the following year in *Frankenstein*. That Percy's Poet "[s]ees his own treacherous likeness there" resonates for Mary as a model for Victor Frankenstein's creation, in which the word "there" becomes especially ironic as a means of the treachery of projecting selfhood outward (*Alastor* 474). The connection between the novel and the poem becomes apparent in Mary's allusion to the lines above, "two eyes, / two starry eyes...," when Victor discovers that the creature has murdered Clerval: "The cup of life was poisoned for ever; and although the sun shone upon me, as upon the happy and gay of heart, I saw around me nothing but a dense and frightful darkness, penetrated by no light but the glimmer of two eyes that glared upon me. Sometime they were the expressive eyes of Henry, languishing in death...; sometimes it was the watery clouded eyes of the monster, as I first saw them in my chamber at Ingolstadt" (131). Victor betrays the "treacherousness" of the male creator's divide between self and his projection "there," the sublime epipsyche.

Looking back from this echo of *Alastor*, in which the subliminal is beginning to surface for Victor, to his first encounter with the creature in the alps reveals Mary's transformation of the male quest for transcendence to a vision of his "own treacherous likeness." In this earlier scene, Victor is gazing in wonder at the sublimity of Mont Blanc's "awful majesty"; a moment later, he bursts into apostrophe: "Wandering spirits, if indeed ye wander, and do not rest in your narrow beds." The creature bursts out of that sublime scene: "As I said this, I suddenly beheld the figure of a man, at some distance, advancing towards me with superhuman speed"; it is however a mock-Wordsworthian moment of being "laid asleep / In body" for, rather than "seeing into the life of things," Victor sees his "own treacherous likeness" there in the form of the creature.

By tracing a trajectory through these texts, one can see both the grounding of the male Romantic ideology in dualism and the proto-feminist warning against the treachery that derives from its insistence on maintaining an identity separate from the phenomenal world. Not all the so-called canonical poets identified with the masculine subjectivity that has defined Romanticism; however, as the epilogue to this book discusses, some were drawn to the nondualism of the east and of the female, defying the gender duality embedded in the aesthetic category of the sublime; in fact, Percy Shelley himself underwent a transformation in depicting the relationship of gender and epistemology that coincided with his discovery of Indian texts.[24] When male writers are viewed through the lens of their female contemporaries who engage with nondualism, the variety of nondual representations by men—regardless of their canonical status—suggests an even greater need for establishing the overlooked relationship between Orientalism and women writers to foreground the role of gender in both female and male British writers' responses to Indian nondualism.[25]

---

[24] See the epilogue's discussion of Blake, Coleridge, and Shelley for their representations not only of nondualism, of their commonality in gendering it female.

[25] See the discussion in Chapter 3 of Owenson's representing Hilarion as a Wordsworthian wanderer in the final chapters of *The Missionary*.

Women Writers, Translation, and *Sati*

Because the resurgence of the aesthetic category of the sublime during the late Enlightenment was so profoundly embedded in the masculinist philosophical tradition of the west, scholars have questioned whether there is a female sublime in women's poetry of the period.[26] Just as the notion of an Indian sublime is paradoxical in projecting a dualist tradition onto Vedic epistemology, so too is that of a female sublime because of the foundation of the sublime in the masculinist tradition of western philosophy. Between the extremes of the early Anglo-Indian impulse to dissolve boundaries and Macaulay's warning against the dangers of the Indian "absorption into the Deity" lies the more typical ambivalence by the British toward the discovery of Sanskrit, in which literary gestures of enthusiastic welcome are qualified by various levels of westernizing. Promising and threatening to be a powerful vehicle of revolt against the western materialist tradition, Sanskrit became associated with the annihilation of a separate and autonomous ego. Hastings anticipated this ambivalent reception when he described the Indian sublime as unpursuable in his introduction to perhaps the most influential Orientalist text, Charles Wilkins's translation of the *Bhagavad Gita*. For British women writing about India, the dissonance between nondual epistemology and gender is intricately tied to their subjective representations of the sublime as a state of translation.[27]

As women writers respond to this new language of Indian sublimity, a yet more intricate interplay among versions of the sublime emerges. One way the vexed relationship between colonialism and Orientalism manifests is through the dissonance within women's writing between their representation of the epistemological and the sociopolitical in India. Though recent scholarship has been interested in literary representations of the Hastings trial, the pattern of responses to Hastings by such women writers as Phebe Gibbes, Mariana Starke, and Elizabeth Hamilton has not been addressed in the fuller context of Hastings's role in the Asiatic Society. Their literary representations of this political crisis are deeply connected to their relationship with Orientalism. Gender, this book argues, enters the Anglo-Indian equation through the epistemological underpinnings of Orientalist anxiety as addressed in women's texts.

While the tendency among postcolonialist approaches to imperialism is to describe a politicized gender binary that feminized the Hindus vis-à-vis the masculinist British empire, Gayatri Spivak's 1988 "Can the Subaltern Speak"

---

[26] One of the earliest interrogations of the relationship between gender and the sublime comes from Anne Mellor; however, in this early phase of challenging the Romantic paradigm, she reduces the male writers to a common objectification of the female which my epilogue complicates by looking at Blake, Coleridge, and Shelley as male poets whose female figures are more powerfully subjective than Mellor allows by equating all male poets under the rubric of the Wordsworthian sublime (*Romanticism and Gender* 90ff). I argue that not only is there a female sublime in women's poetry, but that there is a female sublime in the poetry of these men.

[27] See note 1 above for the *OED*'s entry.

proleptically complicated that binary through its analysis of *sati*. Spivak identifies the paradox inherent in the Orientalist misreading of Sanskrit *sat*:

> The word in the various Indian languages is 'the burning of the *sati* or the good wife, who thus escapes the regressive stasis of the widow.... This exemplifies the race-class-gender overdeterminations of the situation. It can perhaps be caught even when it is flattened out: white men, seeking to save brown women from brown men, impose upon those women a greater ideological constriction by absolutely identifying, within discursive practice, good-wifehood with self-immolation on the husband's pyre. On the other side of thus constituting the object, the abolition, (or removal) of which will provide the occasion for establishing a good, as distinguished from merely civil, society, is the Hindu manipulation of female subject-constitution. (101)

The epistemological paradox behind the Orientalist mistranslation of *sati* that Spivak here identifies has been lost in subsequent discussion of eighteenth and early nineteenth-century Anglo-India, making discussion of women writers' representations of *sati* the more important to distinguish from that of the Orientalists.

In the shift between the Orientalist and Anglicist periods, there is a notable pattern to changes in the attitudes of British women towards *sati*.[28] Earlier women, though universally horrified at *sati*, tend to give subjectivity to the widow, whether they see her as victim or hero, in some cases, using *sati* as a metaphor for their own suicidal marriages. Mary Johnson's 1810 poem, "Hindu Widow on the Funeral Pile of Her Husband," idealizes the stoical widow: "The death I ought to die I dauntless meet; / Its pangs, my children, were your last embrace!" The projection of her subjectivity onto the widow is apparent, contrasted with Maria Jane Jewsbury's 1825 "Song of the Hindu Women" which, as discussed in the epilogue, represents a later poetic movement towards the Anglicist separation between female poet and widow.

This trajectory of British women writers' attitudes towards *sati* is illustrated as well through a comparison of women travel writers across the period who express their first-hand horror at the ritual. One of the earliest of these travel writers, Eliza Fay, contemplates *sati* vis-à-vis English widows in a 1781 letter from India:

> I cannot avoid smiling when I hear gentlemen bring forward the conduct of the Hindoo women, as a test of superior character, since I am well aware that so much are we slaves of habit *every where* that were it necessary for a woman's reputation to burn herself in England, many a one who has accepted a husband merely for the sake of an establishment, who has lived with him without affection; perhaps thwarted his views, dissipated his fortune and rendered his life uncomfortable to its close, would yet mount the funeral pile with all imaginable decency and die with heroic fortitude. (214)

---

[28] For a detailed discussion of the origins of *sati*, see Harlan; for the colonial debate on *sati*, abolished in 1829 by the British, see Mani.

Though Fay here imagines that British women would be as stoical as their Indian counterparts if they were in the same situation, she goes on to imagine the life of a woman "who wages war with a naturally petulant temper, who practices a rigid self-denial, endures without complaining the unkindness, infidelity, extravagance, meanness or scorn, of the man to whom she has given a tender and confiding heart, and for whose happiness and well being in life all the powers of her mind are engaged." Fay says that such a woman "is ten times more of a heroine than the slave of bigotry and superstition, who affects to scorn the life demanded of her by the laws of her country or at least that country's custom; and many such we have in England, and I doubt not in India likewise" (214). That Fay suggests two contradictory *satis* suggests her refusal to objectify these women as representing, from a postcolonial perspective, a single exotic other.[29]

By contrast to the complicating subjectivity that Fay affords to the Indian wife and widow, later memoirists such as Marianne [Young] Postans, Emma Roberts, and Anne Elwood, writing during the nascent Anglicist period, are distinct from each other in ways that are outside the parameters of this book, but whose uniformity in their depiction of *sati* reveals retrospectively how significant the change in attitudes towards Anglo-India and indigenous women were among women writers. These later travel writers focus on outrage at primitive ritual that must be suppressed by the civilized British government.[30] The very difference between attitudes in travelers writing at these formative stages of Anglo-India suggests that attention needs to be paid to the interplay of women's writing about India and Orientalism, both to define the limits of Orientalism's influence on women writers of the earlier period and to note that the codification of colonialism brought with it a change in the pattern of women's responses to India that stands apart from the demise of Orientalism.

This book thus focuses on women writers as a means to extricate them from assumptions behind scholarship that represents them as participating in the cultural imperialism that postcolonialism attributes to both the Orientalists and canonical male writers; this inclusiveness has subjected these women authors to a discourse that limits critical engagement with them alongside the male Romantic writers and the east.[31] My contention is that women's writing connects Orientalism's literalized

---

[29] For various studies of travel writing grounded in postcolonialism, see Moira Ferguson, Ghose, Grundy, Leask's *Curiosity*, Makdisi, and Melman.

[30] See Ghose's discussion of Postans and Graham's later travel writing vis-à-vis their Anglicist context (34–5). Leask discusses differences among the travel writers (*Curiosity* 222). For further contrast to these Anglicist writers, see Chapter 4 for a discussion of Starke's representation of *sati* in *The Widow of Malabar* (1791), in which the English hero's rescue of the Indian widow is preempted by her brother.

[31] My approach therefore reverses Armstrong's earlier advocacy of a "one-sided study of women's poetry in isolation from male poetry" that, she claimed, may be justified before scholarship can take the "next step," namely, the "interaction of the two," a practice that held for many years. This "next step" has begun more recently to produce scholarship founded on poetic sensibility that reintegrates the male poets vis-à-vis their influence by female contemporaries or immediate precursors and their masculine adaptation of these female

gendering of east and west to its ambivalence towards nondualism. Thus, although scholarship has acknowledged that English women writers such as Elizabeth Hamilton and Anna Jones were familiar with Vedic philosophy through their brother and husband, respectively, none has addressed what I argue are epistemological and, by extension, sociopolitical distinctions between the women's relationship with Anglo-India and their male contemporaries. These women—some of whom studied Sanskrit alongside their husbands or brothers, others independently—for all the disparities among them, had in common an engagement with Indian epistemology that differed sharply from the marked ambivalence of their Orientalist counterparts.[32]

Though there has thus been no systematic analysis of how women writers respond to the ways gender and epistemology inform each other in terms of the Asiatic Society's renderings of ancient Indian philosophy, an exception to the pattern of relegating women writers to echoing the claimed cultural imperialism of the Orientalists is James Mullholland's description of William and Anna Jones "as a representative couple for literary Calcutta because each experiments with several versions of the local as a way to transcend geographical and temporal differences"; the approach promises a means for scholarship to extricate itself from the gender duality that has distorted earlier studies.[33]

The translation from India back to England of Anna Jones, who studied Sanskrit and, after the death of William, edited his work as director of the Asiatic Society of Bengal, is the subject of her 1793 "Adieu to India."[34] Her ocean voyage from India back to England becomes a means of exploring her identity vis-à-vis India in the poem. As a farewell to India and her fatally ill husband as well as a reflection on her return to England due to her own poor health, this nuanced poem represents the ambivalence of gender and subjectivity for a British woman whose relationship to India was deeply layered. The poem's first 10 lines, a single-sentence invocation that begins, "Ocean, I call thee," are firmly grounded in a western subjectivity that sees India as exotic, a landscape of imagined wealth. The abundant gems,

---

sources (32). In a recent challenge to the reductivism of earlier postcolonial approaches, Lalita Pandit has emphasized Said's own "distinction between those who did not have a direct colonial investment—such as the Germans, Italians, Dutch, and Swedish—and those who did" (115). This book's epilogue explores the link between nondualism and feminism in representative works by Blake, Coleridge, and Percy Shelley; each engages distinctly with female identity in a patriarchal world through their epistemological crisis that underlies the sociopolitical.

[32] To name a few that are the subject of this book, Hamilton was rigorously involved with her brother Charles's Sanskrit study, Anna Jones wrote her own poetry inspired by the Vedas, and Sydney Owenson's knowledge of Indian philosophy makes reading her novel a radically different experience from the misconception that her Hindu priestess is a mere mask for British or Irish women.

[33] Suleri usefully describes the trajectory of Orientalist texts as "extensive enough to include both imperial and subaltern materials and ... their radical inseparability" (3).

[34] Mary Ellis Gibson has suggested that the poems published under the name "Anna Maria" were not written by Jones; although there are compelling details to raise doubts about the long-held assumption, this book agrees with Mullholland's position that "the similarities between this anonymous author and the biography of Anna Maria Jones are striking" (118).

including the "sapphire Deep" and the "pearl-beds," look ahead to the opening of Charlotte Smith's posthumously published poem *Beachy Head* (1807), in which Smith's view of the English channel opens out to an imagined vista that gradually superimposes an Asian seascape onto the one before her; she translates the British imperial conquest of the Orient's literal jewels to a poetics of the sublime, where "transparent gold / Mingles with ruby tints, and sapphire gleams" (81–2).[35]

While Jones westernizes the seascape with imagined "Tritons and their Nymphs," figures that ground the poem in western mythology, the next sentence creates a dramatic shift from the subjective "I" of the opening line to the third person, "Maria" (11). As though a corrective to the preceding section, the subsequent 20 lines form an embedded poem from the perspective of Maria. Jones strips this voice of the language of western convention, replacing it with images and mythology of ancient India. Maria's is thus a voice that tenderly says goodbye to "fertile" India where "Brahma's holy Doctrine reigns"; though she perpetuates the feminized stereotype of Hindus with "meek untainted Mind," in the context of her poem, it is an honorific, for she now sees England, her "native shore" as a place of ambition in its materialist pursuit of knowledge. She contrasts her life in England before having gone to India, when she was encouraged by "subtle Praise" that "bade [her] hope for Future Fame" in contrast to the "meek untainted Mind" of the Hindu that presumably does not use knowledge as a means for notoriety.

The final stanza returns to the longer lines of the opening stanza, shifting from the embedded voice of Maria to the "I" of the opening stanza. Yet the conventionality of the opening is gone, suggesting that Maria and "I" have become one in a deeply conflicted sense of identity. Saying farewell to India's "sacred Haunts," she is also saying farewell to her identity as a married woman: the personification of "mild Reflection" as a "solitary Maid" hearkens back to the "meek untainted Mind" of the Hindu, suggesting a new identity that awaits her in England without William, whom she knows she will never see again; her solitariness will draw on Hindu meekness rather than the poetic ambition of Anna Jones, the British woman whose identity was changed by India. As the mariners prepare the sails, then, she bids farewell to the double image of the Hougly, "Seat of Commerce" and "the Muse's Pride," an acknowledgement of ambivalence in what she takes from India and what she must leave behind as she returns to England to continue her husband's work. Later described by contemporaries as "dancing minuets and wearing saris," Anna Jones emblematizes the female poet's ambivalent embrace of Anglo-India (Ashfield 107).

Anglo-India and Orientalism through the Lens of Female Subjectivity

To address the many layers of the relationship between women writers and the Asiatic Society's productions, Chapter 1 addresses the Asiatic Society's westernizing of the Sanskrit texts they render, focusing on Wilkins's influential translation of *The Bhagavad Gita* as a means to extrapolate the underlying tensions between the original Sanskrit text's foundation of Vedic nondualism

---

[35] This opening stanza of *Beachy Head* is discussed in more detail in the epilogue.

and the distortions of his translation. Chapter 1 describes the source of tension in Wilkins's *Gita* as two-pronged: his imposition of the male philosophical tradition of the west and his ambivalence about the Orientalist participation in disrupting India's political, racial, and social structure through miscegenation. Focusing on Wilkins's distortions of Sanskrit terms that have no English equivalent, such as *dharma* as jurisprudence, as well as his avoidance of translating others, such as *varna-shankar*, mixed caste, Chapter 1 sets up the implications for women authors in the subsequent chapters whose engagement with these ideas stands in striking contrast to Wilkins's ambivalence that often veers towards aversion.

Elizabeth Hamilton's densely layered, epistolary novel, *Translations of the Letters of a Hindoo Rajah* (1796), is the focus of Chapter 2; its multiply qualified title gestures to the novel's meta-textual relationship between Orientalism and gender, providing a starting point to discuss that relationship among the women authors of the subsequent chapters to Orientalism. Literally marginalizing her authorial voice to footnotes as a fictional editor of the male correspondents' competing points of view on the fictional Orientalists and British women they discuss, Hamilton reflects the common concern among women writers with the relationship between subjectivity and the literal rendering and transmitting of Vedic texts. The dissonance between Hamilton's criticism of India's misogynistic traditions—as scathing as is her criticism of those in England—and her authorial engagement with Indian epistemology as a challenge to the western tradition sets her apart from her male contemporaries, including her Orientalist brother, Charles. Hamilton's novel thus provides a foundation for the subsequent discussions of women writers who represent that relationship more obliquely.

In her "Preliminary Dissertation" to the novel—the only part of the text in her own voice—Hamilton refers to the "narrow and contracted path ... allotted to the female mind," a description that sets her apart from the novel's satirical female characters traveling in the progressive circles of her day (72). Hamilton offers a range of both British and Indian perspectives, all through the apparently unreliable source of her persona's translation, as conveyed by footnotes. Hamilton's satirical approach to her male characters' attitude towards *sati* typifies her treatment of not only the barbaric Indian traditions still extant during her life but, as the novel progresses, of western misogyny that she represents as simply less overt. Upon learning of the Rajah's description of women's education in England, for instance, the ethnocentric and misogynistic Brahmin describes *sati* as a means of keeping Hindi women, "incapable of acting with propriety for themselves..., put out of the way of mischief, by being burned with the bodies of their husbands" (129). Hamilton's is a meta-satire of the traditionally male genre of satire that subverts masculine authority, in this case allowing the Brahmin's voice the potential to undermine the gravity of her own deflected authorial voice.

Chapter 3 focuses on the Anglo-Indian novels of Phebe Gibbes and Sidney Owenson through their subversion of sentimental fiction, a genre that had been codified, by contrast, as feminine. Gibbes's novel creates a striking contrast to, on the one hand, the excitement of Hamilton's Rajah at the prospect of setting foot on English soil, and, on the other, Anna Jones's subjective musing on her Anglo-Indian identity as she leaves India. Sophia Goldborne, the protagonist of Gibbes's 1789 epistolary novel, *Hartly House, Calcutta*, is a young woman coming of age through her gradual immersion in Anglo-India. Gibbes's challenge to the sentimental novel's marriage plot emerges gradually through Sophia's letters to her friend, Arabella. Sophia initially declares her adoration of India through ingenuous hyperbole: as she descends from the ship onto India's coast, she states that "the European world faded before my eyes, and became *orientalised* at all points" (10; italics in original). The statement suggests that Sophia is a *tabula rasa*, whose introjection is naively unconditional by contrast to her increasingly more nuanced responses to the events that transpire as the plot develops.

Sophia's euphemistic treatment of *sati* is a turning point that reveals the discomfort underlying her cheerful façade; in her only explicit treatment of *sati*, she observes that, though the widows "are, no doubt, sanctified ... and pass immediately into the presence of Brumma, to receive their reward," Sophia hints that not all widows acquiesce to the ritual: "[T]hey are conveyed with all imaginable piety, and *often* with their own consent, to the banks of the river, and fitted, by its rising waves, for their *translation* from earth to heaven" (176, italics added). *Translation*, used in such an equivocal sentence, suggests an underlying ambivalence that undermines her proclaimed desire to be "*orientalized* at all points." Underscoring this ambivalence, Sophia elliptically refers to *sati* through a parenthetical reference to the "dying friends" for alligators in the Ganges to "feast on" (175).

Owenson's 1811 novel, *The Missionary*—though written only 12 years after Gibbes's novel—represents a literary-historical context that involves a yet more complex revision of the sentimental genre.[36] Noting that there is "more than a generational shift" between *Hartly House* and *The Missionary*, Franklin compares Gibbes, who "never seems to have escaped a penurious obscurity," to Owenson, for whom "novel-writing brought ... a species of celebrity" ("Radically Feminizing India" 166). Beyond this contrast in their relationship to the sentimental tradition, Owenson's sophisticated engagement with canonical Romanticism is yet more revealing of this literary-historical shift; her indictment of male Romantic subjectivity is manifested through her novel's ostensible protagonist, the eponymous missionary, Hilarion. Despite the influence *The Missionary* had on the second generation of canonical male Romantic writers, the novel itself meta-textually connects Hilarion's narcissism to the early Romantic wanderer.[37] Though previous studies of the novel have regarded Hilarion's voice as authorial, suggesting therefore that Owenson merely echoes Jones, I argue that Hilarion gradually loses his initial power of objectifying both India itself and the Indian priestess, Luxima, whose own voice, extolling the nondualism that Hilarion condemns, emerges with a power that eclipses his subjectivity.

---

[36] See Chakravarty's discussion of *The Missionary* as "an influential Romantic orientalist novel" as an example of the reductiveness of the Romantic paradigm for assessing how Owenson represents India in the novel (81).

[37] See Leask's *British Romantic Writers and the East* as well as Rajan for the novel's textual history vis-à-vis the canonical poets.

Chapter 4 examines the way Marianna Starke's dramaturgical representations of Anglo-India subvert the traditional genres of comedy and tragedy in *The Sword of Peace*, an ostensible comedy, and *The Widow of Malabar*, an ostensible tragedy. In the earlier play, Starke's meta-theatrical reference to the play as a potential "tragical history" due to the gossip about her heroine's purported death echoes her preface's indictment of the gossip that undermines her credibility as an author. By contrast to Wollstonecraft, whose proto-feminism reinforces western dualism by asserting woman's reason and denying her sensibility, Starke achieves a more complex transformation of the binary of masculine authority and female powerlessness by creating two heroines of equal idealization, one characterized by passivity and the other by assertiveness. From a larger social perspective, the comedy's triangulated relationship among race, gender, and trade that the heroines must negotiate further demonstrates Starke's challenge to a range of binaries under the rubric of western dualism.

While Starke contextualizes *The Sword of Peace* in the racially complex world of Anglo-India, the *The Widow of Malabar*'s representation of miscegenation is more problematic: the young Bramin not only preempts the English Raymond's imperial rescue of the widow but voices the play's messages of reason and virtue. By contrast to the earlier play's albeit playful presentation of Starke's authorial embarrassment, *The Widow of Malabar* asserts a providential authorial presence that disrupts subject/object dualism in more overt meta-theatrical terms, including the play's multiple female perspectives that simultaneously project subjectivity onto the *sati*, extol reason from a Hindu perspective, and challenge the heroism of the traditional male rescuer.

With the hindsight of the preceding chapters' discussions of the relationship between female authorship and nondualism, the epilogue returns to the larger questions of field raised by those foundational, iconoclastic studies of the 1980s and 1990s this introduction has described; I reexamine the rigorous poetics of Charlotte Smith alongside Maria Jane Jewsbury, the former as a deist who challenges the reason/sensibility binary with an imaginary journey past the English channel into the perilous waters of colonial oppression, the latter a writer giving up her occupation as a journalist on a literally perilous journey to India. In the same spirit of returning to those earlier challenges to the Romanticism paradigm by those original studies, the epilogue addresses the need to resituate male writers in their literary context during the Revolutionary period. Through analysis of female characters in works by Blake, Coleridge, and Percy Shelley, the epilogue explores a pattern of male writers' embrace of female subjectivity, nondualism, and a powerful female sublime that has not been adequately represented through the lens of either canonical Romanticism or its rejection by recent studies seeking to bring to the fore the noncanonical. In spite of the differences among these male writers, they centralize female subjectivity founded on a revolutionary epistemology their male characters either oppose or lack the vision to embrace. The heroism of their female characters—as distinct as they are from each other—share a vision of nondual female eros that looks ahead to twentieth-century French feminism.

Chapter 1
The Asiatic Society of Bengal: "Beyond the stretch of labouring thought sublime"

This book brings to bear on the transitional period into British colonialism in India the pressure against western binaries exerted textually by women writers who were deeply engaged with India's culture and epistemology. That this volatile, 50-year period of Orientalism is actually precolonial demands a reappraisal of the Asiatic Society's historical context in ways that theories of postcolonialism or even colonialism cannot adequately frame. The intersection of politics and scholarship for the Orientalists is nowhere more dramatically illustrated than in the founding of the Asiatic Society by Warren Hastings, governor general of Bengal, for whom "the study of the Indian tradition and conceptual world simultaneously aided in steering and controlling the Indians within the framework of their own ways of thought" (Halbfass 62). The fleeting phenomenon of the Asiatic Society's transmission of Vedic texts was both defined and complicated by the entanglement of its intellectual pursuits and the political conflict between the hegemony of the East India Company and that of the British government.

During the late eighteenth and early nineteenth centuries, the masculine British response to both the India of their day and to the newly discovered ancient Indian culture and philosophy reflects the double bind underlying their stance towards the political, social, and epistemological ruptures the period was ushering in. That the discovery of Sanskrit coincides historically with the revolutionary period is no mere happenstance, as Raymond Schwab first pointed out and Susan Bassnett and Harish Trivedi (2) have further explored. The simultaneous attraction to and recoiling from a culture and philosophy challenging all that the materialist Enlightenment held dear reflects the ambivalence displayed again and again in spheres ranging from social structure to notions of selfhood. The spread of revolution from America to France as well as the Haitian uprising of 1805 pointed to deep crisis for what C.A. Bayly calls the "symbiosis between Europeans and Indians" which "began to decline [1770–1800] under the pressures of world war and commercial rivalry" (69). Among British intellectuals, the diversity of responses to this shifting relationship to India is represented by the spectrum of positions taken regarding competing notions of social amelioration. The conflict between Indian nondualism and the dualist foundation of the west reflects and extends this range, becoming historically important to the gendered relationship between creativity and authority.[1]

---

[1] The term "nondualism" is chosen over "monism" to convey a dynamic rather than static principle of oneness in order to emphasize the dissolution of subject-object duality. It should also be noted that, although there are dualistic sects of Hinduism, the extent of the

That ancient India was a fundamentally monistic culture was a happy discovery for the Orientalists, who condemned what they claimed to be polytheism in the Hinduism of their day. The Orientalists blurred the line between deism, the belief that the Creator reveals himself through his creation, and pantheism, the belief that the Supreme is a single consciousness pervading the universe.[2] The Orientalists pointed to the Sanskrit texts to support their claim that the ancient Hindus held that a single God reveals himself in and through nature, a central tenet of deism. Yet such texts, in radical difference from deism, state that the Creator is no different from the creation. One of the most striking examples of this eastern nondualism is at the climactic moment of the *Bhagavad Gita*, in which Krishna, an avatar of God, reveals himself as the Creator present in everything, the "origin and the dissolution…, being as well as non-being."[3] The statement illustrates the essential difference between western monism and the nondualism of the Sanskrit texts: while the former connotes a single, static principle, nondualism suggests a more dynamic principle in which differentiation dissolves into oneness that subsumes diversity.

Along with Wilkins's translation of the *Gita*, Jones's *Hymns to the Hindu Deities*, original poetry inspired by his study of Vedic texts, were as influential among British writers as were his translations.[4] Jones's diction betrays his ambivalence

---

eighteenth-century Orientalists' knowledge of this varied tradition is uncertain. By pointing to the conflict in terms of east and west, I do not ignore the nondualist thinkers of the west, such as Jacob Boehme, but rather regard them as working against the tradition of materialism in European philosophy.

[2] Although the Orientalists distinguished themselves from the evangelical deists in India, their own deistic leanings are evident in their writing, characterized by an insistence on a single God separate from but knowable through the phenomenal world. Nevertheless, it has been difficult to label the Orientalists theologically. Jones, for instance, was not a deist as such but, as Halbfass notes, he "nevertheless came close to deistic thinking" (56). For both Jones and Wilkins, the line drawn between Creator and phenomenal world—in spite of their attraction to the dissolution of this line—is what aligns them with deism. See Adisasmito-Smith (2008) on the deism of the Orientalists.

[3] Sargeant (trans.), 394–5. See Chapter 1 of this book for discussion of the choice of modern translations and a detailed analysis of Wilkins's rendering of this climactic moment of the Gita.

[4] Contrasting the scant analysis of the relationship between the newly recovered texts of women writers and Orientalism, the humanist approach of the early twentieth century examines the Orientalist influence on the canonical Romantic poets. Schwab, for instance cites Quinet who, in 1828, noted that Jones's hymns based on the Sanskrit created "a passion for Asia among the poets of the Lake School" (195). Cannon notes that the most widely known of these was "Hymn to Narayana," which influenced Shelley's "Hymn to Intellectual Beauty," and Keats's *Hyperion (Sir WJ*, 70). While early postcolonialist gender studies were premised on a binary of empire as masculine and colonized as feminine, those that followed were more nuanced regarding the "difficulty of negotiating between gender and class" for women writers during the late eighteenth century (Grundy 73). Rajan complicates the position of women of the period writing about India, noting that the differences become more striking than the similarities: "Feminine constructions of India's femininity not only differ from male constructions, but differ in the difference they allow among themselves" (167).

towards the epistemologies of both east and west when he describes the Hindus as more "rational" than the Christians: "I hold the doctrine of the Hindus concerning a future state to be incomparably more rational, more pious, and more likely to deter men from vice, than the horrid opinions inculcated by Christians on punishments without end" (qtd. in Drew 47).[5] Yet in his *Hymns*, Jones draws not only from Indian sources, but from the legacy of western literature: Plato, Pindar, the Bible, Milton, Pope and Gray (Cannon, *Sir WJ, Orientalist* 68). Although Jones's "Hymn to Narayana" itself appears to celebrate the pantheism discovered through the avatar, Narayana, Jones's ambivalence is implicit in his preface to the poem:

> The inextricable difficulties ... induced many of the wisest among the ancients ... to believe that the whole Creation was rather an *energy* than a *work*, by which the Infinite Being, who is present at all times in all places, exhibits to the minds of his creatures a set of perceptions...; so that all bodies and their qualities exist ... only as far as they are *perceived*; a theory no less pious than sublime, and as different from any principle of Atheism as the brightest sunshine differs from the blackest midnight. (Jones, *Poems* 202)

While Jones defends Indian philosophy from charges of atheism by his British readers, what is most uncomfortable for his Enlightenment contemporaries about eastern divinity is the paradoxical simultaneity of its immanence and transcendence. Praising the *Vedas* with the western terms "sublime" and "pious," Jones superimposes deism upon the eastern nondual idea that the Supreme is an energy, not a work. To call the Supreme as energy in all phenomena is essentially pantheistic, distinct from the phrase that follows in which Jones states that the Creator, separate from the creation, speaks through the creation. Jones never says that the Creator itself is this energy, a notion fundamental to Indian philosophy. By limiting this "energy" to the creation, Jones adjusts the idea to impose a deistic separation between Creator and creation.[6]

The most famous of Jones's translations, his 1789 rendering of *Sakuntala* by Kalidasa, best illustrates how his western epistemology distorts his translation of gender and subjectivity in Kalidasa's play. Not only does Jones's anglicizing Kalidasa as the "Shakespeare of India" in the preface to his translation speak to the Orientalists' desire to make the Sanskrit texts marketable in England; Jones's handling of this particular play reveals one of the most extreme examples of the distortions of such rendering (Thapar 203).[7] Jones explains in the preface that he translated it "verbally into Latin, which bears so great a resemblance to Sanscrit,

---

[5] See Chapter 4 for discussion of Starke's characterization of the young Brahmin, whose rational heroism eclipses the role of Raymond, Indamora's British rescuer.

[6] McGann describes Jones's "Hymn to Su'rya" as "the 'Mind' of a certain kind of rationalist neoplatonism—distinctively English, distinctly Enlightened" (128). See Chapter 3 of this book for discussion of Owenson's more engaged relationship with Indian nondualism through the subjectivity of Luxima.

[7] See Thapar's detailed discussion of the evolution of the play and particularly of Jones's translation in its colonial context.

that it is more convenient than any modern language for a scrupulous interlineary version: I then turned it *word for word* into English, and afterwards, *without adding or suppressing* any material sentence, disengaged from the stiffness of a foreign idiom, and prepared the *faithful* translation of the Indian drama" (Thapar 202, italics added). The obstacles to such clarity, however, become obvious even in the course of the prologue.

Not only is it apparent that no such accuracy is possible in the doubly mediated process of translating from Sanskrit to Latin to English but Jones chooses to reduce to a single prose voice Kalidasa's three different poetic styles:

> They are all in verse, where the dialogue is elevated; and in prose, where it is familiar: the men of rank and learning are represented speaking pure Sanskrit, and the women Prácrit, which is little more than the language of the Brámens melted down by a delicate articulation to the softness of Italian; while the low persons of the drama speak the vulgar dialects of the several provinces which they are supposed to inhabit. (Thapar 204)

By reducing the multidimensional voices of Kalidasa's poetry to a single prose voice, Jones averts the complexities of the play's characterization. Yet more problematic is the way Jones forces into the western dualistic tradition Kalidasa's connection among voice, landscape, and divinity; Jones offers a disclaimer about the presences of gods and goddesses in the play that is typical of those Orientalist essays and prefaces anticipating English distaste for India's polytheism. When he introduces the deities in *Sakuntala* as the "machinery of the drama," Jones claims that Kalidasa intended them as "clearly allegorical personages" (Thapar 205). Of Kalidasa's natural landscape, by contrast, the twentieth-century translator of *Sakuntala*, Barabara Stoller Miller, writes, "[I]t reverberates with Siva's presence. Nature functions not as a setting or allegorical landscape but as a dynamic surface on which the unmanifest cosmic unity plays"; Miller goes on to describes the play's representation of Siva, who "identifies "himself with Nature (*prakrti*), the female half of his cosmic totality. Siva is called 'The God Who is Half Female.'... The male and female aspects of existence ... are bound into a single androgynous figure" (7–8). Miller's intention to hew closely to Kalidasa's nondualism helps to illuminate the westernizing behind Jones treating Kalidasa's characters as allegorical figures and reducing the multiple levels of the play's diction to a single prose voice.

A comparison between Miller's translation that seeks to restore the Sanskrit nondualism and Jones's allegorical rendering more specifically illustrates Jones's distortion. In Miller's translation, Kalidasa's nondualism is seen in a conversation of two minor characters, maidens whom Kalidasa calls Cuckoo and Little Bee, names that evoke the natural world. In the original play, one asks the other for "half the fruit of [her]worship" while the other replies, "That goes without saying ... our bodies may be separate, but our lives are one" (Kalidasa 149). Jones's rendering of the conversation between Cuckoo and Little Bee is illustrative of the fundamental ambivalence underlying the process of translation for Jones: the "faithfulness" of the translation is in conveying the one soul shared by two bodies, but the distortion comes with identifying the speakers as "Damsels" without naming them: "'First Damsel: I must have a moiety of the reward which the god will bestow.'" Second Damsel: "'To be sure, and without any previous bargain. We are only one soul, you know, though Brahma has given it two bodies'" (485). Jones's disclaimer in his prologue reveals the epistemological roots of his distorting translation:

> [T]he deities introduced in the Fatal Ring are clearly allegorical personages. Maríchi, the first production of Brahmá, or the Creative Power, signifies light, that subtil fluid which was created before its reservoir, the sun, as water was created before the sea; Casyapa, the offspring of Maríchi, seems to be a personification of infinite space, comprehending innumerable worlds; and his children by Aditi, or his active power (unless Aditi mean the primeval day, and Diti, his other wife, the night), are Indra, or the visible firmament, and the twelve Adityas, or suns, presiding over as many months. (Thapar 205)[8]

In allegorizing Kalidasa's nondualism, Jones subjects it to western subject-object dualism.

Whether limited by the dualistic vocabulary, literary traditions, and philosophical underpinnings of their late Enlightenment context or whether they willfully engage in distortion—two causes that are not mutually exclusive—the Orientalists often conflate Sanskrit *advaita*, Vedic nondualism, with western monism's static principle of unity.[9] The distortion manifests most problematically in their ubiquitous renderings of *advaita* and descriptions of India itself as transcendent or sublime, dualistic terms that connote a threshold to be crossed, illusory from the perspective of the *Vedas*. The question of the Orientalists' complicity in the imperial conquest of India thus becomes more vexed as it splinters into a range of motivations and effects. For Jones and Wilkins especially, this earliest venture into the transmission of Sanskrit is double-edged: what they hold dear in the discovery is that which threatens the very lifeblood of Enlightenment epistemology. The effect of the Orientalists' superimposing the nondualism they find in the Sanskrit "sublime"

---

[8] Jones's choices as translator make clear that his readership is at the canonical crossroads of Neoclassicism and Romanticism: first, his choice to render the play into Latin and then English and, second, to transform Kalidasa into the Indian Shakespeare. As Garland Cannon observed in 1982, Jones "first used interlinear Latin to bridge the exoticness if not potential direct untranslatability for that time, before rendering his Latin into a literal English version that borrowed 118 different nouns transliterated from the Sanskrit. After suitably naturalizing these items and idioms, he minutely polished his English syntax" ("Eighteenth-Century Sanskrit Studies" 199). As a proponent of Orientalist scholarship's humanist period—seen here in his glorifying the "high quality" of Jones's rendering, Cannon is writing before the postcolonialist movement taught us to read Orientalism suspiciously. It is therefore important for the twenty-first-century reader to extract the salient details of Cannon's historical analysis from his own literary-historical context that predates the skepticism foundational to the way Orientalism has been read since Said.

[9] Although Hinduism includes *dvaita*, or dualistic, sects, the eighteenth-century British would not have been exposed to them, especially since the central text that was translated from Sanskrit was *The Bhagavad Gita* by Charles Wilkins in 1785.

onto their Enlightenment tradition is one of profound ambivalence, revealed in the simultaneous attraction to and repulsion from the state they are calling sublime.

That the shifting political landscape is inextricably linked to Orientalism's ambivalence towards nondualism is a phenomenon that can be traced retrospectively, through Macaulay's 1835 "Minute on Indian Education" that reversed the Orientalist promotion of Sanskrit study. On the surface, Macaulay unconditionally condemns as "false philosophy" the major Sanskrit texts, yet he betrays knowledge of the nuances of the Sanskrit of which he claims to "have no knowledge" (727, 722). The circumstances of Charles Wilkins's 1785 rendering of the *Bhagavad Gita* into English reveal this entanglement of the political and intellectual. Not only is it significant that the introduction to Wilkins's translation was written by Hastings, then governor-general of Bengal, but that Hastings's letter introducing the *Gita* was addressed to Nathaniel Smith, Chairman of the East India Company, thus filtering the transmission of Indian texts through the Company. Hastings was made governor-general of Bengal in 1772 after the East India Company had left Bengal in ruins, disempowering the Bengal government and yet refusing to accept administrative responsibility. Horace Walpole denounced the Company, saying, "We murdered, deposed, plundered, usurped—nay, what think you of the famine in Bengal in which three millions perished being caused by a monopoly of the servants of the East India Company?" (Kopf 13–14). Yet Burke's prosecution of Hastings during his lengthy trial, lasting from 1788–1795, so wore on the English public that Hastings was increasingly viewed as a scapegoat and was acquitted. Most antithetical to western thought about these texts, Macaulay claims, is their "absorption into the Deity," or their apparent nondualism (719). Macaulay's speech suggests not only his own ambivalence, but that of his Orientalist precursors whose East India Company connections exemplify the consummate conflict of interest.[10]

Though scholarship has long noted the impact of the Asiatic Society's publications as they arrived from India to England, none has delved into the epistemological accommodations made by British writers as they discovered ancient India through the distorting lens of Orientalist dualism. Nevertheless, scholars have become increasingly divided about how conflicted the relationship between literature and Orientalism was. Those hewing more closely to Said describe the literary productions of Anglo-India through the lens of Orientalism's

---

[10] Just as humanist scholars emphasized that the east is not the sole threat to the dualistic tradition of the Enlightenment citing "coincidences among the intellectual fashions which promoted Boehme, Schelling, and the Upanishads simultaneously" (Schwab 197), so too have more recent postcolonialist studies suggested more nuanced shifts than the stark opposition between imperialism and the subaltern that characterized the first phase of postcolonialism; between 1825 and 1860, for instance, Colebrooke and others attempted to exclude "texts dealing with the canons of sound argument, or with the criteria governing rational assent" as a means of creating the impression of "a radically non-European mode of thought"; the "devaluation of rationalist elements in Indian philosophical thought arose because of 'nativist' trends in the Indian nationalist movement, attempts to find in India's past something radically non-European with which to confront the colonial intrusion" (Ganeri 2).

cultural imperialism. Niranjana, for instance, describes the "outwork" of Jones's translations "to show how he contributes to a historicist, teleological model of civilization that, coupled with a notion of translation presupposing transparency of representation, helps construct a powerful version of the 'Hindu' that later writers of different philosophical and political persuasions incorporated into their texts" (13). By contrast, Lalita Pandit challenges Said's influential claim that Jones and the Orientalists were responsible for codifying the Orient for western readers: "[B]efore William Jones appeared on the scene, Indic scholars had spent hundreds of years codifying and categorizing knowledge and experience...; the Indic system ... was not a diffuse mass of diversity that Jones organized ... for the first time" (115). Regardless of how influential Orientalism was on its contemporary writers, there has been scant discussion of these writers as resisting or engaging with the Indic system beyond merely echoing Orientalism.

Translating Caste, Law, and Selfhood in Charles Wilkins's Bhagavad Gita

In his letter to Nathaniel Smith introducing Wilkins's translation of the *Bhagavad Gita*, Hastings makes explicit his imperialist agenda for cultivating an interest in Sanskrit studies: "Every accumulation of knowledge, and especially such as is obtained by social communication with people over whom we exercise a dominion founded on the right of conquest, is useful to the state" (Wilkins, *Bhagavat-Geeta* 13). That Hastings's letter was written to Smith, Chairman of the East India Company, underscores the political underpinnings of the scholarly project.

Recent commentators have extended the implications of this political agenda beyond its evidence of cultural imperialism to explore the doubleness of the Orientalists' position in India. Steven Adisasmito-Smith, observing that Hastings's concerns were not purely mercenary, notes that "he had absorbed some of the humanistic ideals of the Enlightenment, which were folded in with his commercial interests" ("Self in Translation" 168). Far from apologizing for British imperialism, this exploration of the inconsistencies that characterize the Orientalists has helped scholarship move away from the polarities of humanism and early postcolonialism. In particular, it has reopened the case of William Jones, the figure most variously described between these opposing paradigms.

As director of the Asiatic Society, Jones had long been characterized as a humanist in pre-Said scholarship and, following it, as an imperialist whose motivation for systematizing Sanskrit was to dominate India. Like Said, Tejaswini Niranjana describes the Orientalists' "containment," a strategy that exposes their task of "translating and thereby *purifying* the debased native texts" (3, 16; italics in original). Niranjana studies what she calls the "outwork" of Jones's translations to show how he "contributes to a historicist, teleological model of civilization" that helps to "construct a powerful version of the 'Hindu' that later writers of different philosophical and political persuasions incorporated into their texts" (13). By contrast, Fred Hoerner emphasizes Jones's ambivalence, stating that the reason Jones misrepresents his own poem, "Hymn to Camdeo," as a translation is because "to become a Company man and credible jurist, he first had to suppress his imaginative powers" (222).[11] Observing that Jones supported the American Revolution yet became a judge in India challenges any single-minded description of his political leanings; so, too, the influence on these contradictory positions of his early exposure to the "environment of powerful Whig landowners and the aesthetic of the neoclassical movement in art and architecture" demands these more nuanced readings of Jones's Orientalism (Brine 5).

In spite of these important advances in the critical discussion of Jones, studies of the Asiatic Society as a whole have remained polarized. Postcolonialism, whose interest in demystifying the humanistic emphasis on the Orientalists' contribution (Halbfass 68), has strongly emphasized their cultural imperialism.[12] But the matter is even more complex: as Wilkins's *Gita* finds its way to England, it simultaneously presents notions of selfhood and society alien to the west even as it reinforces ambivalences that define the age.[13]

Wilkins perceives the *Gita* as the religious text of the Hindus that he Christianizes in peculiarly late Enlightenment ways. That this premise underlies the distortions of his translation is illustrated by his announcement of the misleading discovery that the Brahmans from whom he has gained access to the *Gita* are "Unitarians": "they believe but in one God"; he claims that its principal design is "to undermine the tenets inculcated by the *Veds*" and to "bring about the downfall of Polytheism" (24). Wilkins adds a phrase of qualification to suggest that the Hindus are deistic even in their worship of images and their sacrifices: "or at least, to induce men to believe God present in every image before which they bent, and the object of all their ceremonies and sacrifices" (24).

Categorizing the *Gita* as a religious text akin to late Enlightenment Christianity, Wilkins decontextualizes it from its place in the epic, *The Mahabharata*, whose central plot revolves around a feud between cousins over the Kuruksetra kingdom. Opening as the battle is about to begin, the text of the *Gita* is a conversation between Arjuna, one of the Pandavas trying to reclaim the kingdom, and Krishna, his charioteer and teacher. Distraught over the prospect of killing his relatives and friends, Arjuna describes his confusion to Krishna, whose subsequent lesson to Arjuna about attachment culminates with "a vision of totality that liberates [Arjuna] from his prior self-preoccupied identity" (Chapple, xiv).[14] Barbara Stoler Miller comments that Arjuna's dedication to Krishna can begin "only after

---

[11] Compare Letitia Elizabeth Landon's 1824 "Manmadin, The Indian Cupid, Floating Down the Ganges," in which she projects onto Manmadin, or Camdeo, the sensibility associated with the women poets of the period: "Fragrant and yet poisoned sighs, / Agonies and ecstasies" (254).

[12] Niranjana, for instance, includes Wilkins in a list of Orientalists who portray the Hindus as "cunning and deceitful" (26).

[13] See Adisasmito-Smith's 2008 comparison between Wilkins's translation and that of Edwin Arnold in 1885; Adisasmito-Smith traces how the variety of bonds that were "forged" beyond imperialism during that century are reflected in the two translations.

[14] For more detailed synopses, see van Buitenen's introduction to his translation of the *Gita* (1–29) and Miller's introduction to her translation (1–13).

his delusions about the nature of life and death have been dispelled and he has the power to see Krishna in his cosmic form" (9). The *Gita* encompasses many teachings, from nine yogas to the vision of the True Self to the final chapters on detached action. Beyond the *Gita*, in subsequent sections of the epic, it is clear that Arjuna must go through further cycles of learning and spiritual progress.[15]

The sections that follow detail four central tensions in Wilkins's translation: caste, *dharma*, nondualism, and *karma*. In each case, Wilkins westernizes what would be, from the perspective of late Enlightenment England, the *Gita*'s most volatile principles. Regarding caste, Wilkins invests the Indian system with a historically specific emotionalism that the subject of class structure was evoking during the late eighteenth century, thereby participating in the "colonial role in the historical construction of caste" (Dirks 8). *Dharma*, the informing law of the *Gita*, emerges as a tension in Wilkins's translation related to that of the caste system, since British rule in India was problematized by both principles. Thus, while *dharma* in the *Gita* is a philosophical exploration of the individual experience of righteousness rather than a belief system or legal code, Wilkins translates it as law akin to the Mosaic commandments or, in some instances, western jurisprudence. The epistemological problem of rendering Indian nondualism is heightened by Wilkins's eagerness to present to the west an image of ancient India as monotheistic; in doing so, he equates its nondualism with Enlightenment deism. Finally, in his effort to make the *Gita* palatable for his British readers, Wilkins transforms the *Gita*'s description of ritual acts of sacrifice into worship and *karma* into a Christian ethic of sin and salvation.[16]

---

[15] Indologists have offered conflicting perspectives on the text's meaning. Franklin Edgerton sees the *Gita* as dualistic in its distinction between soul and non-soul (38); however, he goes on to qualify this label, acknowledging that the text's third principle of immanence suggests a movement beyond duality (44). Nevertheless, the purpose of this book is less to enter the Indological discussion than to focus on Wilkins's assumptions about the *Gita* and his projected anxieties that surface through his translation of the text.

[16] Because I am not a Sanskritist by training, but rather a scholar of British literature with a working knowledge of Sanskrit, I turn to the expertise of Indologists to help distinguish the meaning of the Sanskrit from Wilkins's rendering when it is particularly colored by his late Enlightenment perspective. These sources include Monier-Williams's dictionary and the modern translations of Franklin Edgerton (1952), R.C. Zaehner (1966), J.A.B. van Buitenen (1981), Barbara Stoler Miller (1986), and Winthrop Sargeant (1994). While my central purpose in referring to multiple modern translations is to avoid suggesting that any one is authoritative, I turn most often to Sargeant, whose rendering in two stages, a syllable-by-syllable gloss followed by a translation of the verse, provides the most useful touchstone. However, I note discrepancies among the modern translators where they are pertinent to Wilkins. Complicating the comparison between these modern translations and Wilkins's is the fact that the Sanskrit text Wilkins used was different from theirs so that a composite comparison offers a degree of latitude for discrepancies between the different Sanskrit texts. See van Buitenen for a history of the principal editions of the text (1:xxx). Regarding references to the sections, or *adhyayas*, of the text, each translator uses a different designation (Wilkins calls them "Lectures," Sargeant, "Books," and Miller, "Teachings"). I have chosen the more commonly used "chapters" and "verses" for the sections within the chapters, though, for clarity, I give page numbers parenthetically as well for reference to translations.

Caste, Class, and Miscegenation

Perhaps the most significant, recent reconsideration of colonialism has been the closer attention paid to its participation in the Indian caste system. "The idea that *varna*—the classification of all castes into four hierarchical orders," Nicholas Dirks notes, "could conceivably organize the social identities and relations of all Indians across the civilizational expanse of the subcontinent was only developed under the peculiar circumstances of British colonial rule" (14). This reassessment of caste as a construction of colonialism suggests a central tension for those British intellectuals struggling with the injustices of class inequities in England. Edmund Burke, perhaps the most significant figure whose position on revolution is far from one-sided, best exemplifies that the class system is a vexed concern. As Saree Makdisi comments, "Burke's attitudes towards India and the Orient oscillate between, on the one hand, an extreme kind of cultural relativism; and, on the other, contradictory claims to and invocations of certain trans-cultural and universal laws and tendencies of humankind" (104). Indeed, Burke supported the American Revolution, condemned the French Revolution, and blamed Hastings for British abuses of India in the impeachment trials.

That there is no simple correlation between class and caste suggests that to attempt to formulate one would be reductive and distorting. "'Empire' and 'state' always remained limited political entities in India," Bayly notes, adding that "this was not because India was a society dominated by caste in which the state could not take root, as many orientalists have asserted, but because there were many sharers in the dignity and power of kingship with overlapping rights and obligations" (13). This observation lends insight into the Indian context on which the British government imposed itself and, as its own power grew, why the British response to the caste system was so fraught with tension.

Robert Southey's account of the Baptist Missionary Society exemplifies the intensity that links the British disparagement of the Indian caste system with their discomfort regarding participation in class hierarchy.[17] Southey recounts the experience of William Carey, a missionary who deplored the caste system as the primary obstacle in attempting to convert the Indians:

> On account of this unnatural distinction of classes among men, all motives to exertion, enquiry, or mental improvement, are cut off: for the most honourable actions, the most beneficial discoveries, or virtuous conduct, would secure no honour or advantage to a person of a low cast: and those of a higher cast being universally revered as a sort of half divinities, lose no reputation by their being ignorant or vicious. The consequence is, a stupid contentment to remain as they are. (*P.A.*, 1803, 214)

Southey's response to the dilemma is curious: "Christianity," he writes, "itself may be represented as a cast. The natives are said to believe that it is written in their

---

[17] I am indebted to Neff's essay for introducing Southey's accounts of the Baptist Missionary society into the discussion of British response to caste; I extend its thesis to underscore the relationship between class and caste.

shasters, that *all shall one day be of one cast*; and some of them begin to ask, if their cast will not be that of the English, whose *shaster* is now come among them" (*P.A.*, 1803, 215; italics in original). Southey here looks for ways to manipulate the Hindu prophecy to suggest Christianity as the one unifying caste. It is thus ironic that, following this passage, Southey identifies the "stumbling block" to civilizing India not as the caste system, but as Hinduism's unifying principle:

> There are rivers from the east, west, north, and south, said a Bramin to one of these preachers, but they all meet in the sea: so there are many ways among men, but all lead to God. This is the stumbling block! This tolerating principle accords too well with the common feelings, and common sense of human nature, to be easily overthrown. (*P.A.*, 1803, 215)

It is not truth or justice being obstructed, this passage reveals, but the conversion of Hindus to Christianity, regardless of ideology.

That Southey assigns religious consequences to class structure further complicates the British perception of Indian society. Caste was "refigured as a distinctly religious system, and the transformation had immense implications," notes Dirks; caste itself "was seen as a form of colonial civil society in India, which provided an ironic, and inferior, anthropological analogue for the colonized world" (12). In the case of Carey and Southey, both ignore the similarity of the tragedies wrought by the caste division to the British class system that made British dissenters such ardent advocates of the French Revolution at its inception.

The Revolution did not come to England—in spite of the British government's paranoia—for two reasons, noted by David Perkins: its class structure, in which members of the middle class "could be assimilated into the governing class," and the rise of the Methodist movement, whose evangelism "distracted and consoled the suffering poor and made the 'atheist' Jacobin an object of horror" (4–5). The intersection of shifting political and religious attitudes in the larger British consciousness during this crucial period of British history is also seen in the ways the Orientalists shaped colonial India through their renderings. The ambivalence of Wilkins towards the caste system, reflecting the simultaneous pulls towards idealism and resistance to change seen on a wide scale during the early revolutionary period,[18] is intricately related to his refashioning of Sanskrit philosophy as religion akin to Christianity.

One of Wilkins's central objectives in exposing the British to the *Gita* is to set the "learned *Brahmans*" against the "prejudices of the vulgar," the lower castes (24). This premise in itself contradicts a central teaching of the *Gita*, that "every aspect of life is in fact a way of salvation.... [I]t is clear that the answers are provided not only for Arjuna but are paradigmatic for people of virtually any walk of life. The *Gita* becomes a text appropriate to all persons of all castes or no caste; its message transcends the limits of classical Hinduism" (Chapple xix). The *Gita*'s emphasis on caste is yet more troubling for Wilkins, however. While ambivalence

---

[18] Wilkins's upper-middle-class background takes on significance in this regard (Kopf, *British Orientalism* 33, Table 1).

towards their own class system seems reason enough for the British unease over their repudiation of the Indian caste system, the miscegenation that gave rise to the Anglo-Indian community is a source of yet deeper anxiety. Benedict Anderson traces the history of the community to its origin in the seventeenth century, in which the East India Company coerced its employees to marry and convert Hindu women rather than marry the Catholic Portuguese and French then living in India (12).[19] By 1750, this community exceeded the British in India; fearing revolution on the part of the Anglo-Indians far more than by either Hindus or Muslims, the British government drew a parallel between the Anglo-Indians and the Haitian mulattos.[20]

The Anglo-Indian community thus conflated, for the British, problems of race and caste. Southey, for instance, disparaged the "the mixed breed" of the Anglo-Indian community by claiming that it "seems to show that the order of nature has been violated" (*P.A.* 1809, 211). Michael Fisher observes that, in late eighteenth-century Britain, the concept of race "had not yet solidified into a strong social boundary. During this period, inter-racial marriages..., especially marriages between white women and non-white men, were not common within the gentry" (902). In her 1812 *Journal of a Residence in India*, Maria Graham reveals the discomfort of the period with mixed-race children in England when she describes an orphanage for half-caste boys in Madras: "I cannot but think it a cruelty to send children of colour to Europe where their complexion must subject them to perpetual mortification. Here, being in their own country, and associating with those in the same situation with themselves, they have a better chance of being happy" (128).[21] Jenny Sharpe describes the "Anglo-Indian/Eurasian" half-castes as "a racially mixed group that formed a separate community of their own. They were mocked for being inherently inferior versions of the British they painstakingly imitated, and it was the common opinion that they had inherited the vices of both races" (19–20). For the British, indictment of the caste system used to rationalize their imperial rule over India had to be reconciled with the growing anxiety over participation in the caste system and its disruption. The government thus barred members of the Anglo-Indian community from studying overseas, from serving in the armed forces, and from entering the officer ranks of the military or civil services.[22] Ainslie Embree notes that "a dominant culture projects onto a minority group all of those qualities and characteristics which

---

[19] For another instance of the bias against the Catholic presence in India, see Eliza Fay's *Letters* dating back to 1779.

[20] According to Hyam, the reason for this change of attitude in the 1790s is "the reaction to the uprising in the Caribbean island of Santo Domingo after 1791. The shock waves generated by the unprecedented explosion against white rule there reverberated around the world.... In India too there were fears that the British might be driven out by Indians officered by Anglo-Indians" (116).

[21] Sharpe observes that they were also called Indo Britons (20), though Hyam notes that the label does not appear until the Victorian period (116).

[22] See Hyam 116. Anglo-Indians were prohibited in 1791 from holding civil or military office with the company and were disqualified from the army as combatants. There were massive discharges in 1795. By 1808, none were left in the British army.

it most fears and hates within itself" (104), an observation that underscores the connection between British obsession with the Indian caste system and its own ambivalence about the British class hierarchy. Indeed, as Bayly notes, by the end of the eighteenth century, the leaders of Bengal created a series of institutions "in the face of rapid political change which might bring about a 'mixing of blood' and degeneration of the caste order" (74).[23]

The mid-eighteenth century is thus pivotal in the changing racial relations between British and Indians, setting in motion "a double current, of increasing contact and knowledge of Indian life, and of increasing contempt of everything Indian as irrational, superstitious, barbaric and typical of an inferior civilization" (Spear 129). Wilkins's translation of the *Bhagavad Gita* betrays this anxiety over miscegenation, the problem of mixed caste arriving at the outset of the *Gita*. In a pivotal episode in the first chapter Arjuna, distraught that he is about to fight a war against his own relatives, tells Krishna of the chaos that would ensue from such an act. Wilkins's translation reads,

> Upon the loss of virtue [*dharma*], vice and impiety overwhelm the whole of a race. From the influence of impiety [loss of *dharma*] the females of a family grow vicious; and from women that are become vicious are born the spurious brood called *Vărnă-sănkăr* [mixed caste]. The *Sănkăr* provideth Hell both for those which are slain and those which survive...; By the crimes of those who murder their own relations, fore [*sic*] cause of contamination and birth of *Vărnă-sănkărs*, the family virtue, and the virtue of a whole tribe is for ever done away; and we have been told, O *Krĕĕshnă*, that the habitation of those mortals whose generation hath lost its virtue, shall be in Hell. (32–3)

Wilkins leaves untranslated the Sanskrit *Vărnă-sănkăr*, which means intermixture of caste.[24] The phrase is key to understanding why Arjuna is in such a state

---

[23] Bayly details the concern over the growth of the half-caste society (70ff). Neff observes that, though scholarship has suggested the turn against the Anglo-Indians after the 1857 rebellion, the problem begins by the middle of the eighteenth century (386–7). While Neff explores the appearance of racism against mixed castes in the literature of early nineteenth-century Britain, this book probes the ambivalence towards caste, beyond the fear of uprising noted in Hyam. Ronald Inden details repudiation of the caste system in 1858: "The fact that the word for this Indian essence is, as almost every introduction to the subject points out, derived from the Portuguese, *casta*, seems not to disturb its solidity as the foundation of an entire civilization." Inden warns against conflating Portuguese notions of race with those of nineteenth-century British, French, and Germans (57).

[24] Monier-Williams's dictionary gives two terms, *varna-samsarga*, a mixture or confusion of castes, and *varna-samhāra*, an assembly or mixture of different castes (924–5). Sargeant and Edgerton, respectively, give "intermixture of castes" (79) and "mixture of caste" (11), while Miller chooses the more general "disorder" (26, line 41). Wilkins uses the term "tribe" rather than caste. Fisher discusses the Hindu *jati* as an alternative to the term "caste" (903). By capitalizing the term, Wilkins suggests a proper noun, so that an English reader with no knowledge of Sanskrit might suppose that *Varna-sankar* is a figure of retribution.

of affliction by the end of this first chapter of the *Gita*, the catalyst, in fact, to Krishna's ensuing discussion of *dharma* which makes up the rest of the text. Wilkins's leaving the Sanskrit term untranslated is particularly conspicuous since he is elsewhere scrupulous about his translation, including lengthy notes following untranslated terms and names. Leaving the phrase untranslated or notated, Wilkins mirrors the growing concern among the British over the unrest of their own created "mixed caste," the Anglo-Indians.

Given the political climate in Europe and America, Wilkins and the other Orientalists would have been keenly aware of the fluidity of the Indian social structure, as Bayly describes it: "Caste ... was not an immutable 'given' of Indian society. Castes were constantly in the process of formation and change, notably in periods such as the eighteenth century when political authority was very fluid" (11–12). The connection between the fear of the Anglo-Indians and the threat of revolution in England is illustrated by Southey's projection of an Indian Buonaparte: "But no century has ever yet elapsed in which Asia has not produced some Buonaparte of its own, some villain, who setting equally at defiance the laws of God and man, collects the whole contemporary force of evil about him, and bears down everything in his way" (*P.A.* 3210). As Neff notes, "Such an Indian Buonaparte ... probably would not be a Hindu," but rather a member of the mixed caste (390).

Particularly during this time marked by flux, the discomfort of the Orientalists with their own participation in the changing social structure emerges in their translations, their ambivalence springing from the realization that they are implicated in India's changing social structure. In the spirit of Sharpe's "case for reading literary and historical documents according to the systems of knowledge of the time of writing" (21), one can regard Wilkins's decision to leave *Vărnă-sănkăr* untranslated as evidence that the British were well aware of their participation in the caste system, not only that brought about by the "death of kings" that had "cleared the way for the transformation of caste under colonial rule," but by their yet more specific creation and subsequent rejection of the Anglo-Indian community (Dirks 12).

Wilkins's evasion at the opening of the *Gita* announces an intersubjectivity that haunts his translation. His awareness that Arjuna's warning could be seen as a prophecy of the "contamination" the British had wrought from the Indian perspective has dire implications from three views, including the Indian perspective on the British as the fulfilment of the ancient prophecy, the British perspective on their creation of a threatening half-caste, and the projection of the British onto the Indian text of its own fear of revolution by England's underclass (Wilkins 32).

Dharma, Judaeo-Christian Law, and European Jurisprudence

Late-eighteenth-century British anxieties over class structure are connected to an underlying ambivalence about Enlightenment epistemology. As J.G.A. Pocock observes about *Reflections on the Revolution in France*, the greatest source of Burke's fear of revolution in England was the British intelligentsia: "Increasingly ... he took the view that the Revolution was a destructive movement of the human intellect, aimed at the utter subversion of the codes of manners and social behaviour which had grown up in the centuries of European history" (xxxiii). Burke's fear of dissenting intellectuals as the vehicle for revolution underscores the link between class structure and epistemology.

This connection between the epistemological and political is seen in Wilkins's problematic translation of *dharma*, a concept complex enough even in the original Sanskrit that its exegesis becomes a central concern of the *Gita*.[25] When Wilkins glosses it at times as religious law, and other times as jurisprudence, his translation multiplies the problems inherent in British reception of a concept with no direct equivalent in the west. In spite of its untranslatability, however, *dharma* was rendered by Baptist missionaries as "religion" (Halbfass 340). Wilkins, in keeping with this tendency, translates *sarvadharmān* (literally, "all duties") as "religion" (133). Thus translating *dharma* as religious law, Wilkins superimposes onto the text the Christian evangelism that his contemporary missionaries were conveying in their translations of the Bible into Bengali and Sanskrit.[26]

Wilkins's rendering of *dharma* into a moral law associated with Anglicist piety can be seen in the passage on *Vărnă-sănkăr* from the first chapter cited in section one above, in which Wilkins translates *dharma* as "virtue" and loss of *dharma* as "impiety." In his eagerness to find commonality between ancient India and Europe and, by extension, his desire to convince his British readers of this commonality, Wilkins fashions the *Gita* as a book of religious law akin to Christianity while evading the social and epistemological construction at its core. In the third chapter, Wilkins once again not only erases the reference to caste in the context of *dharma* but gives it religious meaning. According to Wilkins's rendering, Krishna says, "A man's own *religion*, though contrary to, is better than the faith of another, let it be ever so well followed" (48, italics added). However, the Sanskrit word that Wilkins translates as "religion" is *svadharmas*, literally "own rights" or "own duty." Wilkins converts these passages into endorsements of piety without contextualizing the individual or social law inherent in these notions of righteousness.

The glossing of *dharma* as western jurisprudence has yet more dire implications for its application by the British government in India. A hallmark of postcolonial scholarship has been its indictment of both Hastings, as governor general of Bengal, and Jones, as a judge in India who himself translated Hindu law, through their explicit acknowledgment that ruling an indigenous people according to

---

[25] Eight columns of Monier-Williams's dictionary are devoted to *dharma* and its compound forms. Miller acknowledges its intricacies in her gloss as "sacred duty, order, law.... A concept of complex significance in Indian culture, its basic meaning is 'that which sustains,' i.e., the moral order that sustains the individual, the society, and the cosmos" (157).

[26] As Halbfass observes, "the concept of *dharma* was asserted against the Christian missionaries, and their message was refuted or 'neutralized' within the greater context of Hindu *dharma*" (341).

their own law facilitates the imperial project. Hoerner, for instance, notes that "in signing on as jurist for the East India Company, [Jones] conscripts his poetic voice to a legal project rendered obsolete by historical limitations of the social and conceptual code that contracts him" and that "Jones set himself to a task made impossible, if not immoral, by his assumption that Hindu law and culture derived from timeless forms that authorized him to coerce the deviations of an immature culture" (216, 228).[27]

Indeed, Wilkins's translation provided validation for this cultural and political imperialism, as Rocher observes: the "British orientalists' infatuation with the ancient was legitimized by the fact that the indigenous scholarly tradition presented itself as derivative and commentarial" ("British Orientalism" 229). Not only does Hastings recognize the power of Wilkins's translation of the *Gita* to advocate "home administration for an orientalist form of government," Rocher notes, but Jones's 1794 translation of the *Manusmrti*, the "premier book on Hindu law" and the first to be translated, was a result of his meeting Wilkins in Banaras, when "Hastings had given him 'a taste' of the *Gita*" ("British Orientalism" 228–9).[28]

Linked to this legalistic manipulation is Wilkins's religious gloss of the *Gita*'s central notion of self-inquiry. As in Wilkins's rendering of *svadharmas*, or "own duty," as piety akin to the Christian system of virtue and vice, Wilkins divorces social duty from individual law, inextricably connected in the Sanskrit. By removing from the *Gita*'s central teaching of *dharma* the emphasis on individual law's relation to social and universal law, Wilkins's translation thus authorizes the Orientalists' interpretation of ancient notions of law, lending an aura of legitimacy to the British rule in India.

Vedic Nondualism and Judaeo-Christian Monotheism

The Orientalists' keenness to portray ancient India as monotheistic links epistemological, social, and political agendas. Though it is true, as Adisasmito-Smith notes, that "Hastings and Wilkins ... sought to draw together colonizer and colonized through religious assimilation ... to convince other Britishers that the *Gita*'s doctrines were already practically Christian," the Orientalist translation of nondualism as deistic monotheism points to a deeper level of ambivalence in their transmission of Sanskrit ("Self in Translation" 169).

In his letter to Smith introducing the *Gita*, for example, Hastings warns that its esoteric philosophy is premised on a practice of meditation unknown to the west: the "separation of the mind from the notices of the senses" (9). He adds that "even the most studious men of our hemisphere will find it difficult so to restrain their attention but that it will wander to some object of present sense or recollection" (9). Following this admiring observation, Hastings goes on to

---

[27] See also Makdisi, 107.

[28] As Niranjana notes, Wilkins had already begun translating Manu's *Dharmaśāstra* when Jones communicated his concern that the "interpretations of Hindu Law given by his pandits" be verified (16).

point to what he considers the *Gita*'s "blemish": "I mean, the attempt to describe spiritual existences by terms and image which appertain to corporeal forms" (10). He refers, one may assume, to Krishna's climactic revelation of his divinity in a spectacular visual display to Arjuna in chapter 11. Hastings criticizes the text for what is most fundamentally nonwestern: its nondualism, which becomes fully realized in the text when Krishna catalogues the phenomena that form his identity.

This episode, in which Krishna reveals the embodied form of God as the Self and then commands Arjuna to fight, is key to understanding Wilkins's need to manipulate this fundamental notion of nondualism in the text. In verse 37, in which Arjuna responds first to Krishna's vision of divinity and then to his command, Wilkins omits the reference to nondualism. A comparison to both Sargeant's and Edgerton's translations is illuminating: in both modern translations, Arjuna addresses Krishna as "[t]he imperishable, the existent, the nonexistent, and that which is beyond both [*tatparam yad*]" (Sargeant 489; Edgerton I, 115). Wilkins's version expunges the nondual nature of divinity: "Thou art the incorruptible Being, distinct from all things transient!" (94). Wilkins thus keeps the references that coincide with Christian notions of divinity, namely, purity and permanence, omitting the references to Krishna's nondual state.

Unlike Hastings's letter to Smith, describing the corporeal manifestation of the divine as a blemish, Wilkins treats the *Gita*'s nondualism as a system akin to Enlightenment deism, in which the Maker reveals himself through objects in nature. In his preface, Wilkins colors the reading of the subsequent text by attempting to explain the "unity of the Godhead" in the *Gita* in deistic terms: the "design was to bring about the downfall of Polytheism; or, at least, to induce men to believe *God* present in every image before which they bent, and the object of all their ceremonies and sacrifices" (24). If he cannot wholly eradicate the presence of graven images as he would like to for the acceptance of his English audience, he can at least show, misleadingly, that it is a single, omnipotent God akin to Jehovah that is being worshipped in each instance.

The tension between the nondualism of the Sanskrit and Wilkins's deistic translation is most apparent in chapter 13, which Wilkins entitles, "Explanation of the Terms *Kshetra* and *Kshetra-Gna*" [the Field-Knower and the Field] dealing with the relationship of the subject to the phenomenal world. The epistemological term, *anahamkāra*, which means the absence of "I," the egoless state of nondualism, is translated by Wilkins as "freedom from pride," thus giving the moralistic connotation to Krishna's epistemological lesson (102).[29]

A striking example of this conversion of the Sanskrit nondualism to deism is Wilkins's note to Krishna's statement in the same chapter. Krishna says, "I will now tell thee what is *Gnea*, or the object of wisdom.... It is that which hath no beginning, and is supreme, even *Brahm*, who can neither be called *Sat* (ens) nor *Asat* (non ens)" (103). Wilkins's note reads,

---

[29] By contrast to Wilkins, see the renderings of verse 5 by Sargeant (533) and Edgerton (127).

The opposite meanings of these two words render this passage peculiarly mysterious; and even the commentators differ about their true signification. The most rational interpretation of them is, that the Deity in his works is a substance, or a material Being, and in his essence immaterial; but as he is but one, he cannot positively be denominated either one or the other. (153n105)

Wilkins here struggles to convert nondualism to deism, separating the embodiment of deity from creation; Wilkins's Krishna goes on to describe the nondual experience in such deistic terms as "the reflected light of every faculty of the organs. Unattached, it containeth all things; and without quality it partaketh of every quality.... It is undivided, yet in all things it standeth divided" (103). The Sanskrit notion of *vikārān*, or "modification" (Sargeant 547; Edgerton I, 13), thus becomes "the various component parts of matter and their qualities" for Wilkins (104).

A cause for Wilkins's aversion to nondualism appears when he has Krishna say, "Learn that he by whom all things were formed is incorruptible" (36). However, the "he" is *tad*, translated as *that* by both Sargeant (102) and Edgerton (I, 17); Sargeant renders the Sanskrit as "that by which all this universe is pervaded is indeed indestructible" (102), rather than Wilkins's deistic phrase, "by whom all things were formed" (36). Wilkins's deism becomes yet more striking in his rendering as Krishna continues: "[I]t doth not behove thee to grieve about that which is inevitable. The former state of beings is *unknown*; the middle state is evident, and their future state is *not to be discovered*" (37, italics added). According to both Sargeant's and Edgerton's renderings of this line, however, the italicized words are "unmanifest (*avyakta*) and 'unmanifest again'" (Sargeant 113 and Edgerton I, 21,; verse 28). This case reveals the length to which Wilkins goes to make the Sanskrit fit the deistic belief that the past and future cannot be known; Wilkins is no doubt avoiding the suggestion of reincarnation, which underlies the Sanskrit description of the embodiment and disembodiment of consciousness.

When Wilkins is confronted directly with the term "duality," *dvandva* in Sanskrit, he often translates it as "duplicity," again tinging the epistemological concern of the original with moral judgment; *dvandva* does not signify vice but rather the illusion of polarities such as vice and virtue. In chapter 4, Wilkins translates Krishna's description of a *Pandeet* as one who "hath gotten the better of *duplicity*, and he is free from envy" (53, italics added). Sargeant's and Edgerton's translations of this passage render the term *dvandva* as "polarity of opposites" and "pairs (of opposites)", (Sargeant 222, Edgerton I, 47). Sargeant's translation reads, "Content with whatever comes to him, / Transcending the *dualities* (i.e. pleasure, pain, etc.), free from envy" (222).[30]

---

[30] In chapter 5, similarly, Wilkins's version reads, "Such a one is free from duplicity, and is happily freed from the bond of action" (57) whereas Sargeant renders the lines as one who "neither hates nor desires, / Who is indifferent to the pairs of opposites, O Arjuna. / He is easily liberated from bondage" (245). Wilkins comes closest to the Sanskrit notion of duality when he translates *dvandvair* ("dualities" in Sargeant) as "contrary causes, whose consequences bring both pleasure and pain" (112).

There appears little Wilkins can do to westernize the *Gita*'s most explicit and dramatic moment of nondualism, in which Krishna reveals his divinity in all phenomena in chapter 9. A comparison of modern translations to Wilkins's reveals that he stays close to the Sanskrit. Sargeant's version reads,

> I am the ritual, I am the sacrifice,
> I am the offering, I am the medicinal herb,
> I am the sacred text, I am also the clarified butter,
> I am the fire, and I am the pouring out (of the oblation).
> I am the father of the universe,
> The mother, the establisher, the grandfather,
> The object of knowledge, the purifier, the sacred syllable "Om,"
> ....
> I am the goal, the supporter, the great Lord, the witness,
> The abode, the refuge, the friend,
> The origin, the dissolution and the foundation,
> The treasure house and the imperishable seed
> ....
> And I am both immortality and death,
> Being and non-being, Arjuna. (392–5)

Wilkins's version reads,

> I am the sacrifice; I am the worship; I am the spices; I am the invocation; I am the ceremony to the manes of the ancestors; I am the provisions; I am the fire, and I am the victim: I am the father and the mother of this world, the grandsire, and the preserver. I am the holy one worthy to be known; the mystic figure *Om*...; I am the journey of the good; the comforter; the creator; the witness; the resting-place; the asylum, and the friend. I am generation and dissolution; the place where all things are reposited, and the inexhaustible seed of all nature .... I now draw in, and now let forth. I am death and immortality: I am entity and non-entity (80).[31]

This passage, the most balanced moment in Wilkins's translation, contrasts one of his most self-consciously Enlightenment distortions of the Sanskrit: his substitution of "reason" for Sanskrit terms denoting Self or Consciousness. In chapter 10, Wilkins not only translates *cetanā* as "reason" (85);[32] he also translates *ātman* (the absolute Self, as opposed to limited self) as "reason" in chapter 5 (59). In fact, he appears at a loss for distinguishing the two kinds of knowledge that the *Gita* describes in verse 16. It is clear in Sargeant's translation, for example, that Krishna's words reveal a movement beyond the mind limited by the discursive faculties:

---

[31] The *Gita*'s nondualism survived Wilkins's own deistic alterations, perhaps owing to his close translation of this defining passage for so many western writers. See Schwab on Emerson's poem, "Brahma," inspired by his reading of the *Bhagavad Gita* (201). See Kearns on Whitman's rendering in the "Sleepers" section of *Leaves of Grass* and on Eliot's rendering of the same passage in *The Wasteland* (170).

[32] *Consciousness* in Sargeant (432); *intellect* in Edgerton (101).

But for those in whom this ignorance of the Self
Is destroyed by knowledge,
That knowledge of theirs
Causes the Supreme to shine like the sun. (258)

Wilkins, by contrast, writes, "Mankind are led astray by their reasons being obscured by ignorance; but when that ignorance of their souls is destroyed by the force of reason, their wisdom shineth forth again with the glory of the sun, and causeth the Deity to appear" (59). He creates a contradiction by using "reason" to connote both the absolute and limited self.[33]

Wilkins's discomfort with and mistranslation of this fundamental principle of nondualism, illustrated by the repeated substitutions of western terms of dualism, underscores the materialist basis on which this late Enlightenment rendering rests. Such a foundation further allows Wilkins to construct a westernized *Gita* that can at once celebrate ancient India's philosophy while it vindicates British rule over an India that he portrays as having fallen from its monotheistic origin.

Rendering Action: From Karma and Liberation to Good Works, Sin, and Salvation

Eager to present to the world an ancient India not only more civilized than the India of their day, but an India whose culture and philosophy would rival that of ancient Greece and Rome, Wilkins attempts to make the text more palatable to his British readers; nowhere is this more obvious than in his avoidance and, at times, censorship of the *Gita*'s references to sacrifice, whether it is the implication of barbarity, idolatry, or both.[34] Though Wilkins's translation of the Sanskrit *yajna* as "worship" is in keeping with the definition given by Monier-Williams, which includes both worship and sacrifice (838), it is glossed by Sargeant as sacrifice, a key passage dealing with the subject of ritual acts which specifically refer to the gods eating what is offered.[35] Sargeant renders the words spoken by Prajapati through Krishna in verse 15, "The gods, nourished by the sacrifice, / Will indeed give you desired enjoyments" (169). Wilkins's use of "worship" for *yajna* here evades the ritual act: "With this remember the Gods, that the Gods may remember you. Remember one

---

[33] Another instance of Wilkins's difficulty with *atman* as the Absolute Self distinguished in the original from the limited self comes when he translates the Sanskrit *uddhared ātmanā 'tmānam*—rendered by Sargeant as "one should uplift oneself by the Self" (276)—as "He should raise himself by himself" (62).

[34] As the following examples of Wilkins's avoidance of the term suggest, Hindu sacrifice for Wilkins signifies the sacrifice of another, rather than the Christian ideal of self-sacrifice. See Dirks on the "barbarism and scandal" of Indian sacrifice reported by missionaries (173–5).

[35] Compare also Sargeant's translation of 17.12–13: "But sacrifice which is offered.... Sacrifice devoid of faith" (645–6) to Wilkins's rendering: "That worship which is directed by divine precept.... The worship which is performed with a view to the fruit" (120–21), in which the original reference is clearly to ritual acts of sacrifice.

another, and ye shall obtain supreme happiness. The Gods being remembered in worship, will grant you the enjoyment of your wishes" (45).[36] Wilkins's repeated evasion of the term through the euphemistic *worship* makes unambiguous his concern that his British readers would otherwise reject the *Gita* as barbaric.

Besides cases of avoiding direct reference to ritual acts of sacrifice, Wilkins also recasts references to sacrifice into the language of Protestantism. The problematic Sanskrit concept here is *karma*, which means "action." As Miller notes,

> *Karma* refers to the force of one's actions in determining what one is and will be, to one's role in making one's own destiny.... *Karma* is a store of good and bad actions accumulated over many lives, and it is this store of actions that binds one to phenomenal existence. Only when one acts without concern for the consequences, or fruits, of one's action can one escape the bondage of action. (156)

Wilkins's choice of "works" for *karma* connotes the Protestant ethic of virtuous acts that earn spiritual merit. In verse 12, for example, Krishna tells Arjuna, in Wilkins's translation, "That which is atchieved [*sic*] in this life, from *works*, speedily cometh to pass" (52, italics added). The word that Wilkins translates as "works" is *karmajā*, which Sargeant and Edgerton both translate as "ritual acts" (Sargeant 212; Edgerton 45).

A yet more striking example of Wilkins's weaving of the notion of salvation through good works into his rendering follows: "The ancients, who longed for eternal *salvation*, having discovered this, still performed works" (52–3, italics added). The Sanskrit word that Wilkins translates as "salvation" is *muc*, "liberation" or "release" (Sargeant 215).[37] The concept of salvation is derived from Christianity as opposed to the notion, central to the Vedas, of being released from cycles of *karma*.

At other times, Wilkins tinges *karma* with the Christian notion of sin. For example, in Sargeant's version of verse 17, Arjuna concludes,

> One must know the nature of action,
> The nature of wrong action,
> And also the nature of inaction.
> The way of action is *profound*. (217, italics added)

The term in question is *gahanā*, Sargeant's "profound" ("hard to penetrate" in Edgerton, 45). Wilkins's version, by contrast, reads, "It may be defined—action, improper action, and inaction. The path of action is full of *darkness*" (53). Wilkins thus colors a central tenet of the *Gita*, namely the yoga of action, with ambivalence for the Christian reader.

---

[36] It should be noted that Edgerton also translates *yajna* as "worship" in this instance (35) and that mentioned in note 35 above (Edgerton 157). Zaehner and van Buitenen, like Sargeant, choose "sacrifice" (Zaehner 263; van Buitenen 83).

[37] Edgerton, like Wilkins, gives "salvation" as the gloss here, suggesting that this modern translation is also colored by Christian doctrine (45). Zaehner, again closer to Sargeant and van Buitenen (87), chooses "release" (268).

Wilkins's difficulty with the Sanskrit concept of *karma* reappears in his rendition of Krishna expounding on the relationship between knowledge and action. Wilkins glosses Krishna's threefold impulse to action—*Gnān, Gnēyă,* and *Părĕĕgnātā*—with a note rendering them as "[w]isdom, the object of wisdom, and the superintending spirit" (Wilkins 126 & 155, n. 117).[38] The choice of "superintending spirit" for *Părĕĕgnātā,* or "knower," points to Wilkins's discomfort with human accountability, related to the divorcing of *dharma* from individual law discussed in section 2. Equally problematic for Wilkins is translating the Sanskrit term for the threefold impulse, *karmacodanā*. Monier-Williams defines it as "the motive impelling to ritual acts" and Sargeant glosses it as the "propulsion to action, inspiration to action" (679). Wilkins, on the other hand, glosses the term as "the direction of a work," distinguishing it, as the text does, from the Sanskrit *karmasamgrahas*, translated by Monier-Williams as "an assemblage of acts (comprising the act, its performance, and the performer)," whereas Wilkins translates it as "the accomplishment of a work." Wilkins thus evades the text's direct link between knowledge and action, introducing vague notions of a "superintending spirit" and an unspecified "direction" of a work at the moments in which the text urges human accountability for action, suggesting a deeper level of tension underlying Wilkins's project.

The source of this tension may be gleaned by returning to the *Gita*'s most explicit reference to *karmic* consequences (2.47). Krishna explains to Arjuna that he has a right or claim (*adhikāras*) only to his actions, not the fruits of his actions: "Your right is to action alone; / Never to its fruits at any time" (Sargeant 132). Wilkins renders this passage, "Let the motive be in the deed, and not in the event. Be not one whose motive for action is the hope of reward" (40). This is a significant distinction for one whose action is charged with ambivalence in its simultaneous complicity in British imperialism and eagerness to present to England an India of philosophical and moral greatness.

This connection between the *Gita*'s teaching about *karma* and Wilkins's self-consciousness as translator emerges in an apparently digressive footnote. Wilkins appends this note to Krishna's explanation of the difference between *sannyas* and *tyag*, the former referring to the relinquishing of the fruits of action, the latter to relinquishing action itself (124). In his note, Wilkins claims that the distinction needs no explanation but that he wishes to include the commentary of *Sree-dhar Swamee*. His reason for doing so, however, is not because of the authority of the Indian commentator, but rather because Wilkins finds it noteworthy that

> the commentators of India are not less fond of searching for mystery, and wandering from the simple path of their author into a labyrinth of scholastic jargon, than some of those of more enlightened nations, who for ages have been labouring to entangle the plain unerring clew of our holy religion. (154n114)

Wilkins's note suggests his own need as translator and commentator to reduce the troubling nuances, both within the Sanskrit and between Sanskrit and English, to

---

[38] Besides Monier-Williams's definition of *karma*, see Sargeant's rendering of the phrase (679).

"scholastic jargon" as a means of establishing a uniformity that westernizes the Sanskrit—comparing the "simple path" of Sanskrit authors to "our holy religion," which is "entangled" rather than elucidated by its commentators.

Beyond being a disclaimer for mistranslation, this gesture overrides the imputation of guilt among the British in India regarding its abuses of power, both political and cultural. It is especially significant that Wilkins chooses this moment in the *Gita* to dismiss as "scholastic jargon" the nuances of translation that derive from the inextricable ties of linguistics, politics, and epistemology. Here, he is in the midst of his evasive translation of the passage on *karma* and the renunciation of the fruits of action. The context of such an aside suggests Wilkins's application of the law of *karma* to Orientalism's "labor." By rendering "action" into good works and sin, Wilkins not only abdicates the fruit of his Orientalist labor; he is also free of accountability for the wrongs in which he participates through British rule in India, namely, fulfilling Arjuna's prophecy of the doom of Indian society.

With his rendering of the *Gita*, Wilkins transmits the doubleness of his view as translator, an intersubjectivity keenly aware of both the horror wrought by the British from the Indian perspective and the British self-fashioning as an agent of change, for India as well as Britain. In this historical moment of shifting relations between Britain and India, Wilkins's evasions, disclaimers, and the "entanglements" with which his renderings manipulate the *Gita* expose a dense layering of British anxieties. Revealed is the desire for clear divisions in class structure and race, at odds with the revolutionary energy that seeks to break down those barriers. The same dual impulse at once lays claim to an Enlightenment materialism that draws rigid lines between subject and object but thrills at the rupture of this fundamental western belief.

As the subsequent chapters seek to show, by studying the disparity between dualism and nondualism in writings of the Orientalists and of British women authors writing about Anglo-India, a dissonance within the work of the Orientalists becomes apparent that goes beyond the ambivalence that postcolonialist approaches have described; the focus on women writers engaged with the publications of their contemporary male Orientalists thus becomes a means of illuminating that fundamental, epistemological crisis. This book thus addresses the ways a range of British women writers bring to their experience of India a conflicted relationship with what Mellor has described as "the ideologically dominant construction of subjectivity," represented as a "masculine Romantic self" in contrast to the "fluid" self of the feminine (*Romanticism and Gender* 168). The gendered subjectivities of women writers to Orientalist "narratives of anxiety" prove fertile ground for rethinking the scholarly premise of a binary of male and female writing (Suleri 3). The connection between gender and subjectivity in women's texts complicates their range of responses to Indian philosophy, from directly empathetic portrayals of eastern nondualism to paradoxically deistic perspectives on India. Regardless of how readily they embrace Indian nondualism, however, even the most ambivalent among these women discover in it an alternative to the western philosophical tradition.

Chapter 2
"Out of that narrow and contracted path": Creativity and Authority in Elizabeth Hamilton's *Translations of the Letters of a Hindoo Rajah*

Elizabeth Hamilton's familial connection to Orientalism through her brother Charles has been cause for readers to project onto her text an homage to him and to the Asiatic Society as a whole, beginning with her Dedication to Warren Hastings.[1] This chapter complicates that assumption by focusing on the problem of subjectivity in the novel. In her 1796 dedication to the recently acquitted Warren Hastings, Hamilton uses the appositive "Late Governor General of Bengal" and "Patron" of Orientalism—late, not because he was dead, but because he was impeached. Following the dedication, Hamilton's "Preliminary Dissertation" announces the "extensive plan" carried out "under the direction of the great Governor of the Universe."[2] By connecting Hastings to God through the title of Governor and Patron, not only does Hamilton pay tribute to the maligned Hastings but, proceeding from the actual—Hastings as late governor—to the metaphorical—the deistic God as universal governor—Hamilton suggests that, just as the God of deism unfolds his design from outside His creation, so too will Hastings continue his Orientalist design in spite of his removal from India, "long after the discordant voice of Party shall have been humbled in the silence of eternal rest" (71). Hamilton underscores Hastings's connection to God through the immortal status of his work by contrast to the mortality of his detractors, thus offering consolation for the elegiac tone of "late" Governor.[3]

Hamilton's conceit of governance in absentia does not end with this likening of Hastings to God, however: to show how Hastings's design will continue unfolding, she describes an emerging second wave of Orientalists and in so doing,

---

[1] Charles Hamilton died of tuberculosis in 1792. See Perkins and Russell regarding his encouragement of Elizabeth's Orientalist study (9–11).

[2] Elizabeth Hamilton. *Translations of the Letters of a Hindoo Rajah*. Ed. Pamela Perkins and Shannon Russell. Orchard Park, New York: Broadview Press, 1999. 55. All further references to the novel are in the text. Warren Hastings, impeached in 1787, was on trial from 1788 till his acquittal in 1795, charged with misrule of the East India Company.

[3] See Perkins and Russell on Hamilton's mockery of Burke's attack on Hastings regarding the Rohilla war and her use of Zaarmilla to portray Hastings's "altruistic intervention ... as a deliberate rebuttal of Burke" (26–8). For discussion of Hastings's trial and relationship to Burke, see Chapter 1.

subtly introduces her own project. Through their fiction and poetry, British writers were already building on the foundation laid by those original, ultimately "late" Orientalists—Hastings by impeachment and, more personally, Charles, an East India Company servant as well as Orientalist, through literal death.

Behind her self-deprecating offer of her own novel as evidence that the Orientalist project was alive and well, Hamilton implies a shift from the masculine to a feminine paradigm of creativity. For Hamilton, female authorship is a form of transgression that "may be censured … as a presumptuous effort to wander out of that narrow and contracted path, which they have allotted to the female mind" (72). Hamilton's image of the female author stepping outside prescribed bounds is an ironic variation on her description of God's and Hastings's governance: while God wilfully steps outside his design to govern, and Hastings, forced out, governs through the continued transmission of Sanskrit texts, Hamilton can only author texts when she frees herself from the confinement of the feminine sphere.[4]

The fecundity of female authorship, Hamilton ventures, may generate yet a third wave of Orientalism: "Should my feeble effort lead to further enquiry; should it in the mind of any person of taste give birth to a laudable curiosity, upon a subject where so much is to be learned, my design will be still more fully answered" (56).[5] Here, she echoes the "design" of the Creator and Hastings with her own design, but rather than the patronage of the latter two, her maternal creativity can "give birth"—not to a work in itself, but to a "laudable curiosity"; the phrase underscores the paradox of creativity as a perpetual process of discovering that which already exists rather than siring a lineage of achievements or acquisitions.

The subversiveness of Hamilton's "governing" her novel in absentia lies in its challenge to the assumed purpose of transmitting knowledge. Hamilton observes that she was taught to "view every new idea as an acquisition, and to seize … every proper opportunity for making the acquirement" (72–3). She connects this acquisitiveness of British education to its acquiring "dominions in India," through the "acquired" taste of Orientalist literature (73). Yet the death of Charles, having cut short the possibility that "a competent knowledge of the originals would likewise have been acquired," suggests that the tragic loss renders sterile the masculinist paradigm of acquisitiveness (73).

Implicit in Hamilton's redefinition of "design" is thus a redefinition of education itself: not merely an accumulation of knowledge, education rather requires stepping outside one's own epistemological assumptions. While scholarship on the novel

---

[4] I am extending to women writers more generally Armstrong's argument about poets of sensibility: "They did not take [male] philosophical traditions—the only traditions they had—as an inert model but reconstructed them through critique. This was a way of thinking through their relationship to knowledge" (16).

[5] A striking pattern in Hamilton's syntax is that she tends to use the active voice when she engages with the philosophical paradigm of Vedic nondualism, whereas she tends to use the passive voice, as in this instance, in her roles as both fictional translator and authorial voice objectified through publication.

has often labelled Hamilton anti-feminist, recent studies have challenged the claim by emphasizing Hamilton's influence by Wollstonecraft's 1792 *Vindication of the Rights of Woman* regarding her disdain of contemporary female education as "learning how to entice a man into marriage" (Mellor, "Romantic Orientalism" 156).[6] Unlike Wollstonecraft's polemical prose, however, Hamilton's novel focuses on the education of women writers and, in even more of a departure from Wollstonecraft, the education of men regarding the education of women writers.

Hamilton's choice of genre in conveying the authorial principle of governing in absentia is an important element in her subversion of Orientalism. As an epistolary novel with only male correspondents who mediate Hamilton's voice, *Translations* descends from the "specialized genre" of the Oriental footnote novel through Montesquieu's 1721 *Persian Letters* (Perkins and Russell 22). Though eighteenth-century satire is associated with canonical male writers, Raymond MacKenzie notes that Montesquieu's Oriental footnote novel had a female lineage, including French women novelists such as Madame de Graffigny, whose 1747 *Peruvian Letters* shares Hamilton's trope of governing in absentia.[7] Taking this larger perspective of Hamilton's lineage of European satire helps complicate Hamilton's relationship to British writers on the rights of woman: unlike the polemical prose of Wollstonecraft, Hays, and others arguing for women's equality in education, Hamilton's novel destabilizes any single male perspective of women and, by extension, decentralizes any single masculinist paradigm of female creativity.

Hamilton's ambivalent relationship to India is thus interwoven with her conflicted role as a professional woman writer; the novel's epistolary form, using letters by male correspondents written from radically different points of view, allows

---

[6] Kelly sees no irony in Hamilton's self-abnegation, writing that "she accepts the gendered hierarchy of discourse by referring to her own work as a 'trifle'" (132). Qualifying the Wollstonecraft connection, Perkins and Russell differentiate the "radical Wollstonecraft [who] frames the question in terms of future improvement of society" to the "conservative Hamilton" for whom it "will return society to a happier past" (17). Most recently, Tara Wallace has challenged the "neat dichotomy of Hamilton the apologist *versus* Hamilton the critic of empire," concluding that "Hamilton's mixed feelings about the British Empire may turn out to originate in her depreciation of ignorance rather than colonialism" (134, 141). I extend Wallace's challenge to the facile and often anachronistic liberal/conservative binary to explore Hamilton's radicalism that idiosyncratically subverts both her immediate and ancient precursors.

[7] MacKenzie's observation thus goes a step beyond Perkins and Russell's important qualification of Hamilton's relationship to the genre since her "historically specific India" does not "simply update Montesquieu" (22). In the introduction to her 2011 edition of the 1747 English translation of Graffigny's *Peruvian Letters*, Kaplan notes that "the novel raises questions about the woman as exotic Other, the roles of women, marriage and language, society's expectations and perceptions of women" although Roberts's English translation "takes liberties" that eliminate "part of Graffigny's feminist context" and contain "more religious overtones than the original," by way of "adjustments to the English readership"(xiii, xv).

her to represent a spectrum of ambivalences—eastern, western, male, and female.[8] The paradox of Hamilton's mediating her voice through the male correspondents is compounded through the novel's range of female characters, a doubly embedded composite of a dialectically splintered persona: at the bathetic end of the spectrum are the hysterical Miss Julia and the Caprice Ardent mother and daughter—the former despising the latter's feminism—while the more nuanced, sympathetic characters occupy a range in themselves, including Lady Grey, the Wollstonecraftian companion to her husband and "partner of his studies," and Emma Denbeigh, whose wedding at the end of the novel provides a satirical twist to the sentimental novel's traditional culmination with the heroine's marriage (279). Occupying the farthest pole from such caricatures as the Ardent women is the poet Charlotte Percy, who belatedly utters the novel's dismal sentiment about women's voicelessness in public life: "[Y]ou know how female writers are looked down upon. The women fear, and hate; the men ridicule, and dislike them," a claim that eclipses any potential sentimentality associated with Emma Denbeigh's wedding (303).

Governing her novel in absentia through these two levels of mediation—the three male correspondents as the novel's only direct voices and the women known only indirectly through the letters of these men—Hamilton employs a third device: a vestigial narrator as translator and editor who is literally marginalized to footnotes. This translator's relationship to Orientalism ultimately provides the alternative paradigm through which Hamilton engages with her characters, challenging masculinist authority beyond the effectiveness of any of the positions taken by even the most nuanced of her female characters.

Hamilton multiplies the possibilities for vindicating women's intelligence, creativity, and authority as the male attitudes—east and west—towards women accumulate in the novel. The opening letter of the Rajah, Zaarmilla, is a concentration of multicultural misogyny produced by Zaarmilla's assimilation of Percy's lesson in British education of women. Zaarmilla no sooner makes one claim than he challenges it with another as Percy provides new insights. In a single paragraph, Zaarmilla appears first to perpetuate the stereotype that "the inferiority of women appears so established by the laws of nature" (87). His claim becomes yet more ludicrous when he contrasts what Hamilton, along with her contemporaries, erroneously assumed was a Moslem belief—that women did not have souls—to what he claims to be the more liberal notion that a Hindu woman "who burns herself with her husband" by performing *sati* "shall live with him in Paradise" (87). Yet no sooner does he utter this claim than he questions its absolutism, citing the Pundits who say that "her admission into Paradise ...

---

[8] Hamilton attacks British society by thrusting in the face of her readers their hypocrisy at their condemnation of the Indian caste system, showing how rigid the class hierarchy is through the Indian Pandit's criticism of the Rajah's idealization of British culture and society: "Instead of being all of one Cast, as he imagines, the people are divided into three Casts, all separate, and distinct from each other, and which are commonly known by the several appellations of PEOPLE OF FAMILY, PEOPLE OF NO FAMILY, AND PEOPLE OF STYLE" (122).

depends on her husband's title to an entrance into that state of felicity. Uncertain tenor!" (88). With this final exclamation, Zaarmilla, apparently a quick study, proves to have assimilated Percy's lesson in Christian compassion.

Through this dense fabric of belief systems, Zaarmilla generates the vision of a utopia in which the mythical female of ancient Hinduism morphs into the contemporary "Christian woman" who in turn emerges from her enlightened education as "mother of Krishna" (88). In a satirical denunciation of *sati*, Hamilton has Zaarmilla reason that Christian women are "more fortunate" than Hindu women, for "they may enjoy Heaven without the company of their husbands!" (88). Zaarmilla ultimately envisions an Enlightenment, proto-feminist heaven: neither Hindu nor Christian, it consists of universities as "seats of science," where women emerge with "the torch of reason enlightening their minds" (88). In just two paragraphs, Hamilton demonstrates the potential for a pedagogy in which knowledge is not acquired as much as it is discovered through a process of transmutation. Zaarmilla thus evolves from misogynist to advocate of woman's enlightened education, not by means of the masculinist paradigm of education and "design," but by tracing the lineage of an enlightened matriarchy from ancient Hinduism to eighteenth-century British women.

Hamilton thus embeds her authorial voice by embedding Percy's attempt to educate Zaarmilla in Zaarmilla's own attempt to educate Maandaara, whom Zaarmilla assures that the Wollstonecraftian wife, "friend of her husband," is no cause for dismay (88). Yet Hamilton's own design emerges when Zaarmilla offers for support not the example of the Wollstonecraftian Lady Grey but rather that of Percy's sister, Charlotte, whom Percy introduces as a disembodied, textual voice. Her brief Dedication in Percy's Bible, the "parting gift … to the most beloved of brothers" (89), echoes both Hamilton's Dedication to the "late" Hastings and her subsequent allusion to Charles's death as the "fatal event [that] transformed the cheerful haunt of domestic happiness into the gloomy abode of sorrow" (73).[9] Motivated by Zaarmilla's charge of impropriety that Charlotte Percy not only can "touch the Shaster" but has been "taught to write," Percy explains that Zaarmilla has only known women in "the degrading state of subjection," and so offers to "translate" some of his sister's letters to illustrate the benefit of female education (89).

As he renders Charlotte's letters for Zaarmilla, Percy conflates the explication of poetry with translation from one language to another. The meta-textual dimension that Charlotte's poetry adds to the novel thus underscores a deeper layer to Hamilton's exploring the mediated authorial voice, as may be suggested by a slight emendation to the title: "Translations of the [Women's Writing in the] Letters of a Hindu Rajah." Just as translating the Sanskrit texts holds a key to knowledge for the Orientalists, and just as translating Zaarmilla's letters holds a key to the relationship between east and west for the novel's fictional translator, so too does

---

[9] See both Kelly's and Taylor's commentary in the tradition of reading Charlotte as a persona for Hamilton.

Zaarmilla believe that Percy's "translation" of Charlotte's poetry and Zaarmilla's subsequent rendering of her letters for Maandaara help men understand women. As Zaarmilla marvels, the "sister of Percy has not only learned to read, and write, but is in considerable degree capable of thinking" (90). Hamilton satirizes Zaarmilla's awe of Charlotte as an exemplary female author: for Zaarmilla, Charlotte has not merely been trained passively to acquire knowledge, but rather she "thinks," a claim Zaarmilla no sooner makes than qualifies with the patronizing phrase "in considerable degree" (90).

As translated by Zaarmilla, by extension, Percy's "translation" of Charlotte's poem underscores Hamilton's message that thinking does not equal creating, for the poem itself evades the Wollstonecraftian claim that the goal of woman's education is to cultivate women's reason and eschew sensibility as a means to make them better companions to their husbands and caretakers of their children. By positioning as exemplary the sister-as-writer instead of one of the marriageable or married women that follow in the novel, Hamilton not only eschews the marriage plot of the sentimental novel, but dismantles the gendered binary of reason and sensibility: spurning "Art" as mere "mimic power" in contrast to feminized nature's "conscious power," Hamilton sets Charlotte's verse squarely and unapologetically in the nascent tradition of sensibility and reflection (91).[10]

By including the full poem, Hamilton offers the reader the opportunity to interpret Charlotte's text unhindered, thereby deflecting Percy's literal "translation," a superficial biography that equates the poem's personifications with the orphaned Charlotte's "duty to an aged uncle" who had adopted her. The poem's narrator interprets, or translates, the "sweet voice" of the female Contentment, whom Charlotte sees in nature's "fair bosom" (90). The effect of the slippage from this maternal embodiment of nature—whose "lov'd retreat" the narrator asks if it is possible to leave (91)—to Charlotte's addressing her dead uncle as "my guardian and my friend"—of whom she asks, "Can I forget what to thy love I ow'd"—is to replace the contentment of her "conscious power" with this "more than father" whose "sainted spirit hovers near ... to lead me to the social fire" (90). This odd echo of *sati* adds an ironic twist to the "more than father," for the "social fire" suggests that the west insidiously duplicates Hindu society's immolation of widows.[11] The last words of the poem, "My comfort, and my peace, expire with thee," subvert not only Charlotte's ostensible show of filial piety, but Zaarmilla's own claim that Christian women are better off than Hindu women (92). For Charlotte, society dictates that a woman's life ends with that of the man to whom she is bound, a contradiction to Zaarmilla's excited claim of

---

[10] Until the pioneering studies of Curran, Mellor, and others in the 1980s, scholarship's label of "Romantic" for the genre characterized as descriptive and meditative was implicitly gendered masculine, as the introduction to this book has discussed. Hamilton's voice is thus important in this ongoing effort to redefine and complicate the literary movement of the late eighteenth century as not only inclusive of women writers, but as multifaceted. For more on the sentimental novel and the "cult of sensibility," see Chapter 3.

[11] See the introduction of this book for discussion of *sati*.

eighteenth-century woman's matrilineal inheritance of the power and wisdom of the "mother of Krishna."[12]

Proceeding through layers of translation to the thwarting of female "conscious power," Hamilton's governance of the novel obliquely surfaces when Zaarmilla refers to himself in the third person immediately after Charlotte's poem: "[T]hus far did Zaarmilla write to his friend Maandaara" (93). With this momentary lapse in Zaarmilla's narration, Hamilton gives the reader a meta-textual nudge, challenging any tendency to grant authority to claims derived from masculinist interpretation of the female.

Hamilton blends her nuanced message of thwarted female creativity with the novel's more blatant satire by including Maandaara and Zaarmilla's exchange of sisters through marriage as foil to the (unmarried) brother-sister relationship of Charlotte and Percy. Zaarmilla wishes to leave "in the possession of" Maandaara his own sister, Zamarcanda, who is not only endowed with "ground-kissing eyes" but who has the "blood of a thousand Rajahs [flowing] through her veins" (99–100). As though he were a merchant selling his wares to a potential buyer, Zaarmilla declares Zamarcanda's two-fold value: her filial piety, which will extend to her husband, and her promise to carry on the lineage of Rajahs. A yet more explicit tool than Zaarmilla for Hamilton's satire of both Hindus and British, Maandaara condemns English Christians as "so absurd as to teach learning to their women," thus providing a new link in the chain of men attempting to educate other men regarding women's enlightened education (105). Curious as to the subject of a group of officers' "mirth," Maandaara is told by an interpreter that it was "the dishonor of one of their own countrymen, a Chief of rank and eminence, whose wife had suffered the torch of her virtue to be extinguished, by the vile breath of a seducer," the torch an ironic echo of Zaarmilla's earlier praise of learned Englishwomen for whom "the torch of reason" enlightens their minds (88). Having just witnessed a soldier nearly beaten to death for stealing a few rupees from his officer, Maandaara is incredulous that the dishonored man is given money as restitution for "the degradation of his family," (103–4). Because Percy's education of Zaarmilla regarding enlightened woman reduces her art to female filial piety, Zaarmilla's attempt to educate Maandaara about Percy's views is pointless, each uneducable since the paradigm of male authority is set so firmly in an epistemology common to men of both east and west.

Hamilton's authorial strategy of governance in absentia is thus most evident when she problematizes such moments with multiple points of view—especially that of an "interpreter" whose function is to underscore just how slippery translation is. Agreeing to the Rajah's marriage proposal, Maandaara recounts his dissatisfaction and consequential return of his "ill-favoured" and peevish wife to her father, praising Zaarmilla's sister, Zamarcanda, for being "beautiful, and good

---

[12] This reading of Hamilton's densely layered initial presentation of Charlotte's voice, including the *sati* allusion, differs significantly from Mellor's use of the poem's "psychological self-immolation" to support her claim that Hamilton distances herself from Charlotte (159).

tempered" (105). Hamilton here brings the topic of women's filial piety full circle back to the Orientalists, having Maandaara cite from "Halhed's Translation of Gentoo Laws"; Hamilton's footnote reference underscores the embeddedness of women's miseducation in the process of translation: "[A] man both day and night must keep his wife so much in subjection, that she by no means be mistress of her own actions" (106n2).

By the end of Maandaara's letter, then, each man has a virtuous sister to extol: Maandaara proposes for Zaarmilla's wife his own sister who had "been taught humility and obedience, and has never conversed with any man, except her father and her brother" (106). Zaarmilla's subsequent letter that his wife, Maandaara's sister, has died summarizes his Wollstonecraftian marriage to a woman "who was the companion of my days, the friend of my heart" (145–6), giving Zaarmilla the opportunity to speculate on *sati* from the widower's perspective: "The woman, who is attached to her husband, will follow the spirit of her departed Lord, even though condemned to the regions of punishment; and shall my soul forget her, who waiteth for me in the realms of death?" (145). Hamilton ventures beyond Wollstonecraft's polemic by including moments—however fleeting—of the potential for male empathy, as Zaarmilla's poignantly rhetorical question suggests: in a marriage thus equalized, should not a widower want to sacrifice himself as his widow would have?

The detached authority of Hamilton as translator and editor provides a crucial counterpoint to Maandaara's authority for Hindu values, the Bramin, Sheermaal. Horrified at Zaarmilla's influence by western depravity and sensing the futility of his own attempts, Maandaara has Sheermal write directly to Zaarmilla in an effort to set him straight. Hamilton multiplies her footnotes as the accumulation of skewed male perspectives on women's education reaches this highest claim to eastern authority. As translator, Hamilton satirizes Sheermal obliquely: for instance, unable to track down Sheermal's reference to the Pundit to whom he owes his own education, Hamilton coyly suggesting that Sheermal's meaning "is rather obscure" yet "sufficiently obvious to establish his character as a *systematic traveler*"; "systematic" is an odd modifier for "traveler" that underscores the earlier footnote's deflating comment about Sheermal's Pundit, whose "fame ... has not reached so far as to acquaint [the translator] with his name" (108n1 and 4).

Not merely aimed at Sheermaal's obscure justification for his strongly held judgments against the "Christians of England," however, Hamilton's satire is aimed as well at the British traditions that he attacks. Having railed against Christian hypocrisy, from slavery to England's own caste system, Sheermaal saves his most vitriolic attack for Zaarmilla's praise of "the education and manners of the females of England" (127). Especially in his discussion of art education, it becomes clear that, underlying his condemnation of women's education in England, Sheermal becomes an unwitting mouthpiece for a stance more radical than Wollstonecraft's claim that education will make women better mothers and companions for their husbands.[13] It is not women's ability that Sheermaal denigrates, but rather the

---

[13] See Wollstonecraft's dedication to Talleyrand-Perigord which explains that, if a woman "be not prepared by education to become the companion of man, she will stop the progress of knowledge and virtue" (6).

"wretched imitations of trees and flowers" that suggests "great care was taken, to avoid the possibility of the female pupils ever arriving at any degree of perfection in her art" (128). He offers similar criticism of women's language learning, which he had assumed was a means of preparing them as diplomats to neighboring nations with whom England was at war, instead finding that "few are capable of reading, and still fewer of conversing, with any degree of fluency in his tongue" and the only possible purpose was to enable them "to understand the peculiar terms belonging to the articles of dress imported from that country" (128).

Following this ironic twist on the Wollstonecraftian indictment of women's education in England, Hamilton intensifies her satirical use of Sheermaal as a foil:

> So far all is right. We behold women moving in their proper sphere, learning no other art, save that of adorning their persons; and inspired with no other view, but that of rendering themselves objects of pleasure to the eyes of men. But how shall I astonish you, when I unfold the extreme inconsistency of the foolish Europeans, and inform you, that these uninstructed women are frequently suffered to become intirely [*sic*] their own mistresses; sometimes entrusted with the management of large estates, and left at liberty to act for themselves! (129)

Through Sheermal's stunning misogyny, Hamilton makes sure the reader cannot assume he is more enlightened than those British men he critiques.

Sheermaal's perspective reaches its nadir of illegitimacy when he praises the Hindu tradition of *sati*, through which "creatures, incapable of acting with propriety for themselves, are effectually put out of the way of mischief, by being burned with the bodies of their husbands" (129). Through Sheermaal, Hamilton has thus proceeded from disdain towards British hypocrisy to criticism of its education of women itself to a claim for "women moving in their proper sphere" (129). By the point at which Sheermal advocates *sati*, Hamilton's satire of the logic behind British male authority reaches its most absurd level for, with *sati*, "the number of old women is so effectually diminished!" (129). By ending the early correspondence with Zaarmilla discrediting the "lie-loving" Bramin's authority as founded on "base prejudices," Hamilton begins to construct an alternative paradigm for gender relations to that of the authoritarian British from the unlikely mouthpiece of a Bramin (140–41).

As it appears in her footnotes, Hamilton's editorial persona is most critical when she uses it to counterpoint Zaarmilla's reflections on Hastings's "benignant charity" with "the tale of horrors" that Burke contrived in his prosecution of Hastings (157n1). Hamilton's agenda of exonerating Hastings becomes more overt through Zaarmilla's encounter, at the end of volume 1, with Chait Sing, the Rajah of Benares. Hamilton's footnotes here elaborate her defense of Hastings, accused of mistreating Sing.[14] She points out that his father, Bulwart Sing, was "the son of Monserans, a Bramin, who had been appointed *steward* to Rushem Ally, then *governor* of the province of Banares [*sic*]; he supplanted his master,

---

[14] See Perkins and Russell's own footnote regarding the argument of Hastings's supporters that Chait Sing "had at best a problematic title in the first place" (153n2).

and obtained the province for himself: and this was the origin of a man, called, by some in this country, a sovereign Prince!" (153n2; italics in original). Zaarmilla then naively marvels at what he considers the gullibility of Sing to believe what Zaarmilla claims to be hearsay on the part of the people of Benares, namely, their ability to make Chait Sing "believe that the present Governor General is not without enemies, even in the Supreme Council!" As his letter continues, however, Zaarmilla gradually suggests not that the "English disunion" is merely talk (154n1), but that Hastings did have enemies in the Supreme Council who would "prefer the ruin of a rival, to the glory, and preservation of an empire!" (154).

By shifting the focus from the events themselves to the interpretation of the events—the "tale of horrors" rather than the horrors themselves—Hamilton deepens her subtextual revisionist history (157n1). This conflicted perspective of British disloyalty towards Hastings is followed by Zaarmilla's growing awareness of the decline of Enlightenment science and values. He meets two English friends, eminent in the "divine science" of astronomy and "whose chief motive for visiting Benares ... was to inspect and examine the astronomical apparatus still extant in the Tower of the Stars" (154). Hamilton here complicates the Preliminary Dissertation's laudatory connection between Hastings, maligned governor, and the God of deism, whose governance of the universe can only be known through scientific exploration of nature, "that book of wisdom, where the Supreme hath written his attributes in the most legible characters; even in the golden orbs, whose distant glories delight the eye of ignorance"; she now extends the contrast between the "ingenuity of our ancestors" in constructing the "stupendous engines" and the "degeneracy of their children!" (154). Because Hastings cannot be appreciated "in the current state of degeneracy," he must remove himself from India in order to make "most legible" the Supreme's "characters" through his Orientalist mission, a paradoxical teleology in which revival of ancient knowledge will be the only means to rescue humanity from ignorance (154–5).

Hamilton's indictment of the distorted reactions to Hastings reaches its most ascerbic when she ridicules William Belsham's censure of English misconduct in his 1795 *Memoirs of the Reign of George III to the session of Parliament ending A.D. 1793*. Hamilton satirizes Belsham's idealizing of the "happy times of the Mogul Government" with its "peacocks in abundance," replacing it with her competing vision of how the "English chiefs sustained the lives of thousands" (157). She even challenges Belsham's supporting quotation from Persius, who asks God to punish a tyrant, with one from Pope: "Let not the weak unknowing hand, / Presume thy bolts to throw" (159n1). Having decried the willful distortions of Hastings's governance that Burke perpetrated in his prosecution, Hamilton shows the perils of distortion to be inherent in the very nature of translation.

In an ostensibly comical episode following Zaarmilla's defense of Hastings, Zaarmilla finds himself among a group that includes the fluent Orientalist, Captain Grey. This episode is sandwiched between, first, a description of two British companions—"young Cooper" and a "little fat man" who disgusts his fellow travelers by making "the study of his own ease the principal object of his concern" (160)—and after they leave the village, their discovery of the "poor fat gentleman straining his unwieldy limbs to grasp the trunk of a large tree," the object of Cooper's ridicule who, sitting on a bough above, urges him up to flee a tiger of Cooper's invention (161). The episode occurs on a visit to the Chief of a village, during which they ask where they can get milk. In a footnote, Hamilton's editor-persona translates the response of "Archa Sahib, tomorrow Mulluk,": "Is not this your country—command in it what you please!" (160n2). Grey laughs "very heartily" at the officer for "suffering the casual resemblance between the sound of an English and Bengal word to lead him into such a mistake" (161). The misunderstanding of "milk" as the Indian term for "commander" not only betrays the Chief's intended performance of his "duties of hospitality" as a thin veneer of diplomacy barely concealing his hostility; it also reinforces the novel's counterpoint between masculine and feminine forms of authority, the former suggested by the aggression of "commander," the latter by the nurturing "milk."

Hamilton underscores the novel's pattern of wishfulness that distorts translation in an episode in which Zaarmilla mistakes the British social cues involved in cursing. Shocked at the Christian propensity for cursing, in which "the name of their Almighty Creator" is introduced "upon the most trifling occasions," Zaarmilla worries that, as in this case, his "conclusions, which are formed with precipitance, are almost always retracted with shame" (162). Desiring to reconcile the ease and frequency with which these Christians utter their God's name with the fact that neither Hindi nor Moslem would do so, Zaarmilla decides to admire rather than condemn a group of soldiers cursing a general "who had introduced certain regulations ... by which these gentlemen considered themselves aggrieved"; Zaarmilla's desire to find commonality between the British and what he finds most virtuous about his own culture leads him to a wilful correction of their curses to blessings that, "had the animadversions of these young men been reported to [the general], he would have had the charity to pray for them with similar fervency!" (163).

By this stage in Hamilton's developing satire of the British through the mouthpiece of Zaarmilla, the deeper meta-textual significance of his anxiety about distorting what he wishes to be a "faithful copy of the first impression made upon [his] mind" might easily be lost to the more obvious irony of Zaarmilla's naiveté. Yet Hamilton follows Zaarmilla's bathetic reflection on Christian cursing with his awe at meeting Hastings, expressed through his misquotation from Wilkins's translation of Hetopades's Sanskrit definition of a great man. Specifically, he focuses Hetopades's requirement that the great man "should be resolute, but not rash"; Perkins and Russell note that Wilkins translates the phrase as "resolute but not harsh" (163n1). Although it is tempting to dismiss the difference as an error, when Hamilton's alteration of Wilkins's translation of Hetopades, from "harsh" to rash," is viewed in the context of Zaarmilla's preceding consternation at the consequences of leaping to conclusions, it reveals both a greater logic and a greater irony: it exemplifies Hamilton's pattern of authority in absentia with the deeper implication of that authority's tampering with text that has already been tampered with.

Hamilton ends the first volume with Zaarmilla's description of his ambivalence, his "desires [having] been at variance with each other" regarding his upcoming "European voyage" (180). He reassures Maandaara, who apparently fears "loss of Cast" as "so formidable" that, the reader surmises, he has attempted to dissuade Zaarmilla from stepping outside the strictures of Hinduism. Hamilton has Zaarmilla quote Krishna, from Wilkins's translation of the *Bhagavad Gita*: "[H]e is my servant, he is dear to me, who is free from enmity; merciful; and exempt from pride, and selfishness: who is the same in pain, and in pleasure" (181). He expresses his concern in a rhetorical question: "Can this being, whose animating spirit is spread abroad over the whole universe! Can he behold with displeasure, the attempt of any of his creatures, to explore the varied forms of being which partake of his essence?" (181). The question is indeed a question, lying at the heart of Hamilton's ambivalence as it does for the Orientalists themselves.[15]

In Zaarmilla's voyage from India to England that opens volume 2, Zaarmilla's shift in perspective as he directs his gaze west signals Hamilton's shift in authorial perspective that conflates eastern and western traditions by introducing an Indian sublime.[16] Zaarmilla invokes Varuna, the pre-Vedic sea god, under whose "potent arm" Zaarmilla is "surrounded by the billows of the mighty ocean" (183). Literally transported west, Zaarmilla's very diction becomes westernized as, he notes, "the most sublime objects alone present themselves" to his view. The seascape is simultaneously politicized and aestheticized: it is divided between the "imperial state" above and the congregated waves, like the chiefs of some great republic alternately rise into the majesty of power, and retire into the peace of obscurity" (183). The dialectic of engagement and retirement, an odd substitute for the conventional duality of waves of violence and peace, suggests an aesthetic and political oscillation between involvement and detachment that recurs to Hamilton's opening invocation to the novel, in which she announces her authorial position in the spectrum from involvement to detachment.

In contrast to the ideal expectations generated by the secondhand reports of volume 1, Hamilton uses eastern subjectivity to satirize the hypocrisy of the west. Thus, Zaarmilla's fellow passengers on the "floating castle" form a microcosm of British imperialism, including the insipid wife of a man who has acquired "a fortune" that will "give him distinction in his own country"; while her husband has made off with monetary fortune, she has absconded with a menagerie of India's exotic animals: "Parrots, Lorys, Maccaws small Dogs, Persian Cats and Monkeys of every description" (185). The symbolic danger of exporting the alien fauna unfolds

---

[15] For a contrasting perspective on Hamilton's relationship with Orientalism, see Aravamudan's claim that Hamilton "relies on her brother's 1787 text *A Historical Relation of the Origin, Progress, and Final Dissolution of the Government of the Rohilla Afghans*"; Aravamudan does acknowledge, however, that "[w]hile it is easy to see the sister as fictionalizing Charles Hamilton's treatise into a softer form, her contribution does render a complex background," referring to the novel's epistolary genre (102).

[16] See Chapter 1 on the Orientalist pattern of importing the western tradition of the sublime in their translations and descriptions of India.

quickly: one of the nephews, attracted by the "comical tricks of a Marmozet" is attacked by a Baboon, "one of the fiercest animals" in her collection (186–7).

The ship's microcosm ranges from these caricatures to more complex characters such as the scientist Severan, an uncanny prototype for Mary Shelley's rapacious pseudoscientist, Victor Frankenstein, who "pursued nature to her hiding places" (Shelley 33); Severan, distinguished from "other young men [who] were pursuing the gaudy phantom of pleasure," was "occupied in investigating the laws of Nature, in tearing the choicest secrets from her reluctant bosom, or, in tracing her foot-steps through the various phaenomena of the material world" (207).[17] While Zaarmilla unquestioningly adopts the view of Severan's gushing admirer, Delomond, who extols science as awakening "the most sublime ideas of the great original cause" Hamilton's feminist satire of Enlightenment science is at its most scathing in the portrait of Severan (206).

As it moves towards its literally and ludicrously explosive climax, the novel exposes the misogyny at the foundation of Enlightenment science and deism. Severan contrasts Miss Ardent to the ideal Lady Grey: "Is there a man, who would prefer the vapid chatter of a pretty idiot, to the conversation of such a woman? So good! So wise! So beautiful!" (222). Just as Zaarmilla responds that "the accomplishments and virtues of an ugly woman, can make little impression even on the mind of a philosopher," there is a loud explosion, for in "discoursing on Lady Grey, my friend had forgotten the necessary management of a retort which for want of his attention, burst in pieces" (223). Hamilton's choice of the *retort*, a "long-necked container" that was "used for distilling liquids" suggests a pun on *retort* as *repartee*, the explosion thus literalizing the "suffocating effluvia" of Severan's ludicrous though incendiary epistemology (223n1).

The incident, viewed through Zaarmilla's deistic interpretation and followed by Severan's transformation from melancholy at the experiment's failure to joy at the discovery it reveals, underscores the moment's bathos, Zarmilla admitting, "I was not sufficiently initiated in science, to be able to appreciate the value of the discovery, which gave such ecstatic pleasure the mind of the Philosopher" (223). With Zaarmilla's clumsy attempt to extol the Christian God as the "immortal spirit" who "spread the volume of Nature before his rational offspring," Hamilton satirically gives Zaarmilla's rhapsodic and clumsy praise of the deistic God's "unalterable decree" the volatility of the situation at hand: 'That to the mind, devoted to its perusal, the corrosive passions should be unknown. That it should have power to assuage the tumults of the soul; to foster the emotions of virtue; and to produce a species of enjoyment, peculiarly to its own!'—Such, O! Maandaara! Such are the advantages of Science!!" (223–4).

Hamilton thus recurs to and subverts the Preliminary Dissertation's deism through overt satire, by now destabilizing the framing paradigm of British materialism. Just as the Preliminary Dissertation links Orientalism to deism through the dedication to Hastings, Hamilton here connects the satire of deism to

---

[17] See the epilogue to this book for discussion of Victor Frankenstein vis-à-vis Percy Shelley.

Orientalism in the coffee house scene that follows Severan's explosion. The scene brings to the surface Hamilton's indictment not just of Burke's incrimination of Hastings, but the role of the press in distorting the voice of indigenous Indians in its claims to speak for them. Zaarmilla is accosted by an Englishman who aggressively defends his nation against what the man presumes to be Zaarmilla's hatred of the British, never letting Zaarmilla speak but working him up to an emotional pitch in the course of his projected litany of complaints: "You need not describe to me, the ravages you have seen committed! The insults you have sustained! You need not tell me, that your friends have been slaughtered; your country plundered; your houses burned ... the lovely, the virtuous wife of your affections, perhaps, torn from your agonizing bosom!" (245). With sharp irony, Hamilton has the hyperbolic British man silence Zaarmilla in his self-serving attempt to vindicate the people of India: "I shall make a proper representation of your case. Through me, your wrongs shall find a tongue. I will proclaim to the world, all that I have heard you utter. That mass of horrors, that system of iniquity, which your highness would describe, shall be laid open to the eye of day, and its wicked, nefarious, abominable, and detested author, exposed to the just indignation of the congregated universe!" (245). Though Zaarmilla dismisses the event as a "paroxysm of delirium," it reveals Hamilton's deepening complication of British misrepresentation of Anglo-India, not only in the likeness of the rhetoric of the "noisy orator" to Burke's attacks on Hastings but, more insidiously, in its satire of the press.[18] The source of the rant being an article claiming Zaarmilla had come to England to complain about Hastings's "mal-administration, Hamilton suggests the press's responsibility for perpetuating Burke's false accusation as it is spread to the common reader (246).

Hamilton dismantles the relationship between Enlightenment epistemology and Orientalism more explicitly when Zaarmilla's path intersects with two philosophers who have been robbed and who must appear in court to identify they accused. The first, Mr. Puzzledorf, uses the magistrate's order to identify thief to challenge the Lockean equation of identity and consciousness, citing a litany of British philosophers—from deists to anti-materialists—to challenge Locke (252). The second, Mr. Axiom, elaborates on Puzzledorf's claim that because consciousness is not fixed it cannot constitute identity, adding pseudoscientific support that "the particles of which man is composed ... are necessarily in succession changed" (253). Yet he says there are exceptions to this rule, namely, when there is "stamina," located "in the part of the brain which approaches the nearest possible to the very top of the nose" where it may receive "notices sent to it from the organs of sight, hearing, smelling, &c." (253). Unable to bear it any longer, the magistrate calls upon his "worthy friend," Sir Caprice Ardent, to examine the culprit to determine "whether he be actually the person guilty of the *alledged* [sic] *crime*?" (253). Adding a new layer of hilarity to the satire, Mr. Axiom denies "the existence of crime in any case whatever," claiming that to "the enlightened eye of philosophy," morality is relative, crime therefore "nothing

---

[18] On the comparison to Burke, see Perkins and Russell (245n1).

more than an error in judgment" (253). The prisoner himself speaks directly to Axiom, revealing that he is a servant of Axiom's friend, Doctor Sceptic. Unruffled, Axiom urges the prisoner, Timothy, to "be comforted" even as he is being dragged back to prison for, Axiom tells him, the "age of reason approaches. That glorious aera is fast advancing, in which every man shall do that which is right in his own eyes, and the fear of the gallows shall have as little influence, as the fear of hell" (255). Just as Axiom obfuscates his own inconsistencies to the illiterate Timothy, Zaarmilla assures Maandaara not to be discouraged by the "unintelligible" nature of the philosophers' arguments: "How should our unenlightened minds, expect to understand the language of philosophers, since from all I can learn, they seldom thoroughly understand themselves" (255).[19]

By means of Zaarmilla's effort to comprehend materialist epistemology through the lens of eastern culture, Hamilton thus reduces the western hegemony of reason to its most absurd and ironic: Zaarmilla apologizes to the Bramin, Sheermaal, for what Zaarmilla now deems his ignorance in defending the British philosophers, worshipping at their "pujah" to Systems (257). Enlightenment reason reaches its nadir as it is reduced to the atheist's "infernal deity," suicide, which Sheermal describes as the "privilege of a philosopher," bringing an abrupt end to the novel's denunciation of materialist philosophy (259).

Having thus exposed the Enlightenment model as a sham vis-à-vis eastern thought, Hamilton here recurs to the topic of female education that began the novel, complicating it further with a multiplicity of perspectives. Describing with horror the "female converts" to Atheism who "seldom fail to make an offering to Atheism of their peace, purity, and good fame," Zaarmilla is baffled by Mr. Vapour's eponymously insubstantial claim that the utopian world of reason needs no moral law (259).[20] In such a utopia, Zaarmilla explains, "filial affection would ... be treated as a crime" so that "to prevent the possibility of such a breach of virtue, no man, in the age of reason, shall be able to guess who his father is; nor any woman to say to her husband, behold your son" (260).

Mr. Vapour's argument reaches its most ludicrous as he struggles to answer Miss Ardent's arch question, "[H]ow are the Ladies to be clothed in the age of reason" if "[e]very man shall ... till his own field, and cultivate his own garden"? (260–61). Mr. Vapour's illogic proceeds from claiming that no clothes nor even food would be needed as "the human mind advances to that of perfection" since man's intellectual energy will keep him warm and, in fact, "people will not be so foolish as to die"; the absurd culmination is a haunting prolepsis of Shelley's

---

[19] Hamilton may have been disingenuous in denying Hays's claim that she was satirizing Godwin and Paine, but Hamilton's satire is larger and more subtle than Hays's "complaint" suggests, for it ultimately challenges the dualistic framework of Enlightenment thought (Perkins and Russell 255n1).

[20] In a footnote to chapter 4 of *Vindication of the Rights of Woman*, Wollstonecraft quotes Barbauld's "To a Lady" in full to exemplify how "even women of superior sense" adopt "the language of men" that classes women "with smiling flowers that only adorn the land" (57–8).

Victor Frankenstein: "[W]e shall not then be troubled with—women. In the age of reason, the world shall contain only a race of men!!"(261). By including the reaction of Miss Ardent, Hamilton further problematizes the notion of authority, Miss Ardent herself a caricature of the belief that "the perfection of the female understanding will ... be universally acknowledged" in the utopian Age of Reason (261). More than a straightforward attack on Godwin and Paine, and more even than an embrace of Wollstonecraftian feminism, then, Hamilton wrests away masculinist authority inherent in the dualism that underlies Enlightenment epistemology through her inclusion of multiple voices, emulating the deistic Creator as the author who sustains her creation from the margins.[21]

Having introduced Charlotte's voice at the outset as text mediated by the interpretations of Zaarmilla and her brother, Hamilton's return to Charlotte at the end of the novel in her own person gives the reader the opportunity to revisit the assumptions of the male perspectives that have distorted Charlotte until she speaks. Conversing with Denbeigh about the lot of a woman "who has it little in her power to be useful," Charlotte gives a Wollstonecraftian response to the question, "And is the gift of reason then nothing...? [C]ultivated as [her mind] has been by education ... why should it not exert its powers ... for the instruction, or innocent amusement of others?" (302–3). Charlotte's simple, direct answer, deflates the Wollstonecraftian ideal in its vision beyond the domestic sphere: "Ah! Sir..., you know how female writers are looked down upon. The women fear, and hate; the men ridicule, and dislike them" (303). Zaarmilla, anointing Denbeigh with the patriarchal title, "venerable old man," readily accepts Denbeigh's condescending corrective to Charlotte's dark conclusion about public reception of female authorship (303). Denbeigh qualifies his optimistic claim with a condition that undermines any assurance he intends: "[I]f the simplicity of your character remains unchanged—if the virtues of your heart receive no alloy from the vanity of authorship; trust me, my dear Charlotte, you will not be the less dear to any friend that is deserving ... for having employed your leisure hours in a way that is both innocent and rational" (303). Denbeigh's echoing of the Wollstonecraftian ideals of innocence, virtue, and rationality underscores the gap between the circumscribed Wollstonecraft and Hamilton's representation of the dark fate of the woman author—rational or not—for venturing out of the domestic sphere.

Though it ends with a marriage, the novel paradoxically subverts the sentimental formula, not only in its anticlimactic union between two minor characters, Mr. Darnley and "the blooming Emma" but, in a single phrase, it provides its most damning commentary on marriage as the means by which western society divests women of authority: Zaarmilla stops writing abruptly, "called from [his] pen to witness a ceremony called Signing the Settlements" (307). This detail, as Perkins

---

[21] While Mellor suggests that Hamilton "distances herself significantly" from Charlotte Percy, I see her not so much as Hamilton's "self-portrait," but as a figure closer to Charlotte Smith or Mary Hays, whose authorial identities are informed by a complex relationship between heart and mind rather than a Wollstonecraftian denial of the former and vindication of the former (159).

and Russell note of the "legal documents arranging the financial affairs of an affianced woman and her future children" (307, n.1) embodies the jurisdiction of women's forced surrender of not only her own independence but her authority over her offspring.

A return to Charlotte's mistranslated poem vis-à-vis the novel's trajectory that includes the Dedication to Hastings and the Preliminary Dissertation reveals that Hamilton's subversion of male authority has been embedded even in the most pious of filial praise for Hastings and, more surprising, for Charles. In this way, the process of mistranslation is mutual: Hamilton's authority, embedded in the mistranslated voice of Charlotte, suggests that a woman writer carrying out the Orientalist mission must alter the very premise of Orientalism. That Percy dies before he can complete his education of the Rajah regarding the importance of woman's education is therefore of less consequence than Percy's own inability to read Charlotte's poetry beyond understanding it as a literal tribute to filial piety. Though Hamilton may govern her novel in absentia, she as creator is powerless to control its distortion once in the hands of masculine authority.

Framing the novel with Charlotte—first through her poem, and finally, through her physical presence and spoken though, importantly, still mediated voice— Hamilton thus takes her densely layered text beyond the paradigm of eighteenth-century satire. Following the debacle of the debate among the caricatures of "natural philosophy," Zaarmilla admits, "I deceived myself in extending my notions of Christianity to every Christian, and of excellence to every female, of England, I still see some who amply justify the expectations that were formed by my sanguine mind" (275). By recurring to Charlotte's sensibility in the culminating letters, Hamilton suggests proleptically what late twentieth-century scholarship began addressing: that the revolution in English verse begins with women poets.[22]

The novel's universe, governed marginally by Hamilton, is one in which Orientalists distort their renderings through the lens of their masculinist intellectual tradition. Though the Bramins who taught them Sanskrit prove no less masculinist in their interpretations, they provide women writers, however imperfectly, an alternative paradigm of nondualism. As Zarmilla signs off for the last time with the customary, "What more can I say?" the distance between his request that "his errors" be "consigned to oblivion" and Hamilton's creation suggests that the question "What more can I say?" itself emerges from a wrong understanding of knowledge: the error of the western paradigm is that knowledge is not importable or quantifiable information but the knower herself, that "conscious power" (90).

While Hamilton founds *Translations* on the neoclassical satire of Montesquieu's epistolary novel as a means of exploring the limits of female authorship vis-à-vis Orientalism, the Anglo-Indian novels of Phebe Gibbes and Sydney Owenson discussed in Chapter 3 engage subversively with the sentimental tradition to represent the relationship between female subjectivity and the taboos of miscegenation in Anglo-India.

---

[22] In Curran's pioneering words, "[B]ecause of the powerful shibboleth against the learned woman, an ideological control of remarkable intensity, sensibility was all the more to be cultivated, even celebrated" (195).

Chapter 3
Confronting Sacrifice, Resisting the Sentimental: Phebe Gibbes, Sidney Owenson, and the Anglo-Indian Novel

As Chapter 2 discussed in the case of Hamilton, for a woman writing about Anglo-India, publication means being translated between subjectivities, the fluidity of such subjectivity dissolving into the text. Through female subjectivities that assert a more progressive movement towards nondualism, Phebe Gibbes's *Hartly House, Calcutta* (1789) and Sidney Owenson's *The Missionary* (1811) interrogate the taboo intermixture of race and caste seen in Chapter 1's treatment of Wilkins's *Gita*. Gibbes and Owenson, writing their Anglo-Indian novels at different phases in the rapidly changing eras of both Orientalism and canonical Romanticism, have disparate literary relationships to the sentimental tradition, yet they challenge the foundation of that tradition's objectification of the female in ways that are deeply connected to the conflicting epistemologies at the heart of Anglo-India.

"The colour of his wishes": Subjectivity and Miscegenation in *Hartly House, Calcutta*

That *Hartly House, Calcutta* was, until recently, thought to have been either the memoir of its 16-year-old British protagonist, Sophia Goldborne, describing her experiences in India, or the fiction of an anonymous man with firsthand knowledge of India, speaks to a readership whose expectations of Anglo-Indian texts were either the travel narratives of women or the authoritative texts of male Orientalists..[1] The historical confusion over the novel's authorship is understandable, given the doubleness of a narrative voice paradoxically naïve and authoritative. According to Michael Franklin, *Hartly House* was the culmination of Gibbes's long-forgotten but prolific literary career.[2]

---

[1] Readers from the nineteenth century through the 1980s have offered various suggestions about Sophia as author, including historical travel writer and disguised man (see Clough and Basham respectively). E.M. Forster assumed Sophia Goldborne to be a contemporary of Eliza Fay; in his introduction to Fay's *Letters from India* he quotes *Hartly House*, opining that as a travel writer, "Miss Sophia Goldborn [was] her rival in narrative style" (21).

[2] Franklin notes that "she claimed that she had published no fewer than 'twenty-two sets' of novels" among other writings (*Hartly House Calcutta* xii). All further references to this edition are in the text; when citing Franklin's introduction, the abbreviation *HHC* is given.

The novel represents late eighteenth-century Anglo-India as a welter of political uncertainty through irregularities often dismissed as making for "uneven progress through the book" (Clough viii). The novel underscores the instability of this early phase of Anglo-India through its recurrent references to Warren Hastings, governor-general of Bengal, from his visits to Hartly House to his forced departure and the subsequent arrival of his replacement, Charles Cornwallis. The 1908 edition's added subtitle, "A novel of the Days of Warren Hastings," suggests the historical perspective gained over a century later regarding Hastings's importance to the narrative. For Edmund Burke, who led the charge against him, Hastings embodied the East India Company's abuse of power during this early period of English colonialism in India, before the government itself took control. Many in England were sympathetic to Hastings during the trial, extolling him not only as a shrewd administrator who used the ancient Indian legal system to rule but as patron of the Asiatic Society.

The novel connects this destabilized political context to the irregularities reflected in the equally destabilized sexual and racial mores of early Anglo-India. This dynamic is played out through the mutual attraction between Sophia and the young Bramin who teaches her Vedic philosophy even as the novel appears to follow a conventionally sentimental trajectory with Sophia courted by a variety of East India Company men. The sudden death of the Bramin that had threatened both the marriage plot and British mores allows the novel to return to its sentimental conclusion, leaving Sophia en route to England to marry her East India Company fiancé. More than a foil to the retinue of Sophia's martial and imperialist East India Company suitors, however, the Bramin embodies masculinity as gentle, idealistic, and companionable to the feminine while British masculinity in the novel becomes not only less attractive but, undercutting the sentimental ending, more rapacious as Sophia describes her horror in learning of a British soldier's rape of an Indian girl.[3]

The novel connects these volatile political, racial, and sexual elements through the epistemological dissonance between the western subject-object dualism that informs Sophia's response to her early experience of India and the Vedic nondualism that she absorbs through the Bramin. Gibbes's familiarity with the

---

[3] The attractiveness of the gentle Bramin runs counter to the contemporary stereotypes of Indian men as effeminate. See Rajan's essay, "Feminizing the Feminine," for a nuanced discussion of women whose subjective writing on India predates the British male perception of a passively feminine India. See also Ross on the canonical Romantic poets' "attempt to bring the 'feminine' vulnerability of emotion into the realm of 'masculine' power" (37). Considering yet another dimension of masculinity in the novel, namely, Sophia's avowed desire to be a Nabobess, Franklin notes that the novel perpetuates "the Orientalist stereotyping of feminized Hindoo and virile Muslim"; by contrast, the premise of this book, that Gibbes often uses Sophia to challenge rather than perpetuate such stereotypes, applies in this case as well, first, through Sophia's playful teasing of Arabella and, second, through setting Hindu and Muslim against British and European vis-à-vis race (*Romantic Representations* 4). Germane to Gibbes's treatment of British masculinity is Nicole Reynolds's study of the novel's comparison between English and Indian women, particularly the "nautch girls," as commodities (168ff).

contemporaneous Sanskrit scholarship of the Orientalists who formed the Asiatic Society of Bengal, under the patronage of Hastings, emerges thus not only through the Bramin's overt lessons in the Vedic roots of Hinduism but, more subtly, through its influence on Sophia's most fundamental understanding of selfhood.[4]

Informing the instability of Gibbes's British India is the double role of the Orientalists as scholars of ancient Indian literature and participants in British colonialism. As the novel unfolds, the paradox of *Hartly House, Calcutta* emerges as a challenge to the colonialist dichotomy of Indian as primitive and British as civilized that would be codified fewer than 50 years later. As discussed in the introduction to this book, the Anglicist period of British rule in India, ushered in with Macaulay's "Minute on Indian Education," proclaimed an end to studying and disseminating the Sanskrit language and texts that Macaulay deemed "not merely as useless, but as positively noxious," essentially eradicating Orientalism (730).

At the core of the novel, then, the uncertain political identity of early British India is inextricably associated with the epistemological. Against the western dualism of the otherness of the east, Gibbes sets the Vedic nondualism of these ancient texts that more than influences Sophia—it transforms her.[5] Sophia's premature declaration at the opening of Letter IX, "I adore the customs of the East," is naive in its assumption of safe epistemological and emotional distance that the novel gradually erodes, uncovering an east that threatens the defensive structure of western dualism (33).

Holding Sophia's rapturous embrace of India in tension with her inadvertent projection of British materialism, Gibbes constructs Sophia's growing ambivalence through a pattern of ironic juxtapositions. Sophia rhapsodizes about India often through poetic quotation, a tendency that irritated Mary Wollstonecraft; her 1789 review characterizes the novel as "stretched out by introducing quotations from our English poets—a little too often perhaps," an idiosyncrasy that continues to be the object of critical scorn (Franklin, *HHC* xx). Though Sophia's snippets of British poetry, from Shakespeare to Thomson, appear to be random narrative interruptions reflecting her inflated sense of "the height and depth of [her] intellectual endowments," Gibbes's authorial voice emerges as distinct from Sophia's when the quotations, more than *bon mots* for Arabella's pleasure, are seen to reflect the novel's larger pattern of ironic juxtapositions or *non sequiturs* (34).

This narrative pattern suggests Gibbes's influence by the associational psychology of David Hartley and other eighteenth-century British philosophers

---

[4] The popularity of the novel is indicative of just how much Orientalism was celebrated not only as the first systematic study of ancient India, but as evidence of a common Indo-European linguistic history. See Franklin's synopsis of the novel's historical context of British India, particularly in its contextualization of the novel vis-à-vis Orientalist publications (*HHC* xxiii—xxviii).

[5] See the introduction for a detailed discussion on the Sanskrit *advaita* vis-à-vis this book's use of the term "nondualism" to convey a dynamic rather than static principle of oneness that more accurately represents the dissolution of subject-object duality than the term "monism."

who drew on Lockean philosophy to claim that "one thought is often suggested to the mind by another"; the notion that the "connexion which is formed in the mind between the words of a language and the ideas they denote" was a catalyst to the Romantic interest in the relationship between poetry and consciousness (Dugald Stewart, qtd. in Duthrie 408).[6] In one such moment, Sophia suggests a connection between India's climate and her own emotion when she quotes Thomson's "All-conquering heat! O intermit thy wrath / And on my throbbing temples potent thus / Beam not so fierce"; "the poet's words," Sophia continues, "at this moment spontaneously flow from my pen" (14). Sophia here anticipates Wordsworth's "all good poetry is the spontaneous overflow of powerful feelings" (448). Though the suggestion of literally channeling Thomson's poetic spirit playfully deflects the didacticism that was to characterize Wordsworth's poetics, Gibbes deploys associational psychology by having Sophia "wander wide from [her] intended subject," following the Thomson quotation with her speculation about the possibilities for a young woman surrounded by the "fine fellows ... the East India Company's servants!" (15).[7]

Yet the Sophia that emerges as the plot unfolds is increasingly more complex than the Sophia of these early moments of frivolity. Subverting the bildungsroman formula, Gibbes traces Sophia's coming of age as a trajectory of intensifying ambivalence. Sophia's development takes her beyond both her British suitors and the negative female role models who either capitulate to these men or are victimized by them; as Sophia falls in love with the young Bramin and with Vedic nondualism, she comes to see her identity as formed by India, an identity in which self merges with other. Yet Sophia, whose Greek name, "spiritual wisdom," has both ironic and serious valences at different narrative stages, cannot remain in this state of nondualism, for both narrative and epistemological reasons.[8] She therefore internalizes India as she returns to England, projecting the now-dead Bramin's gentle manhood onto her British fiancé, Doyly.

Progressing through three phases corresponding to its three volumes, the novel is driven by a teleology that can be traced linguistically. At central moments,

---

[6] See Duthrie on Hartley's influence on Joanna Baillie (31). Hartley is a well-established source for the early philosophical poetry of Coleridge and then Wordsworth. As the epilogue to this book discusses, the split between Coleridge and Wordsworth comes about through Coleridge's rejection of the materialist foundation of Hartleyan philosophy that he, ironically, had cultivated in Wordsworth.

[7] In the 1800 preface to the *Lyrical Ballads*, Wordsworth repeats the statement a second time, adding "recollected in tranquillity," a phrase that underscores the associational influence with its claim for the mind's discursive interpretation of the earlier spontaneous overflow of feeling (460). For more on the relationship between these women writers and canonical Romanticism, see both the introduction and the epilogue to this book.

[8] Regarding the possibility for irony, her full name's juxtaposition of "Sophia" with "Gold-borne" suggests Gibbes's wry commentary on the sagacity of England's imperialism in India at the inception of what was to become its long and complex history of bearing its wealth—material and cultural—back to the England.

Sophia echoes and complicates her first breathless declaration that she has become "orientalised at all points," Gibbes creating a diachronic shift from the noun, Orient, to her apparent coinage of the verb, "orientalise" (8).[9] In the first phase, Sophia's early letters reveal a life of insulated privilege so that to declare that she has become "orientalised" is seen as naive when it is retrospectively tinged with pathos and, finally, compromise. Her view of native Indians during this early stage is that of both colonist with "Gentoo" servants, and megalomaniac tourist, amused by what she perceives as a native culture of oddities. She proclaims breezily to Arabella that "to taste the beauties of the poet's pencil ... you must visit Bengal," sounding more like the writer of a travel brochure than one whose being "orientalised" is later quite disorienting in its challenge to her identity as a British woman (28, 8). At this early phase, Gibbes's acerbic anti-imperialism can be gleaned from Sophia's random and undigested observations. In one such case, she abruptly shifts from a description of Mogul "haughtiness" that styles itself "Governor of the Universe, the Ornament of the Earth ... on the assumption of the imperial diadem," to a banal discussion of the East India Company's housing rentals (29). The *non sequitur* elliptically incriminates the entitlement of middle class company men acting the part of aristocracy in India.

The catalyst to the novel's second phase is Sophia's meeting the Bramin who, she remarks, "walks in & out of Hartly House at pleasure," a phenomenon that would be unheard of fewer than 50 years later (51). The implicit ironies of the novel's earlier phase surface as Sophia finds herself drawn to the philosophy and culture that the Bramin imparts as well as to the Bramin himself. A more complex subjectivity now connects Sophia to India both emotionally and intellectually, imbuing her tendency to poeticize, particularly via her references to Thomson, with a deeper significance beyond the early impression of merely displaying her erudition.

Though the Bramin's "orientalizing" of Sophia threatens to transgress both erotic and epistemological boundaries, the final phase of Sophia's development recoups the safe distance of the opening section with a return to the marriage plot: her engagement to the aptly named Doyly creates a homespun image simultaneously pointing to the sentimental novel's return to English domesticity while underscoring Doyly's regrettable lack of the Bramin's exotic appeal.[10] Such a denouement both capitulates to and subverts the sentimental formula, poised on a delicate balance between satire and tragedy not possible in Sophia's earlier letters.

---

[9] According to Franklin, Gibbes's use of the term "orientalised" antedates the first *OED* citation "by more than twenty years" (*HHC* xxxvi).

[10] Franklin suggests that the name may be based on Sir John D'Oyly, an East India Company administrator and friend of Hastings (*HHC* 200); Gibbes may also be playing on doily as "a woollen stuff, 'at once cheap and genteel,' introduced for summer wear in the latter part of the 17th c." (*OED*). The Bramin's gentle masculinity, it suggests, would be merely effete, colorless, and bourgeois without the Bramin's exotic allure. An observation originally made as a criticism of Gibbes can equally be enlisted to distinguish author and protagonist: while Sophia does not "differentiate between her train of admirers," Doyly himself is "an inarticulate paragon" who "wins her father's consent, a fortune and her hand, in that order" (Clough viii, ix).

While Sophia refers with ostensible playfulness to herself and the other British in India as "we Asiatics" and to Arabella as "you English," Gibbes complicates what it means to become "Asiatic" in the late eighteenth century (86, 49). Suggesting that to become "orientalised" involves losing racial identity, Gibbes peppers the early letters with references to miscegenation, ironic when read from the hindsight of Sophia's falling in love with the Bramin in the novel's second phase.

The most pointed early reference to miscegenation follows Sophia's initial claim that the "European world faded" before her eyes and she became "orientalised at all points": among a party of admiring British gentlemen Sophia describes herself in "the language of Southerne's [sic] Oroonoko" (8). In Southerne's rendering of Aphra Behn's *Oroonoko*, the African princess Imoinda is transmuted into a white European while Oroonoko remains a black African prince. Gibbes's interracial reference signals that there is more to being "orientalised" than Sophia may wish to acknowledge at this early stage, especially considering that the choice of Southerne would run counter to the acceptable coupling of British men with Indian women.

Gibbes thus simultaneously points to and masks the subject of intermarriage through Sophia's playful innuendoes; in one such case, Sophia proposes that Arabella come to India and marry a nabob with a "copper complexion" (39). Gibbes deflects attention from the racial implications when Sophia claims, "I should rejoice to see you a Nabobess, that you may surpass me as much in rank" (39). While Sophia suggests that the Nabob's class outweighs his racial difference, she implies that Arabella would never marry for money, concluding with a quotation by Young that, Sophia claims, voices Arabella's disposition: "Can wealth give happiness?" (39). Arabella, being "sentimental," will probably refuse—not because of race, but because love outweighs class, as the second line of the Young quotation affirms: "What gay distress, what splendid misery!" (39). This hint of a potential narrative in which love transcends marrying for social advantage is particularly ironic from the hindsight of the novel's end, which averts Sophia's potential to marry for love rather than for the financial stability, if not aristocracy, of the middle-class Doyly.

The racial tension builds novelistically through a sequence of apparently random observations, beginning with Sophia's admiring description of a military party in mythically idealized terms and culminating in a yet more embedded sequence of references to Shakespeare's *Othello:*

> The party to-day was brilliant—all that pomp and splendor could do, was done, to conceal the ravages of burning suns; and never were military gentlemen more animated, more obsequious, or camp more delightful; but Mars in the East ... has more gallantry than hostility about him. (45)

The overstatement can be read either as girlish giddiness, as readers tended to dismiss all of Sophia's hyperboles preceding the discovery of Gibbes's authorship, or as is now possible to see, it can be read as Gibbes's instrument to satirize British arrogance and imposition of their authority through military force.

Gibbes follows this hyperbolic praise of the "pomp and splendor" by having Sophia refer, with apparent incongruity, to *Othello* in the context of the military presence among the wedding guests:

> You can have no notion of the nonchalance ... with which I conducted myself through the day; but you will recollect that women who are accustomed to live with a multitude of men, acquire a modest assurance (let me call it) private education cannot bestow.—Friendship and respect are the sentiments reciprocally professed, and chearfulness [*sic*] and joy the universal objects: therefore, those who can do the kindest, or say the pleasantest things, are unquestionably the most esteemed companions; for Othello's liberal-mindedness seems to prevail throughout (at least) all my agreeable connections. (46)

Sophia then misquotes act 3, scene 3 of *Othello*. In Shakespeare's version, the passage is the culmination of Othello's dialogue with Iago who, plotting Othello's ruin, has just made the speech beginning, "O, beware, my lord, of jealousy! / It is the green-ey'd monster" (165–6); Shakespeare's Othello, as opposed to Gibbes's, responds to Iago,

> 'Tis not to make me jealous [*sic*]
> To say my wife is fair, feeds well,
> loves company,
> Is free of speech, sings, plays, and
> dances well;
> Where virtue is, these are more
> virtuous.
> Nor from mine own weak
> merits will I draw
> The smallest fear or doubt of
> her revolt,
> For she had eyes, and chose me. (183–9)

By having Sophia preface her recitation by acknowledging, "I am not correct in my quotation," Gibbes calls attention to Sophia's subsequent misprision and elision: "'Tis not to make me jealous, to say my wife is fair, loves company, sings, dances well, &c &c; for, where virtue is, these are most virtuous" (46). In Shakespeare's play, the speech precedes Othello's murder of Desdemona; in Gibbes's novel, Sophia's misprision comes between her description of the wedding of an East India Company man and Sophia's meeting of the young Bramin with whom she will fall in love.

While the *Othello* reference can be dismissed as another of Sophia's attempts to display her erudition, there are enough strategically placed references that signal Gibbes's underlying design of providing and then manipulating the critical moment of what her contemporaries would know as the most famous literary precedent of an interracial marriage, in which the white wife is victim to the violence of a racially other husband. Sophia's preceding claim, that "Othello's liberal-mindedness seems to prevail throughout (at least) all my agreeable connections," underscores the irony of taking the quotation, hardly an expression of liberal-mindedness, from *Othello* just as Othello's suspicion takes hold, leading to his murder of Desdemona (46).

The irony of the odd context in which Sophia makes the reference is problematized further by two lines that she omits from the passage. First, by eliding Shakespeare's line, "fear or doubt of her revolt," in which Othello equates an unfaithful wife with a traitor or rebel, Gibbes demilitarizes Othello's marital metaphor, thus creating a contrast to the British military men at the wedding that Sophia is attending. Gibbes's manipulation of the racial and sexual dynamics of Shakespeare's play, having begun with Sophia's describing Othello as liberal-minded, is apparent as well in the second omitted line, "she had eyes, and chose me." Suggesting that Othello's insecurity stems from his appearance, Gibbes censors Othello's weak rationalization that Desdemona would not betray him because she chose him with full knowledge of his racial otherness. By repressing the line, Gibbes anticipates Sophia's discomfort with the implied active choice behind her growing love for the Bramin, whom she meets shortly after. That Gibbes puts Sophia in the potential role of Desdemona takes on growing irony, for the Bramin is the antithesis of the increasingly violent British men, while Sophia, in turn no mere victim, makes choices that are informed by her increasing awareness of the erotic dynamics that surround her. By calling attention to the elisions, with Sophia's reference to her memory lapse and then the "&c, &c" of the two missing lines, Gibbes signals not only Sophia's discomfort but her own choice to avert one potentially tragic outcome—namely, the death of a white woman at the hands of her black husband—in favor of a different outcome that nevertheless remains latent in the last third of the novel—namely, Gibbes's own choice to dispatch the Bramin before he and Sophia can even consider consummating their love, thereby allowing the Bramin to remain gently and companionably heroic.[11]

Compounding the racial implications of the digression that "spontaneously flows" from Sophia's pen from the military wedding party to the Othello reference, Sophia compares the effects of the sun on the skin of the British and Indians:

> [T]he early maturity of the natives leading down to early decay; insomuch, that you would be shocked to behold a woman of thirty; for her appearance ... is equal, in infirmity and wrinkles, to the oldest looking woman in England at three score. Both sexes marry young, have families, decline, depart, and are remembered only in their offspring—Not so the Europeans, even at Calcutta—having received their birth in the happy zone of your residence, Arabella, their nerves are much stronger strung; their youth, moreover, is passed under the same healthful meridian; which enables them to endure the Eastern sun for ten or twelve years of their mid-life with tolerable satisfaction ; and their days are lengthened into old age by their return to Britain. (47)

Buried in what might simply be dismissed as a young woman's preoccupation with appearance and aging is a logical leap that connects mortality and race. That indigenous Indians look older than their years is causally related to being

---

[11] See Kelsall's discussion of the contemporary importance of *Othello* as "one of the fundamental texts of British Orientalism" (255).

remembered "only in their offspring," while the English attain longevity as their "days are lengthened into old age by their return to Britain." This deepening layer of anxiety about racial identity displaces the novel's subverted marriage plot. Marriage to Doyly will be her ticket to England and a legacy equated with prolonged life in contrast to the potential consequence of marriage to the Bramin, namely Sophia's early death in a symbolic if not literal act of *sati*, the ritual of widow suicide suggested by the return of Sophia's repressed fear of losing her British identity.

Her anxiety rises to the surface as the most banal of her observations, particularly regarding weddings, become laden with subtext. Letter XVI opens with Sophia's description of the "very joyous" weddings among the English in India, but she quickly adds, "It is a festival I have not, however, the smallest desire to treat my friends with; for, even was my choice fixed, and every obstacle obviated, I should have unconquerable objections to making so public an exhibition of myself on so solemn a change of condition" (65). Making this claim in British India as well as in the context of Sophia's attraction to the Bramin belies her ostensible subject of East India Company weddings; Gibbes thus subverts the sentimental marriage plot in which the heroine's coming of age in society leads to her final union with the hero. As becomes more explicit later in the novel, a "public exhibition of myself on so solemn a change of condition" in the context of India suggests not only marriage, but *sati*, the phrase thus conflating the rituals of marriage and death (65).

A yet more satirical juxtaposition illustrates Sophia's increasingly polarized ambivalence. Having expounded on "the wonders of a dessert," namely, "ices, Arabella ... ices" (67), she proceeds incongruously to marvel at Thomson's description of a serpent. How, she wonders, could one who had "never been in India," have "so admirably described an animal that, to be known in all its terrors, must be seen" (67). She then quotes Thomson: "Lo! the green serpent, from its dark abode / Which e'en Imagination fears to tread ... Seeks the refreshing fount" (68). As Franklin observes, the "green serpent" suggests Sophia's jealousy "concerning her father's affections," for she is about to meet Mrs. D— whom, she suspects, her father is courting (*HHC* 190). Yet the serpent also recalls Sophia's previous references to *Othello* coinciding with her own marriage prospects, a connection underscored in the subsequent letter describing the visit to Mrs. D—.

Discovering that Mrs. D— has a son, Sophia confides, "I am more than half afraid there is some plot in this sudden acquaintance and friendship," and with that, Gibbes simultaneously provides and alters the repressed line from the earlier passage from *Othello*. Echoing Shakespeare's "she had eyes, and chose me," Sophia writes, "Let the man have eyes to chuse me, on whom I am ever prevailed upon to bestow my hand, that I may not suppose the question is coolly canvassed whether I shall be accepted by him" (69). Sophia reverses the gender relationship in *Othello* so that she would be object of the man's choice, as opposed to Othello's implication that Desdemona chose him with the knowledge of his racial otherness. Sophia's chilly formality here is a thin mask for the offense she takes at the secondhand proposal, which Gibbes underscores by adding an allusion to the racial dynamic of *Othello:* "Jerry Blackacre (for so my mind would perversely call this unknown young man) never once, however, made his appearance; nor did Mamma glance the way I apprehended" (70). As Franklin notes, the reference to Jerry Blackacre, "son of the litigious and petulant Widow Blackacre" from William Wycherley's *The Plain-Dealer*, is an insult to mother as well as son (*HHC* 191). While the immediate reason for Sophia's huffiness is her own sense of having been insulted, particularly since the son never emerges, Sophia's aside, in the parenthetically stated "for so my mind would perversely call" Mrs. D—'s son, is further testimony to Gibbes's interest in associational psychology. Sophia's dismissing her own name-calling as perverse points to the epithet's deeper implications, namely, Sophia's preoccupation with complexion, particularly vis-à-vis her marriage prospects (70). As another link in the chain of racial images, it builds most directly and problematically to Sophia's idealizing the Bramin as "a Moor of such great dignity" (72).

By this point, the connection between the Bramin and Othello underscores the complexity of Sophia's ambivalence in terms of race, sexuality, and empire. The reference to the Bramin as Moor comes just after Sophia has described British lawyers returning from India "rolling in wealth" (71). Here, she uses the Moor epithet to introduce the Bramin's lesson on the Indian caste system which, she says, is divided into "five tribes" (72).[12] That she follows Dow's 1770 *History of Hindostan* by including the untouchables, or outcastes, as a fifth caste is a significant departure from what surely would have been the Bramin's teaching of the *Vedas*' system of four castes that does not include the outcastes as a caste.[13]

Gibbes's inclusion of a fifth caste, via Dow, reflects the underlying cultural anxiety of the British about participating in the creation of a new caste of Anglo-Indians as Chapter 1 discussed through Wilkins's non-translation of *Varna Shankar*, or mixed caste, as suggestive of his anxiety about British participation in the creation of the Anglo-Indian subcaste. While it is historically accurate to state that, in East India, "marriage with native women was encouraged" as a means to "create a mixed community supportive of British commercial policies," Gibbes's text demonstrates that the subject of miscegenation was fraught with fear and uncertainty in eighteenth-century British culture (Wheeler 166). By 1750, the Anglo-Indians exceeded the British in India; the British government, comparing the Anglo-Indians to the Haitian mulattos, feared revolution by the Anglo-Indians far more than by either Hindus or Moslems.[14] Not only does Gibbes thus explore

---

[12] The *OED* traces the etymology of *caste* to Latin, *castor -a* meaning "pure, unpolluted" through the Portuguese *casta*, or race. The etymological link to *chaste* is especially significant regarding the implication of miscegenation since it conflates racial and sexual purity through unadulterated "stock or breed." The link between sexual and racial purity further complicates Sophia's reference to *Othello* since the issue of his wife's chastity is fraught with the implications of the racial intermixture of their own union.

[13] See Franklin's note on Dow (*HHC* 192).

[14] See Anderson for the history of the Anglo-Indian community, originating in the seventeenth century, in which the East India Company coerced its employees to marry and convert Hindu women rather than marry the Catholic Portuguese and French then living in India (12). For detailed discussions of the Anglo-Indian community, see Anthony, Ballhatchet, and Sharpe.

the nascent taboo of miscegenation by reversing the accepted coupling of white male and indigenous female; adopting Dow's claim to a five-caste society, Gibbes simultaneously mirrors and subverts the undercurrent of cultural anxiety about the Anglo-Indian community itself. In another ironic *non sequitur*, Gibbes has Sophia follow her summary of the Bramin's lesson on the caste system with a recounting of the British Mrs. D—'s tragic story of having been sold at 12 into marriage to a tyrant (73). As Franklin notes, "It is significant that the patriarchal despotism and arranged child marriage are wholly Occidental" (*HHC* 193). Though a seemingly different subject from the Bramin's lesson, the selling of the English child bride underscores the havoc played by British masculine aggression not only in India but in its own society.

Doyly, with his "sensibility so oriental" is the closest Sophia can come to union with the Bramin (91). Yet in one of the novel's most bizarre *non sequiturs*, Sophia begins Letter XXIII with the girlish worry that Doyly "breathes not a syllable" about the "state of his affections, or the colour of his wishes"—a striking allusion to the now-prevalent theme of complexion. She proceeds directly from "I will, Arabella, think ... no more of him" to a graphic description of corpses in the Ganges, so that the oddly phrased "breathes not a syllable" takes on morbid implications made odder yet in a parenthetical aside, in which Gibbes meta-textually alludes to the incongruity: "You have heard of alligators (a pretty contrast for the gentle Doyly!) and their depredations—but it seems, unless you throw yourself in their way, in their natural element, the human species have nothing to fear from them, whilst living" (99). Sophia proceeds with a horrifying description of the laying down of the dead, parenthetically adding, "(or, what is more shocking, their dying friends) at low-water mark, that the flowing tide of the sacred Ganges may bury [them]" (99). She elaborates on the grotesque vision of alligators feeding on the dead or, worse, not quite dead, down to the "mangled limbs and headless trunks, which are daily seen by all who pass that way"; she then speculates on the "impurities [that] must impregnate the air, to augment [the Ganges'] native putridity at certain periods, and endanger the lives of the inhabitants of this place" (99). The "sacred" Ganges is reduced to an embodiment of "native putridity" made pestilent by the corpses it holds, in a narrative tension underscoring the ambivalence that emerges with the splintering of narrator and authorial voice.

Sophia follows this gruesome description of violent death with an incongruously idealized portrait of the bodies that are burned in the ritual of *sati*, "those wives, who, with a degree of heroism that ... would do honour to the female world, make an affectionate and voluntary sacrifice of themselves upon the funeral pile of their departed husbands"; she continues with the enthusiasm of a society page journalist, gushing about the way the wives prepare themselves for their immolation: "No bride ever decked herself out with more alacrity or elegance, than the women about to give this last great proof of their conjugal attachment" (100). Franklin suggests that this "largely positive opinion of the abhorrent gynophobic practice" reveals Sophia's desire to impress Arabella, "anxious to stress ... female courage and devotion rather than to appear the apologist reveals her Orientalist credentials";

I prefer to put the comment in the context of its surrounding observations as a means to filter Gibbes's voice behind Sophia's. (*HHC* 203).[15]

The sequence—concern about Doyly's affection, alligators devouring bodies in the Ganges, and heroic wives performing *sati*—occurs between Sophia's meeting the Bramin and his death. In the letter that follows, complicating the sequence further, she comes closest to avowing her love for the Bramin. Sophia refers to him as "my" Bramin in a passage replete with the language of sensibility traditionally reserved for the heroine's intended: "For love, this young priest affirms, refines the sentiment, softens the sensibility"; the Bramin goes so far, in the presence of Mrs. Hartly, to say to Sophia, "you are the loveliest of women" (104). Sophia tells Arabella, "I was astonished—Mrs. Hartly was silent and the Bramin retired, with more emotion than quite accorded with his corrected temper, as if he felt he had said too much. Wretch that I am, Arabella! This confession, which I shall ever remember with pain, did I ... ardently aspire after" (105). Sophia follows her own confession by meditating on the unnaturalness of a life of celibacy, as though what she believes to be the Bramin's monastic vows were the obstacle to their union rather than the racial and cultural divide that would make any thought of such a union impossible during the Anglicist period.

Gibbes is prescient in anticipating the pivotal nature of this period in the history of British India. The climactic end to volume 2 is an elaborate description of Hastings's forced departure immediately following the narrative sequence of Doyly's departure, the Bramin's near-declaration of his love for Sophia and Sophia's confessing to Arabella her love for the Bramin. Making these associations explicit, Sophia writes, "Doyly's departure has only been a prelude to the loss of our Governor, and every creature is plunged into disconsolation" as they show "their heart-felt respect" (105). The departure of Doyly, the would-be hero of a more formulaic sentimental novel, is merely a "prelude" to the governor's departure, Sophia exuding passion about Hastings's departure that eludes her when describing Doyly. Gibbes's subversiveness comes closest to the surface when she has Sophia speculate on a replacement for the peerless Hastings: "A more uniform good man, or so competent a judge of the advantages of the people, he will not leave behind him; nor possibly can a successor be transmitted, of equal information and abilities" (105).[16] Indeed, when Gibbes has Sophia brush aside the political implications of one who has mastered "the Persian language, that key to the knowledge of all that ought to constitute the British conduct in India, or can truly advance the British interests" she seems to realize that she has come dangerously close to betraying the "British interests" in her claim to having become "Asiatic" (106).

---

[15] While Franklin states that Sophia, though "anxious to stress ... female courage and devotion rather than to appear the apologist ..., reveals her Orientalist credentials" (suggesting Sophia's need to impress Arabella), I would emphasize that Gibbes' voice behind Sophia problematizes rather than merely echoes the Orientalists.

[16] Note the contrast between this idealized depiction of Hastings and the corrupt Resident in Starke's *Sword of Peace* discussed in Chapter 4.

Novelistically, therefore, the Bramin must die. Though Gibbes may be exploring British ambivalence, Sophia herself is hardly a revolutionary, caught in her own illusion that the east-west duality can be transcended. Gibbes nevertheless does not allow Sophia's relationship with the Bramin simply to evaporate. After his death, Sophia muses on how his remains will be disposed of, gesturing back to the earlier letter describing the Indian death rituals: "No funeral pile will, I hope, consume [his remains] to ashes—Yet wherefore that wish?—for then will they be secure from every possibility of insult" (135). In an internalized Hindu ritual, Sophia vows to "raise a pagoda to his memory in [her] heart," linking her to those Indian widows preparing for *sati*. However, she immediately complicates this eastern vision of mourning with what she deems to be a western sentimental tradition. Requesting a lock of the Bramin's hair, "a mental talisman ... against all the irregularities to which we Christians are subject," Sophia worries that such a ritual would be "incompatible with the Gentoo customs" (135). Her "we Christians" is a significant shift from the earlier, playful binary, "we Asiatics" and "you British" indicating the distance she has traveled in the psychic landscape of east and west. In fact, she tempers her ardent avowal of her devotion to the Bramin by telling Arabella that Doyly, now in England, will surely feel for Sophia if Arabella tells him of the Bramin's death.

Gibbes heightens her complication of the sentimental novel by exploring the potential for a tragic outcome beyond the death of the Bramin. Sophia abruptly shifts from the Bramin's death to imagining Doyly dying at sea: "Doyly may, nevertheless, even whilst I am writing his name, have reached the confines of eternity, and found the ocean as merciless, as the cruel disease to which our favourite has fallen a victim" (135). Such an outcome would doubly subvert the marriage plot; instead, Gibbes submerges the novel's disturbances of tradition to allow the sentimental ending, though not without Sophia's tepid response to what should be the climactic news of Doyly's fortune and the prospect of their marriage. Referring to her *deus ex machina*, Gibbes gives Sophia the wryly meta-textual remark, "a pretty plot, this!" The implications of such a resolution extend to the macrocosmic happily-ever-after promised by Cornwallis, who simultaneously arrives "to assume the reins of government," promising to eradicate the corruption of the Hastings regime, and thus ushering in the believed utopian outcome of colonial India (150).

Lest the reader mistake this tidy ending as Gibbes's support for the new British colonialism, she concludes the novel with a haunting end-frame to the hospitality of Hartly House that had welcomed the Bramin early in the novel. Culminating Gibbes's subversion of the marriage plot, Sophia, "all indignation, terror, compassion, and agitation," tells Arabella of a British officer's rape of an old man's daughter and subsequent murder of the father (158). For Sophia, it is a violation on multiple levels, including "the laws of hospitality," for the old man had trusted the soldier by inviting him into his house and, rather than carry her off, he "accomplish[ed] his work of darkness under the paternal roof!" (158). The vulnerability of the Indian's home to British aggression stands in contrast to the welcoming into Hartly House of the Bramin who bestows enlightenment on its British inhabitants .

This culmination of rage at British masculine aggression and Sophia's subsequent dark thoughts about her own fate provide a final ironic juxtaposition. Just before the brief concluding letter announcing their arrival at Portsmouth, she writes, "[S]hould we all be buried in the deep," Arabella should be consoled that "Providence has a right to dispose of us at will; and that, however unable mortals are to penetrate Heaven's design, every seeming misfortune is a disguised blessing" (159). One can hear behind Sophia's recurrence to violent death the voice of Gibbes, the novelist as "Providence," literally disposing of the Bramin and, wishfully, of Doyly, wielding the novelist's power to use misfortune as a means to resolve the ambivalences her characters reflect.

Gibbes's plot resolution, therefore, subverts even as it capitulates to the demand for a sentimental ending. She neither chooses the unrealistic escape of her interracial lovers into a world that can transcend even Hartly House nor does she simply have her heroine forget him and embrace her life with the "inarticulate paragon," Doyly (Clough ix). Sophia, instead, molds the pliant Doyly into an ersatz Bramin, her marriage to him the closest she can come to union with her Bramin:

> Doyly shall figure away as my Bramin and so well have I instructed him in every humane tenet of that humane religion, that he will not hurt a butterfly, nor can he dispatch even a troublesome musketto without a correspondent pang, [concluding that Doyly is] the universal admirer of all Nature's productions. (151)

Gibbes compensates for the potentially facile choice of the British colonist over the native Indian by virtually superimposing the Bramin onto Doyly, whose sensibility could not harm a mosquito.

Though the marriage plot and the new empire of British India prevail over "the smallest fear or doubt of her revolt," in the words of Shakespeare's Othello (if not Sophia's), Sophia's elision of revolt is not that of Gibbes, who gives the reader ample though oblique opportunity to speculate about the alternative fates of her characters beyond the point that Sophia dares consider, including the glimpse of Sophia as Hindu widow heroically offering herself to the funeral pyre of her beloved and the imagined death of Doyly at sea echoing the intended purification of the bodies in the Ganges horribly disfigured by alligators and spreading disease to the living. Amid the late Enlightenment departure from the traditionally martial masculine ideal, Gibbes's British India finds an uneasy balance between horror at its predatory nature and devotion to the Orientalism of the Hastings administration.

"Complexional Enthusiasm": Intersubjectivity in Owenson's *The Missionary*

By contrast to Gibbes, whose subtitle, "A Novel of the Days of Warren Hastings" announces her overt historical context, Sydney Owenson sets her 1811 novel, *The Missionary*, in seventeenth-century India which, this section will argue, thinly veils the Anglo-India of the Orientalist period. Most readers of *The Missionary* have rightly pointed to Owenson's larger concern in this novel with imperialism, "sites of European domination," including Portugal, Ireland, and India, that "are paralleled and mapped onto each other, revealing broad lessons about the cultural, and specifically religious, intolerance that validates and energizes the imperial drive to conquer" (Wright 20). Nevertheless, the broad stroke this perspective uses to describe the novel has tended to reduce the specific nuances of Owenson's engagement with the Anglo-India of her time to a more generalized moral indictment, thereby losing the opportunity to see the novel's deeper radicalism in rejecting the distortions of Orientalism and the nascent ideology of canonical Romanticism.

Owenson, like Gibbes, upends the marriage plot of the sentimental novel by means of experimenting with female subjectivity to voice views that run counter to the hegemony of the late-Enlightenment Orientalism of Anglo-India.[17] Yet while Gibbes subverts the sentimental tradition with an ironic twist on the marriage plot, marking the end of the Hastings era with an albeit rueful unavoidability in not only killing off the Indian object of Sophia's love but replacing him with the insipid embrace of Doyly, her EIC fiancé, Owenson's subversion of the genre involves a more sophisticated interplay of subjectivity. Hilarion's contact with both India and the object of his ambivalent desire, Luxima, is one of ruin, leading to Luxima's death and to his self-exile, which is all the more tragic when the epistemological foundation of their struggling relationship is tied both to gender and the sociopolitical dissonance between them.

In *The Missionary*, Owenson creates in Hilarion a composite of ambivalences that characterize nineteenth-century imperialism and masculinity. Though Hilarion is traditionally seen as the novel's protagonist, Owenson informs her narrative with intersubjectivity between him and Luxima, the Hindu priestess. The effect of this double vision of their perspectives on each other is to complicate and challenge the "archetypal victims" of sentimental fiction: the "chaste and suffering woman ... elevated into redemptive death, and the sensitive, benevolent man whose feelings are too exquisite for the acquisitiveness, vulgarity and

---

[17] While this subjectivity may be seen to align them with the nascent confessionalism that would come to define the Romantic ideology, the differences between Gibbes's earlier influence by associational philosophy—also an influence the early Coleridge and Wordsworth, as the previous section has discussed—and Owenson's later critique of her male protagonist's progressively "hypochondriacal" subjectivity, reveal the significance of the changing relationship between gender and subjectivity during the period. Wordsworth's 1800 preface to the second edition of *Lyrical Ballads*, announcing that "all good poetry is the spontaneous overflow of powerful feelings: and though this be true, Poems to which any value can be attached were never produced on any variety of subjects but by a man who, being possessed of more than usual organic sensibility, had also thought long and deeply," epitomizes the the canonical Romantic appropriation of subjectivity that Curran and others first identified as generated by women poets (448). See the epilogue to this book for a more detailed discussion of the complication of that ideology from the nondual perspective of the women writers, specifically between the early associational influence of Coleridge on Wordsworth to Coleridge's rejection of Wordsworth's memory-based definition of poetics.

selfishness of his world" (Todd 4).[18] Luxima's subjectivity by contrast becomes a lens through which Owenson exposes the *melange* of late Enlightenment repressions and injustices that Hilarion embodies.[19]

Owenson challenges not only the hierarchy of male rationality and female sensibility but even their assumed duality across gender lines; she conceives two radically distinct and gendered types of sensibility, one embodied by the European Hilarion and the other by the Hindu Luxima. Owenson thus exemplifies the phenomenon that Isobel Armstrong describes among early nineteenth-century women writers who dealt with the problem of "affective discourse" by turning "the customary 'feminine' forms and languages" to "*analytical* account and used them to *think* with"; they critiqued the male philosophical traditions that led to a "demeaning discourse of feminine experience" and remade those traditions (15). Casting *The Missionary* in the mode of sensibility as it exposes the conflicts between east and west and between female and male, Owenson challenges the "inert model" of Enlightenment reason so that sensibility becomes "a way of thinking through [her] relationship to knowledge" (Armstrong 16).

Though the novel's setting of Hilarion's seventeenth-century Portuguese mission distances him from Owenson's own historical context, he is conflicted in peculiarly late Enlightenment British ways: the Romantic sensibility underlying his careful self-fashioning of deistic rationalism produces what Owenson refers to as his "hypochondriasm" (202).[20] Eighteenth-century novelists had "found it increasingly difficult to distinguish between the figure of the virtuous hero ... and that of the sadly distracted and isolated hysteric"; Owenson, however, reveals that these are not mutually exclusive characteristics; "creeping 'unreason' haunts Hilarion's supposedly triumphant 'reason'" (Mullan 16). Though Hilarion presents himself as the paternalistic rescuer of Luxima specifically and the Hindus in general, his increasing anxiety over the radical, epistemological shift that India has wrought reaches such a pitch in the course of the novel that his self-proclaimed

---

[18] I use the terms "sensibility" and the "sentimental" interchangeably as does Ellis, who claims that they denote "a complex field of meanings and connotations in the late eighteenth century, overlapping and coinciding to such an extent as to offer no obvious distinction" (7).

[19] Owenson retitled the novel *Luxima, the Prophetess* in her 1859 revised edition, suggesting that Luxima becomes at least as central to the novel as Hilarion.

[20] Eliza Fay's 1779 description of a missionary, a fellow passenger on her voyage to India, is an uncanny prolepsis of Hilarion: "Figure to yourself, a man in the prime of life ... tall, well made, and athletic in his person; and seemingly of a temperament to brave every danger: add to these advantages a pair of dark eyes, beaming with intelligence ... and you cannot fail to pronounce him, irresistible. He appears also to possess, all the enthusiasm and eloquence necessary for pleading the important cause of Christianity; yet one must regret that so noble a mind, should be warped by the belief of such ridiculous superstitions, as disgrace the Romish creed"; when she refuses his entreaty to her to give up coffee as a "libation to the bambino ... Jesus," she writes that he declared "that he was equally shocked at [her] wilful incredulity and obstinate heresy" and "withdrew to another part of the vessel, and [she has] not seen him since" (72–3).

reason gives way to passion that takes "the path of excess," the malady resulting from excess of sensibility; indeed, Hilarion embodies "sensibility in retreat, segregated from a world impervious to it" (Mullan 234, 213).

Owenson thus dismantles, through its self-subverting ties to both sensibility and late Enlightenment rationalism, the Romantic masculine ideal described by Marlon Ross as the Romantic poet's "myth of masculine self-possession" that enables his "historical resituation," in turn allowing him to "adapt psychologically, philosophically, and pragmatically to historical forces that are beyond his control as a human being but that nurture the myth of self-control as the primary means for containing those forces" (28–9). Hilarion, whose self-possession abandons him on each of these fronts in the course of his mission to convert Luxima, becomes afflicted with an excess of sensibility, a paralyzing concoction of rage, arrogance, lust, and repression.

Hilarion is from the beginning of the novel an amalgam of the Romantic poet, imperialist, and Orientalist; his experience of sublimity as he is transported east introduces him as a man who conflates the material claims of imperialism with the visionary: "[T]he imagination of the Missionary, escaping beyond the limits of human vision, stretched over those various and wondrous tracts, so diversified by clime and soil, by government and by religion."[21] Connecting the Romantic imagination and imperial conquest, Owenson does more than demystify the Wordsworthian wanderer-as-outcast: she suggests that Hilarion's imagination tips the balance towards pathology. The sublime scene from Hilarion's perspective "excite[s] man to sow the seeds of great and distant events, to found empires, or to destroy them" (80). Creating a disjunction between aesthetic sublimity and the natural world as a geological, botanical phenomenon, the narrator describes "primeval mountains, whose wondrous formation preceded that of all organic matter" in contrast to Hilarion's struggle with the temptation to conquer this vision (80).

As mentioned earlier, that Owenson sets the novel in the seventeenth century and makes Hilarion Portuguese have been widely recognized as elements of a "thinly disguised commentary on British colonial policy" (Neff 392).[22] The novel takes this "commentary" even deeper, linking imperialism, gender, and Enlightenment deism with its repeated connections between the dualities of east and west and of male and female. Early in the novel, for instance, the Pundit's description of the Hindu widows who perform *sati* echoes Hilarion's own "enthusiasm": "Pure and tender, faithful and pious, zealous alike in their fondness and their faith..., [they] immolate themselves as martyrs to both"; the Pundit adds, "In all the religions of the east woman has held a decided influence, either as priestess or as victim; but the women of India seem particularly adapted to the offices and influences of their faith" (96). Though at this early point Luxima's voice has not yet emerged as an

---

[21] Owenson, Sydney. *The Missionary*. Ed. Julia Wright. New York: Broadview, 2002. p. 80. All further references to this edition are given parenthetically in the text.

[22] Leask (*British Romantic Writers*), Rajan, and Wright also discuss the novel's contention against British imperialism.

alternative to Hilarion's subjectivity, by the end of the novel, as will be discussed later, her sacrifice as she leaps into the pyre meant to kill Hilarion, and her mortal wound by a knife meant for him, underscore the gap between his self-fashioning as a Christian martyr and the emotionally paralyzed Romantic that Luxima's subjectivity shows him to be; that he retires in isolation for his remaining days exposes the underside of Romantic wandering.

More insidious than Hilarion's self-proclaimed rationality, then, is his repressed sensibility which gives rise to a neurosis that Owenson elaborates as he is increasingly forced to acknowledge his self-deception. Homi Bhabha's application of the psychological category of *aporia* to imperialism provides a useful analogue to Owenson's conflation of the sexual and political in Hilarion's ambivalent aggression: Bhabha's notion of the "paranoia of power" which he describes as the "splitting, doubling, turning into its opposite, projecting" characterizes Hilarion's behavior throughout the novel (95, 97). Hilarion's leaving his native Portugal-as-England, the bastion of Enlightenment rationalism and materialism, to go to India, the embodiment for the British of feminine sensibility, is thus double-edged: as the disseminator of such Enlightenment ideals as deism and reason, he goes to convert the Hindus to Christianity, and yet he identifies with what he perceives as India's sensibility and its imperviousness to his Enlightenment dogma.[23] It is religious "enthusiasm" that has alienated Hilarion from his materialistic family (73); the emotionalism connoted by the derogatory Enlightenment usage—enthusiasm literally meaning "filled with God"—reveals British deism peering through the mask of the seventeenth-century Portuguese missionary, complicating the polarities of sensibility and reason.

At the heart of Hilarion's neurosis is his ambivalence towards Luxima, powerful from his first meeting with her: "[W]hen he beheld her receiving the homage of a deity, all lovely as she was, she awakened no other sentiment in his breast than a pious indignation, natural to his religious zeal, at beholding human reason so subdued by human imposition" (101). Hilarion's notion that reason is "subdued" is held in ironic contrast to his suppression of what Owenson refers to later as his "sensibility" (202).

The contrapuntal narrative perspectives of Hilarion and Luxima thus increasingly problematize Hilarion's point of view. As Hilarion's self-subverting impulses do internal battle, Luxima's subjectivity unfolds, the novel complicating sensibility in Luxima's case by linking it to Indian nondualism. For Owenson, nondualism and the feminine together provide an alternative to western epistemology and its ties to imperialism. Hilarion's perspective of a feminine India is distilled through his reaction to Luxima who, as Hindu priestess, wreaks havoc with the assumption of superiority behind his deistic imperialism. With implications for gender, empire, and epistemology, Luxima's nondualism simultaneously exposes the difference between her sensibility and the emotional instability that paradoxically underlies Hilarion's attempt to dominate both Luxima and India. Owenson renders Indian

---

[23] For a detailed discussion of English feminization of India, see Suleri on Burke (60–62).

nondualism, through Luxima's subjectivity, as a divinity permeating all things, distinguished from the monotheism of Enlightenment deism that separates God from the phenomenal world. Hilarion chastises Luxima for her nondualism, claiming that he acts according to God's will, which, he says, "bids me tell thee that the prejudice to which thy mind submits is false alike to happiness and to reason" (112). Hilarion's deism is unmistakable when he claims that they are both children of the same "parent, created by the same Hand" (112). Luxima responds by articulating the alternative nondual view of divinity: "Art thou then an irradiation of the Deity, and like me, wilt thou then finally be absorbed in his divine effulgence?" (112). Luxima here reverses Hilarion's "corrective" vision, asserting that as a priestess she connects to divinity as an "irradiation" or an "effulgence" rather than a "parent" who speaks from on high.

Owenson's knowledge of Orientalist scholarship, particularly the essays and translations of William Jones, the director of the Asiatic Society of Bengal, is evident through Luxima's articulation of Hindu philosophy. Indeed, Luxima's voice reveals that Owenson had assimilated Jones's rendering of the Vedas down to his diction. For instance, Jones translates a passage from the *Sivavedanta* in his essay, "On the Literature of the Hindus": "There the sun shines not, nor the moon and stars: these lightnings flash not in that place; how should even fire blaze there? God irradiates all this bright substance; and by its effulgence the universe is enlightened" (Feldman and Richardson 105). Luxima's diction echoes Jones's when she exclaims, "I adore the effulgent power, in whose luster I now shine, and of which I am myself an irradiated manifestation" (125). Luxima is not only an adorer of nature and of God but, as she states, she is not separate from them, made of the same energy that the sun is and which is God itself.

Studies of the novel that regard Hilarion's voice as authorial have tended to assert that Owenson merely echoes Jones.[24] In their translations and essays, however, the Orientalists often misrepresented Indian nondualism by rendering it as deistic monotheism.[25] It is thus essential to distinguish Owenson from them: when Luxima's voice is given credence, the ambivalence of the Orientalists is all the more apparent in Hilarion's voice, from whom the narrator's ironic distance is underscored by Luxima's unconditional nondualism. Thus, immediately following Luxima's exclamation about being the "irradiated manifestation" of "that effulgent power," Hilarion's "blood ran cold as he thus found himself so intimately associated in the worship of an infidel"; he tells her "I call thee idolatress ... because even now thou didst offer to the sun that worship, which belongs alone to Him who said, 'Let there be light'" (125–6).

---

[24] Wright, for example, regards Owenson as drawing "heavily on an orientalist discourse that tacitly sanctions the imperial project" and that, by representing the east through a woman as a "critique of patriarchy," Owenson does so at a price, "the cost of appearing to reinforce sexist and imperialist claims" (37). According to Leask, the novel idealizes the "monotheism and deism" of Luxima, suggesting that Owenson "follows Jones in reading Hinduism as a form of European deism" (*British Romantic Writers* 102).

[25] See the introduction for my discussion of the Orientalists' blurring of the line between deism and pantheism.

Complicating this conflict further, Hilarion does not merely reject Luxima's non-dualism. Just before her epiphany about the "effulgent power" to which she is connected, Hilarion himself speaks "a language so similar to that in which the devotions of the heathen were wont to flow" that he exclaims, "Daughter, health and peace to thee and thine! May the light of the true religion effuse its luster o'er thy soul, as the light of the sun now irradiates thy form!" (124–5). This sequence of events—Hilarion's exclamation that sounds like Hinduism, Luxima's epiphany of nondual identification with the divine, and Hilarion's condemnation of Luxima as an idolatress—reveal that his condemnation of Luxima's nondualism arises out of his own susceptibility to it.

The simultaneous unfolding of what Owenson represents as Hilarion's neurosis and Luxima's sanity, the latter associated with the sensibility underlying her nondual relationship to the phenomenal world that she both embodies and in which she exists, gives the novel its double vision of the interconnected modes of Hilarion's domination—the political, the epistemological, and the gendered. Hilarion sees not only the Indian landscape, but the Hindus themselves, as primeval: he "was determined to remain until he had made himself master of the dialects of Upper India, where the pure Hindu was deemed primeval" (86). The language of empire is unavoidable: he makes himself "master"; he is able to "conquer the difficulties of the task" (87). In spite of having been influenced by Jones's depiction of ancient Indian writing, Owenson's voice here again needs to be distinguished from Jones's in her warning against gendered imperialism. She decries the epistemological and aesthetic repressiveness of Orientalism by embodying the feminized, colonial voice in the character of Luxima. In spite of his revulsion at the "superstition" of Hinduism, Hilarion's study of Sanskrit, which proceeds so that he reads it "with ease and even with facility," suggests Jones and the other Orientalists (101). Hilarion "had made himself master of the topography of the country—the valley of Cashmire, its villages, its capital, its pagodas, and the temple and Brahminical college, in which the Guru presided," thus associating the learning of language with the imperial project (101).

Owenson's connection to Jones becomes even more problematic through the deistic Pundit who, because of the intensity of his aversion to Hinduism, aids Hilarion's mission by suggesting that Luxima's conversion would be the most effective way to convert the Hindus, advice that turns on itself at the end of the novel when her sacrifice inspires the Hindu revolt (87, 88). The language of Romantic sensibility can be heard in the Pundit's description of the "Vedanti sect" as "a creed finely adapted to the warm imagination, the tender feelings, and pure principles of an Indian woman; and which, sublime and abstracted, harmonizes with every idea of human loveliness and human grace" (88–9). Owenson here links Hinduism to the feminine through the Romantic ideals of sublimity, sensibility, and imagination; that this description is given by the Pundit who opposes his own culture deepens the novel's challenge to Enlightenment dualities of sensibility and reason, and femininity and masculinity.

The novel's intersubjectivity thus reaches a climax as Hilarion's mounting anger and frustration turn to neurosis. Responding to Hilarion's claim that her resistance to his conversion is due to her "illusion," Luxima, undaunted, states, "The light of the Great Spirit has revisited my soul. Even now I am myself become *part of the Divinity*" (175–6, italics in original). Though Hilarion understands this simply as "the delirium of religious fanaticism [that] had seized her imagination," he is nevertheless perplexed, having overthrown reason, the foundation of his deism: "Hast though risen above humanity, or have I fallen below it?" (176).

Hilarion's reaction to the Pundit's explanation of Vedanta, "[t]hat matter has no essence independent of mental perception," thus appears as a deliberate misreading. Hilarion states, "This doctrine, so pure and so sublime … wants but the holy impress of revelation to stamp it as divine" (89). His didacticism quickly turns to revulsion in an ironic juxtaposition, in which he decries polytheism in the form of what he sees as "the grotesque figure of an idol, before whose shrine a crowd of deluded votarists lay"; the irony is underscored in a tableau when, as the narrator continues, "he turned away his eyes in horror, kissed the crucifix which was concealed within the folds of his dress, and proceeded to the vestibule" (91).

Luxima's Bhakti (Love as Religion); Hilarion's Christianity (Love or Religion)

Representing the epistemological challenge of Indian philosophy for Hilarion, Luxima is far more complex than the objectified Indian maiden into which some of Owenson's male contemporaries transformed her.[26] Perhaps the most problematic aspect of Hilarion's sensibility is the conflict he creates between his erotic love for Luxima and his religion, for "passion and honour, religion and love, opposed their conflicts in his mind" (170). Luxima, by contrast, embodies the Hindu notion of *bhakti*, devotional love for God, which Jones describes in his essay, "On the Mystical Poetry of the Persians and Hindus." According to Jones, the Vedas

> concur in believing, that the souls of men differ infinitely in *degree*, but not at all in *kind*, from the divine spirit, of which they are *particles*, and in which they will ultimately be absorbed; that the spirit of GOD pervades the universe, always immediately present to his work, and consequently always substance, that he alone is perfect benevolence, perfect truth, perfect beauty; that the love of him alone is *real* and genuine love, while that of all other objects is *absurd* and illusory. (Feldman and Richardson 219–20)

Owenson reflects these attributes in Luxima's nondual relationship to divinity, which is in turn inextricably tied to her sensuality. When he discovers Luxima worshipping before her private altar, Hilarion, divided between his erotic attraction

---

[26] Luxima was a "character-type to which [Shelley] returned obsessively in his oriental poems" (Leask, *British Romantic Writers* 102). Criticism of the novel has perpetuated the two-dimensional readings of both Luxima and India; Stevenson, for instance, dismisses Owenson's knowledge of Indian philosophy and criticism of the "gaudy colors" in her representation of the Indian landscape (131); more recently, Rajan has claimed that, for Owenson, India is "not a real country but a contrivance, seen through the spectacles of Orientalist books" (137).

to her and his sense of Christian virtue, cannot fathom the *bhakti* tradition of the divine love. To Hilarion, she appears as "a human form," which is "so bright and so ethereal ... that it seemed but a transient incorporation of the brilliant mists of morning" (108).

That Hilarion's disparaging of Luxima is increasingly problematized by his erotic obsession with her is further testimony to Owenson's ironic treatment of male sensibility; at the same time, Luxima's subjectivity emerges as a force with which Hilarion must contend even as his attempts to school Luxima away from her religion and culture become increasingly heavy-handed. This double perspective allows the reader to see the frustration of Hilarion's attempted conversion of Luxima. His desire to translate her into an embodiment of western ideology is sabotaged by his attraction to her freedom from it, so that his growing aggression in his self-proclaimed role as agent of Luxima's salvation is made all the more ironic when he claims that Luxima is "worthy ... to be saved," a phrase he restates soon after as "worthy to be converted" (120, 124).

While Luxima connects love, nature, and divinity, Hilarion, "sigh[ing] convulsively" as he watches Luxima's "perfect form," cannot resolve his overwhelming desire for her with his religious identity (155). Thus, Hilarion's "heart throbbed with a feverish wildness" at beholding Luxima, "the object who had thus agitated and disturbed the calmest mind which Heaven's grace had ever visited" (147). Hilarion's sensibility is neither linked to "moral rightness," the traditional function of sensibility in the late Enlightenment, nor is this sensibility linked to contemplation, but rather to an emotionalism that opposes reason. As Wright notes, the most important way sensibility manifests this ethical challenge is through its "development and contemplation of moral feeling, a pre-psychoanalytic examination of emotion in the context of the needs of society and of the individual" (31). Owenson's authorial irony about Enlightenment ideas of sentiment can be filtered through Hilarion's words as he lectures Luxima, saying that "all sentiments merely of the heart are dangerous, and to be distrusted; whatever soothes the passions, tends to cherish them,—whatever affords pleasure, endangers virtue" (215). Hilarion's separation of love and religion appears with increasing obviousness to run counter to the emerging Hindu perspective of their union.

As Hilarion begins to acknowledge his attraction to Luxima and to India, he comes to fear the possibility that he will subvert his mission. He thus reflects on "how difficult [it was] to eradicate those principles impressed on the character without any operation of the reason.... [H]e whose life had been governed by a dream, was struck by the imbecility of those who submitted their reason to the tyranny of a baseless illusion" (102). That Hilarion considers his quest to convert Indians to Christianity a dream while he dismisses Indian thought as "baseless illusion" suggests his growing awareness that his own idealism may be no more grounded in reason than the illusion he claims Hinduism to be.

This moment is a turning point in Hilarion's response to India; he arrives in a Kashmir whose luxuriant description suggests the emergence of a deeper level of ambivalence in his perspective of India:

> Purple mists hung upon the lustre of its enchanting scenes, and gave them in fairy forms to the stranger's eye. The fluttering plumage of the peacocks and lories fanned the air, as they sought repose among the luxuriant foliage of the trees: the silence of the delicious hour knew no interruption, but from the soothing murmurs of innumerable cascades. All breathed a tranquil but luxurious enjoyment; all invited to a repose which resembled a waking dream (104–5).

The slippage between the Missionary's "dream" of conquest and the "base illusion" he scorns starts to take place for, following this description, Owenson writes, "The Missionary had no power to resist the soft and new emotions which possessed themselves of his whole being" (105). The magnitude of this change is intensified when Luxima reenters, Hilarion left impotent by her presence:

> He had not the power to follow, nor to address her: he crossed himself, and prayed. He, who in the temple of the idol had preached against idolatry to a superstitious multitude, bold and intrepid as a self-devoted martyr, now, in a lovely solitude, where all was calculated to sooth the feelings of his mind, and to harmonize with the tender mildness of his mission, trembled to address a young, a solitary, and timid woman. (111)

Though Owenson here presents Luxima through Hilarion's eyes as a woman of diminished proportions, the novel gives Luxima more than Hilarion's objectified perspective of her. Her trajectory towards subjectivity and, therefore, empowerment reaches a climax when she has a direct vision of Brahma. This episode echoes Arjuna's vision of Krishna in chapter 9 of the *Bhagavad Gita*. In Charles Wilkins's 1785 translation, Krishna explains to Arjuna that his divine form is too difficult to behold through "mortifications, by sacrifices, by charitable gifts; but I am to be seen, to be known in truth, and to be obtained by means of that worship which is offered up to me alone; and goeth unto me whose works are done for me; who esteemeth me supreme; who is my servant only" (97).[27] Owenson reworks the *Gita*'s central moment of revelation to emphasize the epistemological and gender differences between Luxima and Hilarion. Owenson's gothic description suggests Luxima's contact with the supernatural is a revelation unlike anything that Hilarion has experienced:

> The air was breathless, and the branches of this consecrated and gigantic tree alone were agitated; they waved with a slow but perceptible undulation; the fearful eyes of the apostate pursued their mysterious motion, which seemed influenced by no external cause: they bowed, they separated, and through their hitherto impervious darkness gleamed the vision of a human countenance! If human it might be called; which gave the perfect image of Brahma, as he is

---

[27] That Owenson would be familiar with the *bhakti* tradition as well as Wilkins's translation of the *Gita*—if not directly, through Jones—is supported by Franklin's study of Jones's having "enthusiastically devoured" Wilkins's translation of the *Gita* in which "Krishna advocates the spiritual path of *bhakti* or loving devotion" to explore Jones's interest in the "love of Krishna and Radha" which is at once "divine and erotic" (60–61).

represented in the Avatar of "the Destroyer." It vanished—the moon sank in clouds—the vision lasted but a moment; but that moment for ever decided the fate of the Priestess of Cashmire! Luxima saw no more—with a loud and piercing shriek she fell prostrate on the earth. (172–3)

Owenson reverses the *Gita*'s moment of transformation: for Arjuna, the surprise is that his uncle, Krishna, is the avatar of God who reveals himself to be the entire cosmos, whereas for Luxima, the spirit she always experienced as disembodied, in nature, is humanized as a "perfect image" in the vision. Later in the *Gita*, Krishna tells Arjuna the qualities of one who is devoted to him; they include, in Wilkins's translation, being

> patient of wrongs, contented, constantly devout, of subdued passions, and firm resolves, and whose mind and understanding are fixed on me alone. He also is my believed of whom mankind are not afraid, and who of mankind is not afraid; and who is free from the influence of joy, impatience, and the dread of harm. He my servant is dear unto me who is unexpecting, just and pure, impartial, free from distraction of mind, and who hath forsaken every enterprise. (99–100)

Hilarion's passion, anxiety, intimidation of and by others, and ambition are likewise seen from the perspective of Luxima as qualities that go against the essence of Indian tradition.

This moment underscores the complexity of Luxima's sensibility. Far from being associating with weakness, as Hilarion suggests when he muses over Luxima's potential to be saved from "her wandering mind," Luxima's sensibility contrasts Hilarion's erotic love for her (120). This is also the moment in which she embraces her identity as priestess. Through Luxima's "religious ecstacy" upon her vision of Brahma, like Arjuna's vision of Krishna's divine form, she both experiences and embraces nonduality: "I am myself become *a part of the Divinity*," she proclaims (176). Her voice through this section is strong: instead of meekly addressing Hilarion as "Father," she calls him "Christian," equalizing her role as Hindu priestess with his as missionary. More important, she understands that she has given up her identity in order to follow Hilarion: "From the moment I first beheld thee," she says, "I have ceased to be myself.... [B]ut the dream is over! The God whom thou didst teach me to abandon, has this night appeared on earth to reclaim his apostate" (177).[28]

That Luxima is given such a powerful role of direct communion with God underscores the importance for Owenson of linking Indian epistemology with a feminine sensibility, a radical revision of her male contemporaries' feminizing of India. Hilarion has no understanding of the profundity of Luxima's direct communion with Brahma; the "mystery" of Luxima's "sudden distraction was unfathomable" to him (173). Hilarion, mystified when she expresses her growing doubt about her

---

[28] Luxima's pointed correction of her earlier addressing Hilarion as "Father" suggests Owenson's ironic reference to "the father-daughter tie" characteristic of the cult of sensibility (Todd 18).

conversion, asks, "Who will dare to disobey the mandate of a God, who comes in his own presence to save and to redeem us?" (177). He hears her with "uncontrolled emotion," deeming the "fancied event ... but the vision of her own disordered imagination" (177). Hilarion's deistic perspective of Luxima's divine revelation is ironic from the perspective the novel has given of his "hypochondriasm."

Owenson thus takes the feminine India of Orientalist translation and renders it so that its subjectivity is reclaimed. By feminizing the *Gita*'s narrative of Arjuna's subjective experience, Owenson underscores her concern particularly for Hindu women at the hands of European imperialism. Whereas, for Arjuna, the vision of the divine crystallizes his knowledge of yoga and *dharma*, for Luxima, the vision comes, tragically, after she has cast herself out of her community by committing herself to Hilarion, who has given her the ultimatum, "we meet to part *for ever!*—or—*to part no more!*" (179). For Luxima, the only action she can imagine now that Brahma has revealed himself as the "Destroyer" is that she and Hilarion honor their "respective vows" and immolate themselves," foreshadowing the novel's culmination with the Inquisitors' attempt to burn Hilarion at the stake (179). That it is Luxima who dies while Hilarion survives underscores Owenson's message that it is the Hindu woman who suffers the consequences of imperial dominance; after her excommunication, Luxima sees that her "days are numbered—sad and few, they will wear away in some trackless desert; where, lost to my cast, my country, and my fame, death, welcome and wished for" will come (190).

Caste, Race, and Exile

The disastrous consequences of Luxima's decision to follow Hilarion unfold because of what Owenson shows to be the inextricable link between caste and epistemology. That Owenson assigns the role of guru to Luxima's grandfather, who "holds a high jurisdiction over all which relates to his cast," underscores the importance of caste not only for the Hindus in general but for Luxima particularly (88). Indeed, Hilarion silences her along with the larger Indian community, as seen in the reaction to Hilarion's first sermon: "He ceased to speak, and all was still as death" (94). We find out here, as we do later with Luxima, that the Hindus' "dreadful fear ... which *loss of cast* inspired" overshadows any inspiration of "truths, so bright and new," that Hilarion offers (94, italics in original).

It is increasingly clear that the prospect of becoming an outcast underlies Luxima's fear of Hilarion, whose stern paternalism towards her reduces her eloquence to silence and dismay. When he tells her, "Oh my daughter! True religion, pure and simple as it is, is yet awful and sublime—to be approached with fear and trembling, and to be cultivated, not in fanciful and tender intimacy, but in spirit and in truth," Luxima looks "timidly in his eyes, and sigh[s] profoundly: the severity of his manner awed her gentle nature; the rigid doctrines he preached subdued her enthusiasm. She was silent; and the monk [was] touched by her softness and trembling" (140). By contrast to Luxima's conflict about loss of caste, Hilarion idealizes his self-exile from his wealthy family; his religious austerity is the means by which he justifies repressing all worldly desires associated with the upper class. Thus, "his religious discipline became more severe; his mortifications more numerous; his prayers and penance more rigid and more frequent" (75). Losing touch with "all social intercourse, from all active engagement," Hilarion's "ardent imagination" thus becomes his "ruling faculty" (76).

Hilarion's sensibility is described as "complexional enthusiasm," a phrase used twice by the narrator in a single paragraph. That enthusiasm is modified by "complexional" suggests not only "characteristic," but skin color, thus yoking race and religion; the secondary meaning is reinforced later, when the Hindus know him "by his complexion for a native of the West" (102). At the heart of Hilarion's conflict with Luxima is his anxiety over his own sensibility, or enthusiasm, which draws him to Indian epistemology; as the phrase "complexional enthusiasm" connotes, it likewise draws him away from the white ruling class into which he was born. Hilarion, a self-exile from the European community in India as well as that which he left behind in Portugal, has no comprehension of what community means in the Indian context of caste. Solyman, the Moslem prince whom Luxima and Hilarion happen upon in their exile, tells Luxima that she has given up more than her religion by following Hilarion: "Unfortunate Indian...! Thou art then a Christian, and an apostate from thy religion, and must *forfeit cast*" (italics in original). Hilarion, however, sees Solyman simply as a rival lover, not understanding the deeper levels of both connection and disconnection during the conversation among the three. In this turning point for Luxima regarding the impact of forfeiting cast, her response to Solyman reveals her own ambivalence towards Hilarion: she shrieks, falling at the feet of the Moslem, saying, "I am not *all* a Christian! Not *all* a Christian! His God indeed is mine; but Brahma still receives my homage: I am still his Priestess, and bound by holy vows to serve him; then save me from my nation's dreadful curse" (167). The final phrase of this speech is ambiguous; on one level, Luxima is saying that the curse of her nation is on her head, but it can also be read as a nation that is cursed, since Luxima becomes increasingly marked as a signifier for India in the novel. The irony thus deepens, for it is the European Christian male who is enacting the curse, leading to India's as well as her own downfall.

Hilarion's reaction to this emblematic scene which he both witnesses and in which he participates is that "for the first time his secret [is] revealed even to himself" (168). That secret is what Solyman, condemning Hilarion, voices directly: it is the "imprudence" of this "obscure and unknown Christian wanderer" that exposes her to the "rage of Brahminical intolerance" (168). Not only is Hilarion warned of the consequences of his actions for the first time here, but Luxima's own complexity reaches the nadir that leads her to contemplate suicide, for she believes that it would be better to die now that Hilarion has torn her from "the solace of [her] own religion" to have her "wander wretched and an alien in distant wilds, [her] nation's curse and shame," again a contrast to Hilarion's romantic wandering (170).

Luxima, dressed in the clothes of a *Chancalas*, or outcast, inspires fear and revulsion by those they meet on their journey to Goa. To Hilarion, Luxima becomes an ambivalent signifier: "equally resembling in her look, her dress, and air, a Christian Magdalene, or a penitent Priestess of Brahma" (184). Hilarion chooses to read her indeterminacy as signifying the need that she give herself up "exclusively to Him," the Christian God, through Hilarion's service as missionary. Thus he adds another symbol, the Bible, to pull the increasingly indeterminate Luxima towards Christian signification. Yet here again Owenson provides intersubjectivity, giving Luxima's perspective along with Hilarion's. While Luxima—who has just spoken eloquently about the power of her vision of Brahma—is once again made meek, taking the "book in silence" and meeting his eyes "with a look so tender, and yet so despairing," Hilarion too is reduced to silence and divested of his power, feeling "how fatal to every resolution he had formed, another such look might prove" (184).

Owenson suggests that Hilarion's disempowerment results from his egocentrism and its attendant neurosis; Luxima's rationality, which she retains in spite of her powerlessness, stands in contrast to Hilarion's sensibility which has built to a complex set of psychological conditions:

> No thought of future care contracted her brow, and the smile of peace and innocence sat on her lips. Not so the Missionary: the morbid habit of watching his own sensations had produced in him an hypochodriasm [sic] of conscience.... [H]is danger arose less from his temptation, than from the sensibility with which he watched its progress, and the efforts he made to combat and to resist its influence. (202)

Luxima's response to this neurotic behavior reveals the contrasting sanity Owenson associates with her:

> [R]efer not to thy faith alone, a sentiment inherent in thyself....If thou art prone to pity the wretched, and aid the weak, it is because thou wast thyself created of those particles which, at an infinite distance, constitute the Divine essence. (214)

Owenson here suggests that, distinct from Enlightenment deism, reason arises from an epistemology that recognizes the same "divine essence" constituting the self and others, including "the wretched." Owenson links eastern nondualism with the feminine and with what Armstrong describes as a nineteenth-century feminine epistemology of sensibility that challenges the western tradition.

Once Hilarion realizes that he has seduced rather than converted Luxima, his "hypochondria" gives way to a more extreme neurosis, one that would be labeled hysteria if applied to a woman.[29] Indeed, by displacing this "feminine disorder" onto the embodiment of patriarchy, Owenson underscores the latent sensibility that has been driving him all along (Mullan 225). At this point in the

---

[29] See Mullan's discussion of the eighteenth-century characterization of hysteria in which he quotes the Enlightenment physician Robert Whytt: "[I]n women, hysteric symptoms occur more frequently, and are often much more sudden and violent, than the hypochondriac in men" (217).

novel, Hilarion has become "feeble" due to the exertion of their trek through the "desolate wild" (220). As Luxima lies dying in his arms, "madness seized the brain of the frantic lover, and he threw round a look wild and inquiring, but looked in vain"; when he discovers that she is alive, he lets out a "frantic shriek, and falls lifeless beneath his precious burthen" (221). Hilarion displays the symptoms of the hysterical woman diagnosed in the eighteenth century, "seized with faintings, during which they lie as in a deep sleep.... Others, along with faintings of this kind, are affected with catchings and strong convulsions" (quoted in Mullan, 217).

Luxima's Sacrifice: Sati and Martyrdom

Most surprising about Luxima's emerging subjectivity is the discovery that, rather than choosing Hilarion or her Hindu identity, she has held firm to her beliefs in spite of her love for Hilarion and her willingness to die for him:

> Oh! Give me back to my country, my peace, my fame; or suffer me still to remain near thee, and I will rejoice in the loss of all.—Thou sayest it is the law of thy religion that thou obeyest, when thou shalt send me from the:—but, if it is a virtue in thy religion to stifle the best and purest feelings of the heart, that nature implants, how shall I believe in, or adopt, its tenets?—I whose nature, whose faith itself, was love—how from thee shall I learn to subdue my feelings, who first taught me to substitute a human, for a heavenly passion? (230–31)

Luxima, regarding her conversion as leading inexorably to *sati*, contrasts Hilarion's refusal to acknowledge his own sensibility as well as his stifling of hers.

Luxima's excommunication only heightens her identification with all that has alienated Hilarion from India: Hinduism, nature, and sensibility. By contrast, Hilarion's excommunication brings his internal dividedness to the surface:

> [N]ature stood checked by religion!—passion submitted to opinion, and prejudice governed those *feelings*, over which *reason* had lost all sway.... he, who till now had felt only as a man, remembered he was a *religious*; he who had ... acknowledged the precious influence of human feeling, now recalled to mind that he had vowed the sacrifice of *all* human feeling to Heaven! (234–5)

Hilarion's ambivalence gives the early scene of his meeting the derisive Pundit greater irony: the narrator, reflecting Hilarion's perspective in that early scene, refers to "loss of cast" as "an excommunication which involves every worldly evil" (87).

Intensifying this irony, when Hilarion asks Luxima, "[A]re we then to be *eternally disunited*?" he is still trying to convert her. Luxima's response is simply "a look of life and love," the pure spirit of religion that Hilarion has lost sight of in the zeal of his mission (256). Her faith, indeed, never wavers, and her last words, "Brahma ... Brahma," echo her reaction when the dagger enters her heart (258–9, 249). Here is perhaps Owenson's most radical critique of the "heroic female plot of suffering" which is "untenable without the deep Christian context ... considered essential for [the] sacrifice of woman" (Todd 128). In spite of Luxima's sacrifice for Hilarion, her last words unambiguously cry out against his attempt to convert her. Her love of Hilarion, in other words, has never compromised the *bhakti* nature of her love, which she has consistently linked to the "irradiating" nature of the universe.

Owenson's decision to have the uprising associated with Luxima's final rejection of Christianity has several narrative implications, one of the most significant involving the public setting of her death. Owenson contrasts Luxima's body as a signifier for Hilarion to what she comes to represent for the Hindus attending the *auto da fe*. Deepening the implications of Luxima's sacrifice, her spiritually triumphant prayer to Brahma becomes the catalyst that triggers the uprising by the Hindus against their Christian persecutors:

> Brahma! Brahma! was re-echoed on every side.... [T]he sufferings, the oppression they had so long endured, seemed now epitomized before their eyes, in the person of their celebrated and distinguished Prophetess—they believed it was their god who addressed them from her lips—they rushed forward ... to rescue his priestess—and to avenge the long slighted cause of their religion, and their freedom;—they fell with fury on the Christians. (250)

The revolt is inspired by the Indian epistemology that Luxima embodies for the Hindus, itself becoming retribution for Luxima's loss of caste that had resulted from her conversion to Christianity. Indeed, Luxima's appearance at the stake where Hilarion is about to be burned is seen through the eyes of Hinduism as one that transcends the human: she is "a phantom," "a form scarcely human, darting with the velocity of lightning through the multitude," whose "long dishevelled tresses" are compared to "the rays of a meteor on the air" (248).

Owenson nevertheless complicates the Hindus' subjectivity by having Luxima convey the cross as the signifier of Christianity. Causing her to be misread as a Christian martyr, the appearance of the cross adds to the irony behind the "superstitious wonder" with which the Hindus behold her, who see the conflicting signification, the "sacred impress of *Brahma*, marked on the brow of his consecrated offspring" announcing "vengeance to the enemies of their religion" (249). The "energy of madness, which nerved [Hilarion's] powerful arm" in spite of its "supernatural strength," does not have the power to ward off the dagger aimed at his heart, "received" instead "in the bosom of the Indian" (249).

The trajectory of Luxima's subjectivity culminates with her complex associations of the *auto da fe* with *sati*. When she sees Hilarion on the pyre, Luxima is not only reminded of her previous rejection of suicide when she was widowed, but in her confusion she recreates her widowhood, reclaiming her opportunity for martyrdom:

> [I]n every thing she beheld, she saw a spectacle similar to that which the self-immolation of the Brahmin women presents:—the images thus presented to

her disordered mind produced a natural illusion—she believed the hour of her sacrifice and her triumph was arrived, that she was on the point of being united in heaven to him whom she had alone loved on earth; and when she heard her name pronounced by his well-known voice, she rushed to the pile in all the enthusiasm of love and of devotion. (251)

This moment underscores the transformation of point of view through the course of the novel; rather than idealizing this sacrifice, the narrator describes Luxima's "disordered mind" as producing an understandable "illusion."[30] Luxima's double role as Hindu woman and icon of India are dramatically fused here: her ambivalent signification culminates with her memory of having rejected *sati* as a young widow to take up the powerful position of priestess, now martyring herself as both widow and as priestess.

With the very public and emotional climax of this paradoxical union and disunion of Luxima and Hilarion, and of Hindus and Christians, Owenson also brings to a climax her complication of the convention of sensibility, whose "construction of the body" is of "more than literary significance," constructing a "sensitive and socialized body—the site where the communicative power of feeling is displayed, but also where sensibility can become excessive or uncontrollable" (Mullan 16). Hilarion's attempts to save Luxima are seen through an irony of deepening consequence, for it is she who saves him through the sacrifice of her own life. Rather than having Luxima perform a kind of westernized *sati* in which both die on the pyre, Owenson chooses to have Luxima die later of her wound in saving Hilarion:

> [S]he had heard him with a soul ignorant of human passion, and opening to receive that sacred truth, to whose cause he had proved so faithless: the religion he had offended, the zeal he had abandoned, the principles, the habits of feeling, and of thinking, he had relinquished, all rushed in this awful moment on his mind, and tore his conscience with penitence, and with remorse. (255)

The underlying irony of Luxima's sacrifice is complete when Hilarion sees that her eyes "were ardently fixed on the rosary of her idolatrous creed, to which she pressed with devotion her cold and quivering lips, while the crucifix which lay on her bosom was steeped in the blood she had shed to preserve him" (256). Hilarion's objectification of Luxima here culminates in the metonymy of her rosary, which Hilarion misreads according to the novel's increasing privileging of her subjectivity: he equates the rosary with Luxima's "idolatrous creed," a perspective whose irony is underscored with Luxima having sacrificed herself to save Hilarion out of love, in spite of her refusal of conversion.

---

[30] The choice of the term "enthusiasm," to describe her state as she throws herself into the fire is ironic, because of its etymology, being "filled with God"; it is this very "enthusiasm" which has been such a source of contention between herself and Hilarion in the course of the novel.

By the end of the novel, Hilarion's identity, literally cloaked throughout the novel by his monastic trappings, comes to the surface: he is the "wild and melancholy man," the "obscure and unknown Christian wanderer" that Solyman had warned Luxima was Hilarion's true nature (168). Hilarion's sensibility, repressed throughout the novel, has returned at the cost of Luxima's life; his choice to be outcast stands in further irony next to Luxima's being forced into exile because of him. That he becomes the embodiment of the masculine Romantic recluse thus underscores the paradox of sensibility and domination (259).

The final description of Hilarion as one who was "in the character of a Christian Missionary," suggests his Christian paternalism had been a part acted rather than his true identity. The final irony is represented through his altar, discovered upon his death, which holds the crucifix stained with Luxima's blood: even after her death, he insists on believing that he converted her. Owenson has laid bare the hypocrisy behind Hilarion's conviction that his dream of converting the nation differed from "the imbecility of those who submitted their reason to the tyranny of a baseless illusion" (102). By submitting his sensibility to the tyranny of reason's baseless illusion of control, Hilarion himself brings about tragedy for a woman and a nation.

While Hamilton, Gibbes, and Owenson complicate subjectivity through their engagement with three distinct subgenres of the eighteenth-century novel, as Chapters 2 and 3 have discussed, the playwright Mariana Starke, whose two Anglo-Indian plays are the focus of Chapter 4, presents a more elliptical subjectivity. Though the absence of a narrative voice is a function of dramaturgy, the elusiveness of her authorial presence has made for critical assumptions about Starke's complicity with imperialism that the following chapter challenges.

Chapter 4
Female Authorship in the Anglo-Indian Meta-Drama of Mariana Starke's *The Sword of Peace* (1788) and *The Widow of Malabar* (1791)

Female authorship is a lose-lose proposition for Mariana Starke, as she proclaims in the preface to her first play, *The Sword of Peace*: "I have not confidence to stand the public gaze, nor vanity enough not to feel embarrassed as an avowed authoress."[1] The usage of "embarrassment" as an emotional state and an antonym for the "confidence" that Starke lacks before the "public gaze" was new in the late eighteenth century. For its primary definition of embarrassment as "of (or with reference to) affairs, circumstances … often in pecuniary sense," the *OED* cites a seventeenth-century reference as the earliest usage, whereas the first usage of the secondary definition, "constrained feeling or manner arising from bashfulness or timidity" is not until the late eighteenth century.[2] Starke plays on the two meanings—the first, struggling to subsist on the earnings of her plays; the second, thrusting her own authority out of the subject position, as the passive "avowed" suggests—to show semantically that her embarrassment will not permit her to avow her avowal of authorship. Such embarrassment is a phenomenon that extends the implications of what Catherine Gallagher identifies as the "vacillating materiality of the signifier" for women writers of the eighteenth century (xxiv). Indeed, Starke's humility goes beyond the *humility topos* of the confident author: she feels like an impostor.

Central to the embarrassed Starke's dilemma is that the "public gaze" before whom she stands in judgment includes rumormongers who function as both audience and the fraudulent authority over her own narrative. Well before she confesses her embarrassment at avowing her authorship, Starke dramatizes the female author's stymied creative energy by preempting her own voice in the

---

[1] Mariana Starke. *The Sword of Peace; or, Voyage of Love* (1789). In *Slavery, Abolition and Emancipation: Writings in the British Romantic Period*. Vol. 5, *Drama*. Ed. Jeffrey Cox. Brookfield, VT: Pickering & Chatto, 1999. 132. All further references to this work are in the text.

[2] The *OED* cites a speech by Burke in 1774, "If my real, unaffected embarrassment prevents me from expressing my gratitude to you as I ought". In the *OED*'s gloss of *embarrassed* as "confused, constrained (in manner or behavior)," the first quotation with emotional valence suggesting humiliation is L. Sterne's 1768 *Sentimental Journey* II. 198 ("As much embarrassed as the lady could be herself."). The first *OED* reference to the modern definition of the verb to *embarrass* is 1828: "To make (a person) feel awkward or ashamed, esp. by one's speech or actions; to cause (someone) embarrassment."

preface to *The Sword of Peace* with a conversation among inane and vicious gossips. Among them, Mrs. Gabble claims to have been "confidently assured" about the juicy tidbits of Starke's life from a friend of a friend of a friend whose son "is continually among those literary geniuses, who know every author in the kingdom" (131). The use of "genius" as a person of "esteemed greatness" was new in the late eighteenth-century and was considered a masculine trait; indeed, Starke's ironic usage of the term anticipates Virginia Woolf's 1929 observation that genius was never ascribed to woman.[3]

Starke sets the embarrassed female author against the confident rumormonger; this "most undoubted authority"—the source of hearsay—semantically eclipses "every author," underscoring the impossible situation for the female writer brought down through sexual scandal (131). While the "authoress" has no chance of vindication against the claim to credibility of such overt male rumormongers as the decorated Colonel Prattle or the anonymous son of the friend's friend's friend, Starke suggests that the destructiveness of female gossip lies in its contrasting insidiousness. Starke caricatures the eighteenth-century matron through such figures as Mrs. Languish, whose name conveys that antithesis of female creative energy and whose ennui paradoxically fuels her gossip-mongering; the play itself echoes this motif in the "fine indolence" of Mrs. Tartar, the hostess of the heroines' temporary residence in India (142).

"Thus can she neither speak, laugh, nor be serious, with impunity": *The Sword of Peace* (1788)

Starke's conflict between the embarrassment of female authorship and the confidence of gossip is a binary that the heroines of *The Sword of Peace*, not being authors, do not have to address. Yet they must navigate the treacherous world

---

[3] "If a woman in Shakespeare's day had had Shakespeare's genius" she "would certainly have gone crazed, shot herself, or ended her days in some lonely cottage out to be sure that a highly gifted girl who had tried to use her gift for poetry would have been so thwarted and hindered by other people, so tortured and pulled asunder by her own contrary instincts, that she must have lost her health and sanity to a certainty" (Woolf, "A Room of One's Own," http://ebooks.adelaide.edu.au/w/woolf/virginia/w91r/). According to the *OED*, the definition of genius (only in sing.) as the

> native intellectual power of an exalted type, such as is attributed to those who are esteemed greatest in any department of art, speculation, or practice; instinctive and extraordinary capacity for imaginative creation, original thought, invention, or discovery…, appears to have been developed in the 18th c. (It is not recognized in Johnson's Dictionary.)… The difference between genius and talent has been formulated very variously by different writers, but there is general agreement in regarding the former as the higher of the two, as 'creative' and 'original', and as achieving its results by instinctive perception and spontaneous activity, rather than by processes which admit of being distinctly analyzed.

A sampling of the *OED*'s quotations shows the ubiquitous use of the term—all extolling male creativity—in the late eighteenth-century. *OED*, 2nd ed.

of Anglo-India in their quest to retrieve and re-sign the sword from a symbol of the phallic power of war and conquest to one of peace and righteous rule; their heroic quest is to retrieve and re-sign confidence itself, wresting it from the gossips and claiming confidence for their own. Starke achieves this shift in power, from confident gossips to confident heroines, by deconstructing the binary of female virtue and promiscuity fundamental to the western male literary tradition. Starke's usage of *virtue*, deriving from the Latin "*virtūt-, virtus* manliness, valour, *vir* man," that originated during the Middle Ages,[4] is all the more ironic when contextualized with the contemporaneously emerging tradition of the canonical male poets' "internalization of quest romance that made the poet-hero a seeker not after nature but after his own mature powers" (Bloom 15). Starke's meta-textual quest is to wrest "virtue" from the stranglehold of its usage as female chastity, sexual repression, and consign it to female valor.

The complexity of Starke's revolt against the female virtue/promiscuity binary is striking in its contrast with *Vindication of the Rights of Woman*. Published four years after *The Sword of Peace*, Wollstonecraft's polemic against sexual manipulation blamed women as well as men for women's lack of virtue. As Mary Poovey first pointed out, Wollstonecraft attempts to argue against male criticism of female sexuality by sexualizing men: "The root of the wrongs of women, according to Wollstonecraft, is the general acceptance of the idea that women are *essentially* sexual beings....Wollstonecraft's response to [Rousseau's] sexual characterization of women is simply to reverse the charge: not *women*, she argues, but *men* are dominated by their sexual desires (71). Starke, by contrast, takes terms that connoted female promiscuity in the late eighteenth century and creates a dissonance between their intended defamation of woman and her usage that empowers them.

Starke's challenge to the assumptions behind the negative feminizing of words with positive masculine valences becomes yet more nuanced when Colonel Prattle dismisses Starke as a failed "adventuress"; he reflects the double standard of the active male as virtuous and the active female as "vicious" (131). As the feminized form of "adventurer," a term that in itself had connoted masculine self-interest for centuries, "adventuress" had been coined fewer than 50 years earlier, a feminine form by which Colonel Prattle equates female authorship with sexual profiteering (131). The *OED*'s entry for "adventurer" describes an evolution from its first appearance in the fifteenth century as one who "plays at games of chance" to the yet more mercenary, including one who undertakes, or shares in, commercial adventures or enterprises" and one who is "on the look-out for chances of personal advancement," both the latter fitting for East India Company employees.

In Starke's play, whose heroines' journey is no less than a quest to redeem a symbol of righteous power, Starke anticipates the medievalism manifested in the poetics of internalized quest romance from which the Romanticism label would be derived as a late nineteenth-century coinage for early nineteenth-century canonical male poets. Starke's preface not only anticipates Romantic medievalism but, in

---

[4] *OED*, "virtue." http://www.oed.com/view/Entry/223835?rskey=rwUcOm&result=1&isAdvanced=false#eid.

its sly references to Starke herself through the network of gossip, deconstructs medieval romance. In so doing, Starke anticipates the plight of women poets of the era. Mrs. Gabble, for instance, attributes Starke's running off with a "strolling player" to her "romantic turn," a euphemism for sexual deviance (131).[5] By framing the play according to the preface's polarities of embarrassment and confidence, Starke replaces the opposition between virtue and promiscuity at the heart of medieval quest romance with a more complex binary, a linked creativity-activity against a linked insidiousness-passivity.

While Mrs. Gabble's innuendo that Starke has "hawked this Sword about from theatre to theatre" connects Starke to her heroines, the contrast between Starke and her protagonists speaks even more significantly to Starke's project: Starke's *Sword* is her creation, vulnerable to public scrutiny as she herself is, whereas the comedic heroines are able not only to reclaim the object of masculine aggression, but to transform it into a symbol of peace, thereby exacting no less than a revolution in the paradigm of patriarchal authority (131). By contrast to the trajectory of her heroines, who must travel to India from their native England to wrest power from masculinist aggression, Starke, born and raised in India, is a foreigner in England. Silencing the gossips before they have even seen the play, Starke cuts off the scandal-mongering as with a sword of ultimate authority: interrupting their network of rumors that began the preface to appeal to the English audience, Starke addresses this "GENEROUS PUBLIC ... capable of speaking truth amiably," praising their "delicate politeness..., friendly interesting manner of address, and inexpressible liberality of soul," she attempts to mold the audience's response to her play through flattery (132–3). The contrast with Wollstonecraft is again striking: Wollstonecraft would no doubt revile such education by flattery as a form of manipulation by the disempowered Starke, whose dilemma as a female writer cannot be addressed by Wollstonecraft's polemic. Starke, by contrast, reaches deeper into the foundation of Enlightenment thought in her attempt to transform the duality of masculine authority and female powerlessness.

Starke's efforts, however, are thwarted when it becomes evident that the embarrassment-confidence binary undermines Starke's claim to her own subjectivity. Making clear that she has little control over the identity of her audience, Starke reinforces her embarrassment by following her preface—the introduction of the play's "avowed authoress"—with a prologue by a male author. A triply mediating, multilayered male voice, it is written by the Haymarket Theatre's manager, George Colman, and spoken by Mr. Palmer, the actor who will play Lieutenant Dormer, Louisa's object of desire (132). The voice of Colman-Palmer-Dormer echoes and extends Starke's comparison of the play to a sword by warning that the play proves not

---

[5] See the introduction for discussion of McGann's dismantling of Romanticism as a category that belied the New Critical exclusion of writers outside the canonical paradigm as well as Mellor and Matlak's introduction to their 1996 anthology avoids the label because of its gendered exclusivity. Since the field has expanded to include women writers who antedated the male poets one can see as in the case of Starke that they were already deconstructing the myth.

to be "edgeless" (136). The plot, Colman warns, has a double edge: he compares the heroines to "Syrens" who are yet "harmless" (136). By labelling the young women "advent'rers," a term that both recalls and contrasts the misogynistic connotation of Colonel Prattle's defamatory label for Starke as "adventuress," Colman puts Louisa and Eliza in the Homeric subject position of the adventurer, the questing hero—subjects of the highest order (136). Yet by labelling them "Syrens"—howsoever benign their charms—Colman conjures those fatal objects of desire who shipwreck male heroes—in this case, the position of the audience (136).

By challenging the audience to question the Homeric binary—male adventurer, female temptress—in the context of the East India Company's capitalist venture, Starke and Colman ridicule the Anglo-Indian marriage market in which women exchange virtue, or *good*ness, to be commodified as goods. On the surface, Colman's prologue contrasts the heroines' honorable quest—the sword's redemption (in both senses of the term) with that of the typical Englishwoman going to India in quest of marriage:

> India they seek, but not with those enroll'd
> Who barter English charms for Eastern gold;
> Freighted with beauty, crossing dang'rous seas,
> To trade in love, and marry for rupees (135)

Yet the contrast between the heroines and these other women breaks down under linguistic scrutiny: the *litote*s in the subordinate clause that begins "but not ..." underscores the ambivalence of the heroines' position: are they virtuous or are they cunning manipulators?

Colman's prologue brings to the surface the irony of the etymological distance between the Latin *virtus* as virility and virtue associated with female chastity, particularly as the basis for the medieval hero's quest that entails protection of female chastity. He ends the preface with the proclamation,

> Our heroines, tho' seeking regions new,
> To English honor both hold firm and true;
> Love-struck, indeed, but yet a charming pair,
> Virtuous and mild, like all our British fair! (136)

That the heroines are virtuous by traditional standards is called into question when their "honor" is qualified by the phrase "tho' seeking regions new"; the second phrase compounds the doubleness of the message: that they are love-struck may promise the audience a chaste romance that will end in marriage, "but yet [they are] a charming pair" (136). Rather than questioning the heroines' purity, Colman endorses the play's destabilizing of the traditional association of female chastity with virtue; the heroines are adventurers whose "charm" is a feminized *virtu* capable of promising them success in their quest.

Yet Colman's comparison of the heroines to Syrens echoes Starke's own attempt at seduction in the preface as she flatters the audience to win them over. In the traditional request for the audience's smiles that actors "live upon," the prologue's speaker-author associates such smiles with the conceit of the sword: "Smiles and a sword...! A bowl and dagger would no less surprise" (136). The relationship between audience's smiles and play-as-sword is the symbiosis of "a bowl and dagger," a sexualized metaphor that brings Colman's prologue full circle back to the split introduced in Starke's preface: to which audience is Starke playing—the gossip-mongers or the "generous public"? Taken together, Starke's preface and Colman's prologue suggest that, by challenging the duality society has created regarding women and sexuality, the play ambivalently frees and imperils not only the heroines but the play itself. The prologue playfully announces the drama's political connection to the Hastings controversy: in case the audience is too willing to enjoy the play for mere escapist pleasure, Colman-Palmer-Dormer satirically vows, again through litotes, that there will be "not a breath of politics," for "Grave politics wou'd here appear a crime,— / You've had enough, Heaven knows! All winter time"; the reference to the trial of Hastings instead alerts the viewer to the significance of the play for its Anglo-Indian political context (135).

Giving the play two heroines rather than one, Starke thus complicates the marriage plot of traditional comedy: the cousins create their own dialectical relationship to patrimony in its various forms: their fathers, their lovers, and the phallic object of their quest, the sword. Though the heroines are financially "embarrassed" at the outset of the play by patrimony, their confidence regarding the virtuousness of their quest is split between the reticent Louisa and the assertive Eliza. When Louisa— the more reticent of the two cousins—reflects her sense of helplessness in the passive voice by wishing they "were safe shipp'd off again," Eliza urges her to stay to receive their fortune, pointing to "the difference between women who come here to *make* their fortunes, and those who only come to *receive* them" (139).[6] The heroines tread the razor's edge of the gender binary: merely receiving their due is virtuous while imperial conquest translated into female adventure is scandalous, yet they are anything but passive, as Eliza's acerbic play on words suggests: "Money, girl, is the universal *good*" (139, ital. added).

Silencing the gossips is no easier for the play's heroines than it is for Starke, who frames the play with observations by Eliza and Louisa that counter a simple dualism between coquetry and prudery. In an early confrontation with Mrs. Tartar, Eliza defiantly states, "though I despise prudery, I cannot bear anything which degrades my sex .... [N]o one has a greater show of spirits, or more laughing chearfulness than myself, by some ill-naturedly term'd coquetry; but call it caprice, affectation ... while it tends to modest decorum and reserve, let no one of my sex be so wanting to herself as to condemn me" (144). By multiplying and interweaving the binaries of chivalry and commerce and of masculine aggression and female passivity, Starke creates a world that her heroines can rearrange and from which they thus emerge victorious.

The play's opening mirrors and complicates the revolt against masculine heroism in both Starke's preface and Colman's prologue. Eliza and Louisa land

---

[6] See Chapter 3 regarding the contrast with Sophia of *Hartly House*, orientalized from the beginning though with a deepening sense of the term.

in the double bind of precolonial Anglo-India, a context that resonates with irony through the bifurcated subjectivity of the two heroines, the forthright Eliza, the daughter of a man whose will controls the fate of her more reticent cousin, Louisa. Creating a foundation for the play's deconstruction of patrimony, Starke has Eliza's father dictate the conditions of Louisa's inheritance while the "mercenary rigid parents" of Edwards, Eliza's lover, banish him because they think Eliza "friendless ... pennyless" (139). Setting the patriarchal attempt to disempower the two heroines in the context of their retrieving the sword, Starke complicates this archetypal symbol of masculine aggression through its association with the dead Clairville, the play's disembodiment of "deceased merit"; having failed to claim entitlement by seeking "a fortune here" in India, Clairville's quest can only be redeemed by the heroines (140). The association between worth as inheritance and worthiness of character becomes further complicated later in the play when Louisa explains that Northcote is the executor to Clairville's will. The Resident disparages Northcote's idealism, claiming that Northcote will "counteract every thing that don't tally with his ridiculous notions about honor, generosity, benevolence, and stuff: as if that had any thing to do with trade" (148). For the Resident, trade and honor are mutually exclusive.

Starke brings the subversion of medieval romance to the surface when Louisa responds to Eliza,"[R]eceive your fortune, and then begin your pursuit of your true knight, like any princess of ancient heroism, and I, your female Sancho, shall doubtless accompany you" (139). Louisa's reference to Cervantes is doubly ironic: as for Cervantes, any belated quest for a romantic ideal is an illusion; these female adventurers on the cusp of the Romantic era contest the very notion of quest; Eliza's response underscores this double irony: "In the true spirit of romance, let me say then, hail! Hail! Thou land of mercenary interest, where love of gold destroys its thousands; where woman ... for wealth and grandeur comes from far to sacrifice beauty, health, happiness! (139).[7] Starke does not merely upend the assumption of female passivity; as Eliza observes, the ball in which they are expected to make their social debut is like a market: "what d'ye please to buy, gentlemen?" (144).

The re-signing of the sword culminates with a tableau in which Dormer bequeaths the sword on Eliza. By choosing the name Dormer for this protector of the sword, Starke underscores the need for her heroines to assume its guardianship, ironically reversing the gendered duality of domesticity and heroic action. According to the *OED*, the word dormer had multiple meanings dating back to the seventeenth century, including "sleeping chamber," "resting place" or "repository."[8] Dormer embodies a chivalric protectorship that is narcoleptic in

---

[7] Cox identifies Louisa's suggestion as a reference to Charlotte Lennox's 1752 play, *The Female Quixote* (388).

[8] According to the *OED*, all three definitions were extant in English beginning in the seventeenth century:
> Etymology: < Old French *dormeor*, *-ior*, *-or* (= French *dortoir*) < Latin *dormītōrium* sleeping-room, dormitory, < *dormīre* to sleep....
> 1. a. A sleeping chamber, dormitory. *Obs.* exc. *Hist.* 1605 G. Chapman *Al Fooles* iv. i, Or to any shop.chamber, dormer, and so forth. b. *transf.* A resting place; a

its current state, the name suggesting the "sleep" of passivity or lack of insight. The last of these connotations emerges most dramatically in Dormer's resistance to transferring the sword: "What, madam, sell it! Part with it—not for millions; unworthy shou'd I prove myself of his dying tenderness! No, Madam, if it cannot more nobly get me bread, it shall deprive me sooner of existence"; Eliza offers a more enlightened narrative: "You do not see the affair in its proper light, Sir; it is not selling, it is exchanging it, and for the noblest purpose" (159). That Dormer confuses Eliza's offer as commerce gives Starke the opportunity to enlighten her audience regarding the ethical possibilities for inheritance in the hands of her female characters since her male characters are, as is Dormer, either lost in the old world of chivalry or, as are their fathers, manipulating their wealth as a means to control their daughters.

Eliza's educating of Dormer in the disparity between selling and exchanging culminates with an ironic ceremony. Exclaiming, "To *you*, then, Madam, I resign the sword, which not the most potent enemy shou'd have forc'd from me but with my life," Dormer proceeds to kiss the sword "with enthusiasm" then "kneeling, presents the sword to Louisa" who is "hiding her tears with her handkerchief.— Eliza also weeping—Dormer rising, hurries off" (160). That chivalry is literally dead and *virtus* is asleep provides a vacuum for the heroines to fill, though Starke does so paradoxically: Clairville's bygone masculine virtue is one of "sensibility," a term that signals the blurring of the gender binary of masculine *virtus* as military prowess and feminine feeling (140). Starke not only feminizes the masculine, but she simultaneously upsets the gender binary from the opposite direction, the heroines distinguishing themselves from the women who come to India to find a husband, and who thereby perform a female version of the masculinist colonial enterprise.

Starke sets her heroines in an Anglo-India in which not only is traditional quest romance imperiled by nascent capitalism; these forces intersect in the marriage market through which Starke deepens the ironic distance between commerce and honor. The heroines contemptuously compare the marriage market to the slave trade, undercutting the potential jingoism suggested by the play's elevation of the English heroines above the Anglo-Indians. Terms like "nobility" take on new meaning when, after Mrs. Tartar demands that Eliza and Louisa receive suitors at a ball, as was customary, Eliza rejects the tradition "with the most sovereign

---

repository. *c*1640 *Capt. Underwit* ii. ii, in A. H. Bullen *Coll. Old Eng. Plays* (1883) II. 342 The gold.he put in his hocas pocas, a little dormer under his right skirt.
2. A projecting vertical window in the sloping roof of a house. Also dormer-window.[Orig. the window of a dormitory or bed-room.] 1592 'C. Cony-Catcher' *Def. Conny-catching* sig. B4^v, If there were a dormar built to it.it would make the properest parlour in al the house. 1703 R. Neve *City & Countrey Purchaser* 129 *Dorman, Dormer*, In Architecture is a Window made in the Roof of a House, it standing upon the Rafters.

Starke's name choice here bears comparison to Gibbes's choice of the homey and rather effeminate name of Doily for the EIC suitor who ultimately wins the hand of Sophia in *Hartly House*. See Chapter 3.

contempt," adding, "I sincerely hope the traffic will be abolished, as still more disgraceful to our sex than that of the poor slaves to a nation" (142). The statement would clearly resonate with the familiar language of the abolitionist movement.[9]

Starke uses the visual power of theater to underscore the relationship between English imperialism and trade. When the Resident makes his first entrance in act 1, his words and appearance speak in specific terms to his assumption of power in Anglo-India. He is wearing a Banyan which, as Cox notes, is "a loose gown ... worn in India and derived from the dress of traders from the province of Guzerat" (388). While this visual signifier suggests the Resident's assumption of Anglo-Indian empowerment through trade, his words to the heroines reveal the way he both objectifies and subjugates them in terms of their being in the ambiguous geography of Anglo-India: "Well, my little beauties of our hemisphere, how d'ye do?" (143). The phrase "our hemisphere" can be read in two ways simultaneously, pointing to the doubleness of the Resident's position of power regarding gender and empire: he praises the heroines for the Englishness of their beauty as opposed to what he infers is the lack thereof in the indigenous women and half-castes of India while he simultaneously co-opts the royal "we" in "our hemisphere" to suggest the English nationalism that will surface more emphatically as the play progresses.

The trade wind is not only a metaphor for the intersection between the demise of romance and nascent capitalism; human trafficking becomes more than a metaphor in the subplot in which Jeffreys, Eliza and Louisa's servant, buys Caesar in order to free him. When Jeffreys later echoes the Resident visually in his donning of a "loose Banyan," the Indian traders' dress and symbol of authority, Starke underscores her indictment of Anglo-Indian assumption of power through trade. By having Jeffreys's Banyan visually echo the Resident's, Starke shows the ease with which this English servant's desire for power is fulfilled by assuming the clothing of authority in Anglo-Indian culture. The stage directions emphasize this irony when his entrance is followed by that of Caesar, whose imperial Roman name given by his previous owner underscores the irony of cultural exchange: an English servant in the garb of Indian rule and black slave with the name of Roman emperor (150).[10] Just after he enters, Jeffreys makes a catty aside about Mrs. Tartar that is significant in its echo of Starke's preface that refers to the gossip about Starke herself. Jeffreys remarks that Mrs. Tartar was "originally the daughter of a tallow chandler in England," but in India, she has a "crowd of attendants" waiting on her in spite of her humble beginnings (156).

---

[9]   For the nascent rights of woman debate, the association between female subjugation and the slave trade becomes a familiar pattern, as seen in Wollstonecraft's *Vindication of the Rights of Woman* (see, for example, references to women's "slavish dependence" (12) and the description of fashion as a "badge of slavery" (20).

[10]   Starke's characterization of Jeffrey's buying Caesar to free him bears comparison with Aphra Behn's *Oroonoko*. See Gallagher's compelling analysis of the novel's "pattern of freeing a slave to keep him" which she links to female authorship through Behn's "heightened consciousness of the connection between self-possession and self-alienation because of her experience as a woman in the literary marketplace" (86, 87).

The play's representation of the triangular relationship among race, gender, and commerce is found not only in Jeffreys's emotionalism in buying and releasing Caesar, but in the variegated skin colors of the inhabitants of the settlement, where English social rules are scrambled. The Resident, who sees himself as "the *first man* in the settlement" distinguishes the typical "poor devils" from his "secretary," the unscrupulous Supple—a name that suggests a protean ability to mold himself to this new world—paradoxically as a man of "ancient family" now a maître d'hotel who is "the most rising man in the settlement" (145). Mrs. Tartar's attempt to defame Eliza, whom Mrs. Tartar accuses of using her "rank and fortune" to defy the Resident, takes on greater significance when Mrs. Tartar's own racial and social ambiguity is taken into account: as a half-caste, she is a reminder that the world into which the heroines have landed scrambles the English binaries that would have treated them conventionally as virtuous English maidens in the sentimental tradition.

This triangulation reaches its climax at the opening of act 3, a scene fraught with sensibility in which Jeffreys frees Caesar, a figure whose diction suggests a composite African and indigenous Indian slave ("massa"; "v" for "w"). They enter from opposite sides of the stage, representing the instability of this transitional phase in Anglo-India's history: Jeffreys as the English working class, now in the clothes of an Indian trader, in an ambivalent master-liberator of an enslaved indeterminate but clearly non-English origin, who "faints away in Jeffreys's arms" (164). When Caesar begs Jeffreys to teach him how to be an Englishman, Jeffreys's speech is Starke's satirical criticism of the jingoism that masquerades as nationalism: "for a true-born Englishman, if he provokes him, damme, he'd knock his best friend's teeth down his throat ... but never lifts his hand against the oppress'd" (166).

Jeffreys's caricatured emotionalism is a foil to the sensibility of the heroines who represent a new order of nationalism, a difference which helps explain the problematic center of the play at the opening of act 3. Starke distils this jingoism in an elaborately staged tableau representing the racially diverse "Country born" world of the gossips. The stage directions underscore Starke's agenda of scrambling and blurring the traditional binaries, with women and men of varying complexions ranging from colorfully garish to anemically colorless set against the white heroines.

> Mrs. Garnish, with her natural brown Complexion, her dark Hair dressed out with a Number of Jewels ... overloaded with Finery as possible in the Indian Stile, lolling in her Chair, holding her Cards, and a black Slave standing by her, playing them for her as she speaks them, or points to them.... Another lady "to be a contrast to Mrs. Garnish in every Degree, looking pale and sick, peevish, ill-natured, and unhappy; dressed fine and awkward.... A great fat woman, very brown, sitting full front to the Audience, as fine as can be, but dressed as ridiculously as possible: this is Mrs. Gobble. The other Lady the Colour of Yarico. Miss Bronze dressed with elegance, in a silver or gold Gauze, Flowers, Jewels, etc. (167)

Mrs. Gobble echoes Starke's Mrs. Gabble of the preface, a means of connecting the caricatured world of the play to Starke's life as an author: Anglo-India is a world of grotesque extremes into which the audience anticipates the heroines' entrance. Starke's reference to Colman the Younger's play, *Inkle and Yarico* is significant not only because Yarico "appears to be a native American" but because of the allusion to intermarriage (Cox 388). Starke's ridicule of the men portrays enervation embodied in the "brown sickly Skeletons" and the "elderly Men very Fat" for, she writes, "these two extremes prevail most in India" (167). The binaries are shuffled in this tableau: caricatures male and female, rich and poor, indulged and impoverished. The elaborate description ends with the Nobodies seated at "the two tables next to the Ballroom Door, purposely neglected…; where such Folks are generally placed to keep the Wind off from their Betters" (167).

Just before the heroines enter this grotesque scene, Starke's stage directions end with a single sentence of commonality among the elaborately differentiated gathering, with "the whole Group as much in the Bunbury Stile as possible" (168). As Cox notes, the reference is to "the style of Henry William Bunbury (1750–1811), a well-known but amateur caricaturist of the period" (389). However, complicating the implication of Starke's use of the term, the name may also allude to the 1642 "Bunbury Agreement" to keep Cheshire neutral during the English Civil War; as it turned out, it was strategically impossible thereby becoming a parable of national interests overruling local interests.

The significance for the play comes immediately following, when Eliza and Louisa enter. Whereas earlier their differences were accentuated in their reactions to the other characters, here, the visual effect is to set the two white, English heroines—entering "dress'd with the utmost Simplicity and Elegance of Taste and Fashion; but their Hair without Powder, in Curls and Ringlets, flowing in Abundance down their Backs to the bottom of their Waists"—against the various races of the Anglo-Indians who range from dark brown to sickly pale may appear jingoistic on Starke's part, but the Bunbury allusion suggests rather a critique of jingoism, as was case in the scene in act 1 in which Eliza's nobility challenges the established hierarchies of race and class inherent in Anglo-India (169). At this central moment in the play, Eliza and Louisa have yet to prove themselves as heroines: it is the tipping point at which the binaries are tested: the heroines could remain objects of admiration or transform the choice that tradition would have heretofore offered them between virtue and viciousness.

As it turns out, the scene of the gossips' backbiting stage whispers about the heroines is interrupted by false news—gossip—that Edwards, Eliza's lover, is dying, at which Eliza faints. Act 4 opens with news that Edwards is imprisoned by a "black merchant" for a debt that the Resident, trying to get rid of his rival for Eliza, won't help him to pay off. The Resident uses the situation to punish the heroines regarding the valuable sword. Gossip reaches its nadir with news of Louisa's death. The "black merchant," Mazinghi Dowza, is a Moslem moneylender whose sensibility echoes that of the other indigenous figures. When he is told that he must arrest Edwards for his debt, he is torn between his legal and ethical duties: "Me swear by de great Prophet, it make me heart ache" (175). He later urges the bewildered Eliza to take the money to release Edwards, making her promise not to tell his attorney that Mazinghi gave her the money for "if you do, me ruin—doe me de black man, lady, me ave *heart*"; as he exits, he "puts his hand on his breast" (178).

With her characteristic nobility of spirit, Eliza overturns her father's will, to the horror of the leering and lecherous Resident who is a friend of Eliza's father; she takes the moral high road when he denounces her for rescuing Edwards, "throwing away yourself and fortune upon him into the bargain" (182); Eliza responds, "Resident, don't mistake me—I honor you, as a friend of my father's—your kindness to him first help'd to raise his fortune—an obligation once conferr'd, in my opinion, *can never be cancell'd*" (183). She continues, 'I am very much oblig'd to my father, Sir, but thus stands the case—I am the mistress of my own actions, if you will not sanction them with your approbation, Sir, I am sorry for it; but as you have no right to control them, I must beg you not to attempt it" (183).

The attempts by the Resident and Mrs. Tartar to defame not only the heroines but Northcote as Resident-elect culminate in Act 5's reversal; the Resident threatens to "write home" to complain that Northcote has "set the whole settlement in an uproar! There's no governing them—blacks, whites, Gentoos, and Hindoos, all alike running mad after you, and your vagaries" (189). Northcote, echoing Eliza's noble diction, responds, "Yes, Mr. Resident, I feel for human nature of whatever colour or description; I feel for the name and character of an Englishman. I feel neither the power of gold, prejudice, nor partiality; and where the lives and properties, or even happiness, of others, are concerned, I have ever regarded the impulse of *humanity*" at which point Supple enters with news of Northcote's replacement of the Resident (189).

The comic ending of the play in Northcote's house resolves the gossip theme that began the play in the Resident's home and that had culminated with the presumed deaths of Edwards and then Louisa. Northcote, reassuring Edwards of Eliza's faithfulness and encouraging Dormer in his admiration of Louisa, represents Starke's vision of an Anglo-India predicated on sensibility that overrides the fraudulent authority of rumor (171).[11] In the play's final scene, Louisa emerges baffled from the news of her own demise, telling Eliza, "So now, my dear, you may either play off a thousand coquettish resentments before you grant him a pardon, or generously at once confess he has been master of your heart, from the first hour you convers'd with him" and she adds slyly, "I only just advise you, cousin, as you ought certainly to act as you think proper" (195).

Eliza understands the double entendre of "proper" as fitting or chaste, referring to Louisa as, "my dear, wild cousin," a term that echoes Louisa's own response to Eliza when, in act 4, Eliza reveals her affection for Edwards with what Dormer calls "charming sensibility" and Louisa, when Eliza includes the mutual affection

---

[11] The motif of residences along with Dormer's name again emphasizes the revolution the heroines enact in transforming the patriarchal estate in Anglo-India, a parallel to the central metaphor of Hartly House in Gibbes's novel.

between Louisa and Dormer, calls her "my dear, wild girl! With the tears in your eyes, and the smiles on your cheeks! Such lively sensibility and spirits sure never were so sweetly contrasted," Dormer quickly editing the comment, "rather say so charmingly blended"; Eliza responds, "I suppose my partiality for Edwards has made me a fine feast for scandal here" (180). When Dormer replies that Supple and the women "cry shame" but the men "adore you," Eliza refers to herself as a "wild blundering creature," yet protected from such "censures" by the friendship of Dormer and "the worthy Northcote" (180). Because the reverberation of the word "wild" in the play consistently challenges the duality of female propriety and sensibility, it demonstrates how central the authorial voice of women writers to the new paradigm of early Romanticism, anticipating, for instance, Wordsworth's celebration of the shooting lights" of Dorothy's "wild eyes" in *Tintern Abbey*, in which Dorothy embodies a sensibility that is linked to goodness in contrast to William's own hyper-self-consciousness.[12] By the end of the play, Starke's challenge to the traditional genres of tragedy and comedy is unavoidable: the structure itself confounds the distinction between the death of a male protagonist in the former and the marriage plot of the latter.[13]

Eliza's ironic meta-textual reference to the "tragical history" that the gossips create about their death as opposed to the "reality" of Starke's play as comedy in which the heroines not only marry but carry the day in overturning the patriarchal will and having the sword "re-signed" to one of peace in this subtly rendered classless society (195–6). The sword as a "trophy" thus becomes an empty signifier, whose devaluation is literalized when the Resident advises bargaining with Dormer regarding the sword's worth. After Eliza explains, "Sir Thomas Clairville has commission'd Louisa to expend the whole five thousand pounds that his nephew's grateful heart left him as a legacy, rather than not procure it," the Resident responds, "Let me contrive it, and I don't doubt getting it for a mere nothing" (147). Starke may be playing on the bawdy connotation of "nothing" as female genitalia: after Louisa responds indignantly to the Resident's recommendation that she take advantage of Dormer's poverty, saying "You have bound me to offer him nothing less than all; for perish that prudence that can take advantage of another's distress," the Resident picking up the association between monetary value and chastity with, "at this rate ... you wou'd ruin yourself in a month" (148). For a woman to offer nothing is everything: Eliza and Louisa re-sign the phallic sword, and in so doing, re-sign the notion of legacy as the exclusive domain of patrimony.

---

[12] Wordsworth, *Tintern Abbey*, ll. 18–19; p. 110. See the introduction for more on the poem vis-à-vis gender and the sublime as well as regarding the recent critical history that has shifted the paradigm away from the canonical male poet's visionary quest to one founded on female sensibility.

[13] Note the pattern of Romantic women dramatists' use of dual female protagonists, such as Hannah Cowley's two sisters in her 1783 comedy, *Bold Stroke for a Husband*, and Joanna Baillie's female cousins—though Agnes is clearly the dominant figure while Marianne is her sidekick—in *The Tryal* (1798).

"A theatre of horror": *The Widow of Malabar* (1791)

As the culmination of Starke's career, *The Widow of Malabar* moves from the authorial embarrassment that Starke had set against her heroines' triumph over masculinist tradition in *The Sword of Peace* to a providential female authorship that dismantles binaries of gender and empire even while it acknowledges its continued vulnerability to public opinion. Like *The Sword of Peace*, *The Widow of Malabar* asserts its subjectivity through a gradually complicating meta-drama framed by the play's relationship to its front- and back-matter. While the play has traditionally been read as "an exercise in ideological imperialism, an expression of 'civilized' Christian outrage at the Hindoo practice of sati," Ann Mellor's reading of the play's "anxious commitment to a cosmopolitan, international peace sealed by an interracial romance" has helped challenge what has been read as Starke's ostensible jingoism ("Embodied" 294).[14] By probing Starke's authorial presence in the play, its yet more radical resistance to patriarchy emerges through Starke's meta-theatrical references to her providential design that dismantles western binaries.[15]

As in *The Sword of Peace* Starke's connection between the play and its framing front and back matter creates a more complex Anglo-India than has been attributed to her. That Starke's advertisement declares the play is not merely her "translation" of Antoine le Mierre's French tragedy, *La Veuve Du Malabar*, but rather "a Drama in some measure her own" signals her resistance to replicating le Mierre's voice, the Advertisement thus functioning as an invitation to read her revisions suspiciously.[16] Framing the play as well are T.S. Fitzgerald's prologue and the epilogue by her father, R.J. Starke, the two masculine voices both reinforcing and contrasting Starke's authorial voice. There is no doubt that Fitzgerald and the elder Starke reinforce the play's ostensible subject of decrying *sati*, Fitzgerald's prologue functioning as the first signal of this affinity between the framing prose and the drama. Thus, that the prologue declares *sati* to be a "custom ... which harrows up the soul" is both an unsurprising opening to a play performed at Covent Garden in 1791 and understandable in having led to interpretations that the play is programmatically imperialistic (11).[17] However, several complications suggest a more subversive reading of the prologue. That Mr. Holman, the actor playing the

---

[14] Dakessian helped pave the way to Mellor's complication by claiming the play "supports even as it censures British patriarchy ... through a striking blend of national chauvinism, religious elitism, and colonial reformism" (111).

[15] That Starke rejects the very dualistic foundation of those binaries by dismantling them complicates the notion that the play "incorporates a number of classic binaries which gradually develop along with the widow's struggles" (Dakessian 114).

[16] For a detailed comparison of Starke's play to le Mierre's, see Dakessien. O'Quinn points out that La Mierre himself was "indebted to Voltaire's writings on the subject" (67). The term "reading suspiciously" was coined by Ricouer; though Felski argues that the concept, if not the term, dates back to the Middle Ages.

[17] Dakessian addresses the colonial history of India vis-à-vis *sati*, noting that by the 1780s the colonial government "began addressing issues of sati" (111).

young Bramin, delivers the prologue immediately challenges the binary of civilized English/barbaric Indians, his condemnation of "Bramin Law" gesturing ahead to his character's embodiment of the play's most forceful rejection of the custom (11).

Yet the colonizer/colonized binary is not merely reversed by giving the young Bramin these lines. Gender necessarily enters the equation in considering the triple male gaze of Fitzgerald/Holman/young Bramin on the female victim. What most horrifies Fitzgerald/Holman/young Bramin is the death of a young woman at the peak of her sexuality, whose erotic union with her husband is displaced by a perverse emotionalism bordering on necrophilia: "Her heaving bosom must repress the sigh, / And learn with Stoic apathy to die" (11). In this context and with the double entendre that was extant in the eighteenth century in mind, to "die" on the pyre suggests a grotesque transmutation of sexual climax that she will have to suppress with "stoic apathy." (11). The significance of this prototypical widow's sexuality through the male gaze can be contrasted to Owenson's erotically charged descriptions of Luxima in *The Missionary*. As Chapter 3 has discussed, Luxima cannot fathom the sexually repressed Hilarion's inability to reconcile her embodiment of eros and *bhakti*, or spiritual love. The widow of Fitzgerald's prologue, by contrast, is a nameless prototype rather than a character, her dilemma in choosing immolation or exile showing her utter helplessness. Choosing to be an outcast, she "wanders on the Earth, / Disown'd by those to whom she owes her birth," her death suggesting suicide as "the only refuge from Despair!" (11). By contrast, Owenson makes doubly complicated Luxima's choice between *sati* and exile: even before the opening of the novel, the Bramins offer Luxima the choice between becoming a priestess rather than immolate herself and, later, Owenson creates a striking contrast between a cowardly Hilarion, facing the prospect of immolation at the hands of the Inquisition and the heroic Luxima, dying as she tries to rescue him. For the prototypical Widow of this play's prologue, by contrast, the two choices—immolation or exile—set up a tragic formula that the play itself will dismantle.

Just as it is the young Brahmin who "invokes the Enlightenment's glorification of reason and universal humanity," what follows in the preface sets up an unsettling context for Raymond to enter the play as Indamora's hero (Mellor, "Embodied," 295). The binary of colonizer/colonized becomes more problematic as the prologue shifts from the description of *sati* as a barbaric custom of India to the ravages of war wrought by the British. With considerable irony, Starke has the young Brahmin first pay homage to his English audience in Covent Garden: "How bless'd the Natives of this happier Land, and flattering the English as "A Nation fam'd for arts, in arms renown'd," only to be subverted in the subsequent paragraph:

> Would Europe's sons, who visit Asia's shore,
> Where plunder'd Millions can afford no more,
> To nobler ends direct their future aim,
> And wipe from India's annals Europe's shame. (12)

The prologue thus proceeds from an indictment of India's ancient rituals to one of Europe's own violent part in India's tragic history, creating a deeply problematic framework for Raymond's victory over the Indians and his rescue of Indamora in the play.

Starke's relationship to the play can thus be discussed as one of the multiple perspectives on Indamora's anticipated immolation, beginning with the prologue's prototypical widow. Within the play itself, Starke makes many references to the miracle of providential design whose context becomes ironic, her meta-theatricality serving as a reminder that Starke herself is that providence as the creator of the play. Starke's meta-theatricality has a double function; first, it connects the spectacle of *sati* with the audience's relationship to the play and playwright. The second function of Starke's meta-theater is linked to the first: with Raymond's warships in view, the "theatre of horror" is likened not only to the Indian ceremony of sati, but to the many wars fought on Indian soil.[18]

Beyond the play's use of traditional devices of meta-drama, Starke suggests a yet more nuanced relationship between the playwright and her characters. She represents a disruption of traditional subject-object dualism by complicating the relationship between English author and Indian object. That providential, authorial presence stands in contrast to the author as widow at the end of the elder Starke's epilogue, in which the speaker begs the audience not to "light our trembling Author's Funeral-Pyre (14). Like Hamilton, who asserts her authority by removing herself from her novel, Starke creates a meta-theater in which she controls the movements of her characters but, as Hamilton also suggested, as a woman author, she is plunged into a relationship with theater which puts her at the mercy of the audience as tribunal.[19]

Through a comparison of the heroic role of the young Brahmin in *The Widow of Malabar* and the young Brahmin with whom Sophia falls in love in Gibbes's *Hartly House* as discussed in Chapter 3, Starke's authorial relationship to her text can be seen as more complex than previously described. On the most fundamental level, there is a contrast between the way Starke challenges the binary of white rescuer/female Indian victim through the young Brahmin's anticipation of Raymond's rescuing Indamora and the authorial choice Gibbes makes, whose young Bramin, beloved by Sophia, must die so that she can have the proper

---

[18] Starke does not use the phrase "theater of war," the term not coined until 1831 by Clausewitz, a Prussian soldier and war theorist, his usage predating the first entry in the *OED* (twentieth century): "1.—*Theatre of War*. '... a portion of the space over which war prevails as has its boundaries protected, and thus possesses a kind of independence. This protection may consist in fortresses, or important natural obstacles presented by the country, or even in its being separated by a considerable distance from the rest of the space embraced in the war.—Such a portion is not a mere piece of the whole, but a small whole complete in itself" (J.J. Graham translation, London, 1873.). http://www.clausewitz.com/readings/OnWar1873/Bk5ch02.html.

[19] See Chapter 2 for a detailed discussion of Hamilton's authorial relationship to her text.

sentimental ending to her novel by marrying her white Doyly. Gibbes, however, subverts the formula even as she surrenders to it by literally making Doyly pale by comparison to the Brahmin. For Starke, her young Brahmin, as brother to Indamora, is the object of the play's meta-textual "romance"; in his expression of the humanistic ideals of benevolence and reason. Contextualizing *The Widow of Malabar* with *Hartly House* thus exposes the play's depiction of an uneasy erotic relationship between English and Indian characters that is not necessarily true of Starke's authorial relationship to her young Brahmin. Though the plot of the play, revolving around the love of an Englishman for an indigenous Indian woman, does not negotiate *Hartly House*'s more taboo topic of an Englishwoman's love of a Hindu man, Starke's own young Brahmin embodies a similar attractiveness, here not objectified as is Sophia Goldborne's Brahmin, whom we only know through her letters, but as the strongest voice that articulates the central tenets of late Enlightenement England: reason and virtue. By comparison to the young Brahmin, Raymond appears a two-dimensional plot device, an observation scholars have used to criticize Starke herself.

The play's opening scene brings together a composite of binaries to be dismantled in the course of the play. That there are two generations of Brahmins representing a contrast of indigenous attitude towards *sati* has been observed by Daniel O'Quinn, who notes that "the struggle between reason and superstition is staged as an intra-caste conflict between a Young and an Old Bramin" (67). The Chief Brahmin's rigid hewing to orthodox law contrasts with the young Brahmin's flexibility to alter decisions based on the situation, which we find out from the start is that the English army has arrived and the ritual of *sati* will imperil the Indians. The young Brahmin then expresses concern to the Chief Bramin that the widow did not promise to commit *sati* since her husband died in battle. While the young Brahmin compares the widow to a slave, the Chief Brahmin is only concerned with custom and appearance regarding how it would look for them to cancel the immolation. That the young Brahmin embodies morality and reason challenges the composite opposition between western, masculine enlightenment and eastern, effeminate emotionalism.

Starke further complicates the composite of east/west binaries by adding a double female perspective when the scene shifts to Indamora in conversation with her Persian chambermaid, Fatima, who offers a female perspective on sati that is eastern but outside the Hindu culture. Like the young Brahmin, Fatima follows the path of reason: "Man, who boasts the glorious light of reason, / Adds the various ills entailed on Woman. / wreaks his cruelty beyond the grave" (6). Her comment, "Unjust, inhuman law!" counters that of the Chief Brahmin in the first scene in which he claims that adhering to law is all-important. Yet another layer of the binary, the conflict between Love and Duty, is dismantled when Indamora reveals that she never loved her husband; her duty to a father who forbade her to marry Raymond, a Christian, is a perspective that Starke's English audience would understand through the well-established norm for British EIC men to marry Hindi women and convert them. Starke creates a situation in which such a conversion would be unthinkable to Indamora's father. The situation is striking in its contrast to that of Gibbes; Sophia enshrines her Brahmin in her heart after he dies and she marries Doyly while here Indamora refers to Raymond as "the Husband of my heart" in contrast to the "hated Tyrant," Indamora's husband. As Sophia, Gibbes's English female protagonist, is in love with a young Brahmin that Gibbes must dispatch, the contrast with Starke is striking since the taboo for Gibbes could not have been evaded as it comes to be here.

Starke brings gender to the surface when Indamora prays to Brahma to "drive the Woman from my soul" and "[a]rm it with more than manly fortitude"; it is important to contextualize these statements in the Anglo-India that Starke creates as making women powerless from both sides of the hyphen, by contrast to Hamilton who depicts Luxima's femininity as powerful in its embrace of Vedic nondualism by contrast to Hilarion's Christian dogma (8–9). Immediately after Indamora wishes to have her weak femininity driven away, the young Brahmin enters, displaying traditionally female sensibility at beholding the widow, whom he does not yet know is his sister, about to be sacrificed. Telling Indamora of his being an outcast due to his having refused his mother's milk as an infant, he personifies the ritual of infanticide as "Tyrannic Custom" (11). After Indamora and he, in an awkward plot device, too quickly arrive at the conclusion that they are indeed siblings, they debate the possibility of fighting Brahmanical law, Starke's young Brahmin standing in contrast to Gibbes's young Brahmin, who embodies all that Sophia adores about Indian philosophy. That Starke keeps the young Brahmin nameless is an interesting choice since she chose to give Le Mierre's nameless widow the name of Indamora. By keeping her brother nameless, he remains a prototype though, as the reading of the play that follows suggests, not indicative of debasement of his representation, but rather of Starke's hope for the new generation of Brahmins that he represents.

Starke's choice to delay Raymond's appearance until act 2 is one of many that serve to undermine his heroism. Raymond's opening soliloquy bemoaning his separation from Indamora is interrupted by news that "a spectacle of horror" is about to unfold (18). Though the news is, of course, about the ritual of *sati*, the visual cue of the British fleet in the background creates an ironic inference that the "spectacle of horror" could also refer to the British part in the devastation of India. Raymond's first reaction when he hears that the obstacle to his invasion is a ritual immolation is to blame the Rajah for using the ceremony as a "pause from war" (19). That Raymond's reaction is strikingly unheroic would be an understatement, reinforced by the fact that he merely echoes or reacts to this news from Albert who turns out to be wrong about the Rajah. Starke thus uses dramatic irony to expose Raymond's lack of insight; he seems most upset that Hindu law will "allow self-murder" as he refers to the widow's "suicide," not knowing that it is Indamora who is heading for the funeral pyre. Even Raymond's subsequent plan to forgo his plan to attack Malabar and "save the Victim" becomes less heroic than questionable when Albert makes a reasonable point that Raymond is an "inconside'rate youth … / Ardent to save a single life he goes / Perhaps, to spill the blood of thousands," putting the audience in the uncomfortable position of being divided between the sympathy for Indamora and the criticism that her life is being saved at the expense of thousands (19, 20). The dividedness over Raymond's heroism that Starke elicits in the audience becomes yet more pronounced when the young Brahmin responds with "rapture" when he discovers that Raymond has gone to rescue Imoinda for, he tells Albert, "Our crafty Bramins, anxious to avert / From their solemnities, each Christian eye, / Send, ere I fled the walls, a daring Band / To fire yon stately ships" (21). That Raymond's defeat by the Hindus is averted because of his decision to save the widow casts more doubt on Raymond's idealization. When the young Brahmin returns to Indamora with the news that Raymond is on his way to rescue her, he proclaims the heroism of "Britannia's Chief," though Starke continues to erode Raymond's power even as she gives it: news follows that Raymond now must be saved from the "insatiate Bramins" (60).

That the phrase "insatiate Bramins" comes from Indamora casts her in a negative light as well, especially that she is interrupted by the young Bramin with the enlightened advice, "O, stop!—Reflect!" (26). That Indamora uses the term "insatiate" to describe the Bramins while claiming to her brother that this is "no time for thought" creates an ironic connection between her impulsiveness and theirs. In case there is any doubt on the part of the audience about this contrast between them, Starke has Indamora respond, "This is no time for thought," adding that her heart "exults / To die for him who risks his life for me," at which the young Brahmin urges her again to stop (26).

As the providential manipulator of her characters, Starke brings British imposition in direct contact with the human by having Raymond's path intersect with the young Brahmin:

> Young Brahmin: You little know me
> Raymond: Thou art a Bramin.
> Young Brahmin: Yes, I blush to own it:
> But, tho' a Bramin, I am still a Man;
> A Man oppres'd by sorrow—Read my soul.— (27)

When Raymond hears him out, the young Brahmin's lucid description of his love for his sister convinces Raymond of his sincerity: "Thy Accents, Priest, / Accord not with deceit" (28). Starke, the "Myserious Heaven" who designs the universe of the play, gives the young Brahmin the meta-theatrically ironic lines, "kind Heaven, / Has sent a pitying Angel, in thy form, / To save my dearer self—my Indamora" (30, 29). As she has shaped his character thus far, he is no pitying Angel: with the revelation of Indamora's identity as the lover thwarted by "cruel wedlock" Raymond is in a "sudden rage": "My brain's on fire— / O'urge me not to madness!" he responds, now "a desp'rate Lover" (29–30). It is Starke's authorial role as "Heav'n and Earth!" to bring about change and to reveal the ironic dissonances among their claims, their thoughts, and their actions (29). Thus, as he does to Indamora, the Young Brahmin urges Raymond "Reflect" at which point Raymond tells him, "O, thou hast made a Coward of me!" (31). By the end of act 2, Raymond does rally to assume his position as the leader of the British army, but his imperious words are more disturbing than inspiring:

> By Heav'n I'll sweep their bloody Race from earth!
> Their Friends, their altars, nay, their very Idols,
> Shall feel my utmost rage.—This splendid Temple
> I'll make a smoking heap of dust and ruins,
> And the whole city one huge Funeral-Pyre!" (32)

The speech is shocking in its violent desecration, in part because Starke has humanized the younger generation of Hindus through Indamora's brother and Narrain, Raymond's merciless rampage threatening to destroy the beauty of a civilization he cannot understand, embodied by the temple.

The multiple levels of meta-theatricality converge in act 3 with the competing spectacles of *sati* and war reaching their climax (42). Act 3 begins with an elaborate stage set that includes both the Funeral-Pyre at the center of the Quadrangle and "the English Fleet standing out to Sea," a visual reminder of the play's tension between the internal and external threats. It is now the Young Brahmin who is given a soliloquy, "reflecting," as he urged both Indamora and Raymond to do in act 2, now on his plight when the false news of Raymond's death arrives—a rumor created not from the Rajah or Bramins as earlier, but from Raymond himself to mislead the Indians.

Starke centralizes the irony produced by the double spectacle of the British ships arriving as the play's elaborately staged spectacle of *sati* is about to commence. This visual backdrop is an important means to underscore the irony of the Chief-Brahmin's triumphant speech as he is about to immolate Indamora, "The Monster, War, is fled, and lovely Peace ... descends from Heav'n" (36). That "Heav'n" is neither the Christian God nor Brama, but the dramatist who speaks through the young Bramin: refusing to follow the dictates of the Chief Brahmin, who asks "What madness prompts thee?"; the young Brahmin answers, "The clear light of Reason" (38). By this point the significance of Starke's choosing to keep him nameless becomes clearer: she has made him representative of a new generation that transcends binaries, not heroic because of British influence which he himself must keep at bay, but because of his courageous resistance to custom, or what the Chief Brahmin calls "that ancient Cypress," that the young Bramin says he will fell with "Reason's strong axe" (38).

Lest the binary between custom and reason appear clear-cut, however, this argument between the Chief Bramin and the young Bramin is complicated when Indamora appears in an elaborate train; the stage directions include two women, "the one bearing a Mirror, the other a dart"; the symbols are suggestive of several possible choices for Indamora, including a literalizing of the mirror "to reflect," as her brother has continually bids her do, or to violently oppose "that ancient Cypress," custom (40). The symbols thus represent a duality that Indamora later overcomes thanks to her brother's counsel, for she is ultimately able to see them not as antithetical, but as mutually enabling her to escape her own death and, when Indamora discovers that her brother is to be killed, to rescue him.

When escape or rescue appears impossible at this stage, however, both Indamora and her brother want to die, each restraining, thus reflecting, the other. Indamora, however, thinking Raymond is dead, wants to join him in an ironic *sati* of her own choosing: "to mix my ashes with his, whose mem'ry I abhor!" By contrast to her brother, she says, "Reflection, worse than death itself, appals me!" (42). As both Dakessian and Mellor have observed, Indamora's role in "renegotiating the meaning and performance of her suicide" grants her subjectivity that earlier readings did not account for; however, it is important not to equate her subjectivity with heroism, as becomes clear not only through Starke's own multiply qualified perspectives of Indamora in the play, but through comparison to the heroic death of Owenson's Luxima in attempting to save Hilarion ("Embodied" 294).

There is further irony when Raymond commands them to stop their ritual, only to find out that this is Indamora's attempt at using the ceremony to join what she thought was the dead Raymond. Raymond's victorious speech, too, is full of irony by this point:

> Love, Bramin!
> And, henceforth, let your holy doctrines teach thee,
> That the peculiar Ministers of heaven
> Shou'd scatter peace and comfort o'er the world;
> Turn savage cruelty to gentle love,
> Disarm the hand of vengeance of it's [*sic*] steel (45)

His speech echoes the Chief Bramin's earlier ironic claim, just before the ceremony was to begin, that peace had come; Raymond's admonition to him that the "Ministers of heaven" should scatter peace is thus a reminder of the connection that has recurred since the prologue between the violence of the ancient ritual of human sacrifice and the wars waged by Europeans like Raymond, claiming to do so in the name of Christianity.

Thus, when Raymond urges the Brahmins to convert to Christianity, Indamora's question, "If such its doctrines, / Who wou'd not be Christian?" resonates not as rhetorical, but as ironic. Indeed, the play has created a gulf between its meta-theatrical message and Raymond's vision of "the conversion to Christianity of his future wife as well as his brother-in-law, who will in turn enact a mass conversion of the natives and therefore provide the spiritual leadership of the land" (Dakessian 114). In his final speech, Raymond oddly refers to himself in third person, asking for Indamora's "fruits" to "bless Raymond and thy Country," followed by the patronizing depiction of the young Brahmin "who, 'spite of Error's mists, / Discovered and purs'd bright Virtue's paths," as his rationale to "fix the Christian Cross" on the altar of his Temple.

The audience perceives the distance between her leaving the young Brahmin nameless and Raymond doing so, since it is a jarring inconsistency to have Raymond name himself but not Indamora's brother; Starke thus drives home the ironic distance between her authorial perspective and that of the would-be hero. Though from Raymond's point of view, the Chief Brahmin's suicide ends the tyranny of his generation, Starke has dismantled the binaries that have set him against Raymond, instead linking Raymond's conquest of India and of Indamora with the Chief Brahmin's hypocrisy. While the play's final placing of a cross on the Hindu altar has been read at face value as Starke's perpetuating this consummate act of imperial imposition, it can be read ironically when the emphasis is not on the comedic ending of the marriage between Raymond and Indamora but rather on the young Bramin's heroic role in subverting that of Raymond. The play's ending is thus not a moral lesson in British conversion of the heathen Indians, but a final tension between Raymond's imperial conquest and the subversive message of a new generation of Brahmins, represented by the nameless young Bramin, that take reason and benevolence deeper than their conquerors.

Reinforcing this subversive reading of the play is the rhetoric of the elder Starke's epilogue, which is revolutionary in tone in spite of the relative lightheartedness of its ostensible subject, namely, the actress's concern that the audience endorse the play:

> For your dread anger our small Realm can shake;
> Even your frowns can make its basis quake;
> The superstructure then comes tumbling down,
> And buries fancied Fame and castle-built Renown:
> Then, helter-skelter, plumes and pinions fly,
> And blasted laurels 'mid the ruins lie;
> While Envy, smiling grim, her visage shews,
> And fills the World next morning with the news. (13)

This apocalyptic language—overblown if merely used to describe the desire for good reviews—takes on a revolutionary cast when related to the lines that follow immediately: "But how shall I about my arduous task, / if neither you nor I must wear a mask?" (14). That the actress Anne Brunton delivered the epilogue in brown-face is a historical detail Mellor connects to reviewers using "the occasion to attack the increasing number of marriages between British men and Indian women spawned by the East India Company's settlements in India" ("Embodied" 297). Indeed, the message of Starke's play is echoed in the plea for the audience's racial tolerance at the end of her father's epilogue: "Mercy prevails, even o'er distant Climes, / And makes the human Race her fondest care, / Whether their hue be tawny, black, or fair," the sentiments of both Gibbes in Sophia's passion for the Brahmin and Owenson, who subverts the traditional subjectivity of the hero seeking to instill Christian values in heathens through the relationship between the missionary, Hilarion, and the Hindu priestess, Luxima (14).

In spite of the gain in Starke's confidence regarding the assertion of her providential authorship between the two plays, there is a sad irony about the critical reception of *The Widow of Malabar* as Daniel O'Quinn observes that, in spite of Starke's "attempts to analyse the place of custom in the regulation of female subjectivity, the press used the play as an occasion for scrutinizing upper-class women and the threat their sexual agency posed to the maintenance of 'tradition'" (67).[20] The final lines of the epilogue thus bring to the surface what has been implicit throughout the play, namely that the audience is connected to the Brahmins who decide the fate of Starke:

> Then, since the Age is thus to mercy prone,
> In this Tribunal, you can fix her throne:—
> Break Criticism's shaft, quench Rancour's fire,
> Nor light our trembling Author's Funeral-Pyre. (14)

The implication is that, if the "Christian" audience becomes an inquisition as it watches the play with smug superiority, they must answer to a charge of hypocrisy if they forego mercy in their reviews of the play. But the epilogue educates this new age by flattery, urging them to follow the teaching of the young Brahmin, to reflect and thereby "quench Rancour's fire," ending a tyranny against women writers akin to the brutal custom of the elder Brahmin.

---

[20] I take issue, however, with O'Quinn's reading of Starke's allegorical intention in linking Indamora to English widows since Starke has created in Indamora too conflicted a character to signify a type.

Epilogue
Lost and Found in Translation: Re-Orienting British Revolutionary Literature through Women Writers in Early Anglo-India

This book has sought to challenge the engrained scholarly perception of passivity on the part of late eighteenth-century women writing about Anglo-India, particularly in their relationship with the male Orientalist tradition.[1] That perception, I have suggested, derives from a paradigm of western dualism that these women resisted, if not overcame, in their texts; it is thus with the hindsight of the previous chapters' discussion of these texts that I reopen Gallagher's challenge, "How can we explain the continuities, as well as the historical ruptures, in the rhetoric of female authorship?" (xx). The wide range of representations of Anglo-India by British women reveals the larger revolution in female authorship that gestures to even more than a poetics of sensibility. It is a rigorous engagement with a non-western epistemology whose trajectory can be traced from early texts such as Anna Jones's poetic rendering of her departure from India, expressing grief not only that she will probably never see her husband again, but that she is leaving a place the world she anticipates reinhabiting cannot fathom at the core of its epistemology.

Yet it is important to underscore that there were writers in England who were drawn to the nondualism of the east, some in spite of the distortions that plagued Orientalist translations, others reflecting Orientalist ambivalence towards Vedic nondualism. One of the most striking examples of the latter is Charlotte Smith, who reflects this double view of India in her last volume of poems, published posthumously in 1807. Of this volume, Curran notes that "its variety of natural treatments—from the opening meditative reminiscence through fable to allegory to didactive moralism and religious exemplum, all attended by an array of botanical, geological, and ornithological learning—testifies to an alternate Romanticism that seeks not to transcend or to absorb nature but to contemplate and honor its irreducible alterity" (xxvii–xxviii). The perspective from the Anglo-Indian texts complicates this perspective by both highlighting Smith's awareness of eastern epistemology and suggesting an attempt to bring together its nondualism with her foundation in Enlightenment deism.

---

[1] Regarding the masculinist assumptions about these women's passive extension of the Orientalists' work, see for example Aravamudar who founds his otherwise sympathetic reading of Hamilton on the assumption that she "relies on" the Orientalist texts of her brother, Charles, a position that Chapter 4 argues against (102).

Smith begins *Beachy Head*, her long, narrative poem with a challenge to the heart of late Enlightenment dualism as it manifests in the Burkean sublime that, as Armstrong has noted, "short-circuits the connection between representation and its object: the less sublime language is connected to an object, and the more it is connected with associative feeling rather than image, the more sublime it is" (28). By superimposing an imagined Asiatic sublime onto her didactic anti-imperialism, Smith represents an alternative subjectivity projecting onto the object world a visionary imagination embodied by the east that simultaneously condemns British imperialism. Smith thus opens *Beachy Head* with an ambivalently rendered eastern sublime that decries England's enslavement of the colonized in deistic terms while self-consciously drawing on India as a repository of aesthetic riches that she, as a poet, exploits.

Shifting her gaze from the quaint and unthreatening foreground of English fishing boats to the horizon, Smith focuses on a "dubious spot" in the distance. A new subjectivity arises, imagining the spot to be a merchant ship returning from the exotic and "torrid" Asia of multitudes. Smith thus creates the metamorphosis of seascape from English harbor to the merchant ship's port of entry in India, "where the sun / Matures the spice within its odorous shell" (44–5). This subjectivity can perceive odors impossibly distant and sights invisible to the human eye: "There the Earth hides within her glowing breast / The beamy adamant" (50–51). The vessel of commerce becomes an increasingly ambivalent vehicle of imperialism: Smith condemns the British exploitation of "the sacred freedom" of "Asia's countless casts" by creating an eastern sublime that takes her under the sea that houses "the round pearl / Enchased in rugged covering; which the slave / With perilous and breathless toil, tears off / From the rough sea-rock" (59, 51–2, 54).

This early description of an imagined India becomes complicated as Smith self-consciously projects those images from the eastern land- and seascape onto the present view of *Beachy Head*:

> … transparent gold
> Mingles with ruby tints, and sapphire gleams,
> And colours, such as Nature *through her works*
> Shews only in the ethereal canopy.
> Thither aspiring Fancy fondly soars,
> *Wandering sublime thro' visionary vales*. . . . (81–6, italics added)

As the "gold" and "ruby tints" of the sun sink westward, they give way to an apocalyptic image of flood and the last sun ray that "fires the clouds / with blazing crimson" (94–5). Smith's transcendent vision emerges out of and dissolves back into an ordinary moment.[2] "Nature through her works" is the creative source of revelation. That the sublimity of the seascape is gradually colored by the riches gotten by the imperialist plundering of Asia in the earlier passage suggests that

---

[2] Such a moment challenges the assumption of a gender binary behind such statements as Curran's claim that Smith's romanticism "seeks not to transcend or to absorb nature but to contemplate and honor its irreducible alterity" (xxviii).

Beachy Head represents the questioning that Suleri articulates regarding the myth of surplus in the east: "[W]as legislative discourse itself exempt from the mythmaking of that era's cultural imaginings, in which the distant exoticism of the east could be conceived and represented only by a metonymic extravagance with descriptions of the miraculous fashion in which money was seen to reproduce itself in the remoteness of that land?" (25). The deistic God Smith imagines at the outset is replaced by "Nature" as a female artist, who "through her works / shews" what lies beyond the threshold. While the image does not contradict the masculine "Omnipotent" who "Stretch'd forth his arm" in the poem's opening lines, it shifts emphasis from the deistic God to an empowerment of nature, now not acted upon but, herself, creating (6–7).

Published in the same volume as *Beachy Head*, Smith's lyrical poem, "The swallow [*sic*]," bears the hallmarks of women's Anglo-Indian texts this book has traced. If one were to read Smith through the lens of the Romanticist ideology, the first two stanzas introducing the swallow appear easily described through the genre of the Romantic ode, with a pastoral invitation to the bird to come and sing, "Low twitt'ring underneath the thatch / at the gray dawn of day" (14–15). Ironically, William Wordsworth, co-opting Smith's sensibility and subjectivity, prophetically described Smith as "a lady to whom English verse is under greater obligations than are likely to be either acknowledged or remembered" (Curran 202). Yet the following stanzas overturn the Romantic paradigm by giving an alternative interpretation of the bird through Indian mythology:

> As fables tell, an Indian Sage,
> The Hindostani woods among,
> Could in his desert hermitage,
> As if 'twere mark'd in written page,
> Translate the wild bird's song. (17–21)

Moving between these two stanzas, the former a familiar voice of a projected subjectivity, the latter an appeal to the Indian sage to "translate the wild bird's song," suggests our need as readers to adapt to a complication in subjectivity, for the bird's song is understandable to the eastern sage but not to the English poet. Thus, Smith continues,

> I wish I did his power possess,
> That I might learn, fleet bird, from thee,
> What our vain systems only guess,
> And know from what wide wilderness
> You came across the sea. (22–6)

Smith rejects the western "systems" for knowing in favor of the Indian sage's lack of separation from nature that allows him the direct apprehension of the bird's song.

Later in the poem, Smith brings together the eastern fable with the western myth, alluding, in her own footnote to the stanza, first to the "Ovidian fable of the Metamorphosis" of Philomel, turned into the nightingale by the gods after she was raped and her tongue cut out by her brother-in-law, whose wife, Procne, was turned into the swallow, and then to the "oriental story of the Loves of the Nightingale and the Rose":

> Were you in Asia? O relate,
> If there your fabled sister's woes
> She seem'd in sorrow to narrate;
> Or sings she but to celebrate
> Her nuptials with the rose? (36–40)

Smith's note includes her own preference for the "elegant extravagance" of the Indian myth, but leaves the question open to the reader regarding how one will interpret the bird's song. Displaying her frustration at not knowing how to understand the song, she concludes the series of questions with a stanza that rejects the Enlightenment assumption of human potential to know the nature of the universe through scientific inquiry; yet she embraces the deistic notion of a God whose laws determine the answers to nature's mysteries:

> Alas! How little can be known,
> Her sacred veil where Nature draws;
> Let baffled Science humbly own,
> Her mysteries understood alone,
> By *Him* who gives her laws. (66–70)

As in the opening stanza to *Beachy Head*, Smith here both celebrates the potential for an eastern subjectivity that breaks down its barrier to the phenomenal world while maintaining a deistic belief that the human is separate from the divine.

The tension between women writers and Orientalism waned in the 1830s, suggesting an affinity between a new generation of writers with the Anglicist movement in Anglo-India that rejected Sanskrit study and, by extension, Vedic nondualism. A poet who bridges these two eras is Maria Jane Jewsbury; by contrast to earlier writers such as Anna Jones and to Gibbes's fictional Sophia, who declared she has become "orientalised" upon landing in India, Jewsbury has an unwilling "translation" to India, never to return to England. Jewsbury's relationship with India is one of suffering; she informs her description of Hindu widows performing *sati* with a subjectivity that projects her own despair at sacrificing a public life of literature to follow her husband to India in what she rightly anticipates will be her literal death. Jewsbury writes with the same resignation about her journey to India in the collection of poems that comprise *The Oceanides*, as she does in "Song of the Hindu Women" about *sati*. As a British woman literally transported east who had had aspirations for a professional life of writing in England, Jewsbury's alienation and fear through emerge through her concern with *sati*.[3]

---

[3] As her biographer, Norma Clarke, notes, Jewsbury was "at the height of her career as a journalist when she left England, and, like a true professional, she had taken clippings of all her published pieces with her" (11). According to Clarke, Jewsbury "was excited by the prospect of travel ... and only sorry that she could not 'carry with her half the books in the British Museum.' Once on board ship she began a journal, extracts from which were

The Oceanides reflects Jewsbury's dread of leaving behind the world that had defined her to face one of uncertainty and probable illness. In one of *The Oceanides* poems, entitled "The Spirit of the Cape," Jewsbury compares the ship headed toward India to a woman, writing,

> Grim destruction hath its way,
> Till the vessel beautiful
> As with woman's nerve and heart,
> Downward sinks with groan and start.[4]

Like the Hindu widows in her "Song," Jewsbury stoically faces the indeterminate future represented by the blank ocean:

> Hail to thee, thou surging foam!
> Hail to thee, thou screaming blast!
> And hail the drowner's thought of home,
> His saddest, fondest, last!
> And a few more days and leagues a few,
> Hail to *thee*, Ocean, calm and blue! (208)

Characteristic of women emerging out of the "cult of domesticity," Jewsbury domesticates even the most unlikely settings so that by the time the ship makes landfall in the final poem of *The Oceanides*, entitled "The Haven Gained," the ship itself becomes the home she has to surrender:[5]

> And I have learned to read the face
> Of many a rude yet kindly tar;
> So loves the human eye to trace
> The lines of brotherhood afar;
> So longs the human heart to love
> Something, beneath, around, above. (209)

Ironically, as her biographer notes, though Jewsbury was alienated from the "Anglo-Indian community, there is every likelihood that they were equally unenamoured of her" (Clarke 161). The fact that Jewsbury "found the social atmosphere 'entirely antipathetic'" itself reveals how disconnected she felt from India by contrast to the British women who preceded her.[6]

---

published in the *Athenaeum*. She continued to write poetry. Her letters, from the middle of the ocean,... and from the 'biscuit-oven' of Bombay—'alias brick kiln, alias burning Babel, alias Pandemonium, alias everything hot, horrid, glaring, barren, dissonant, and detestable'— were lengthy and vivid and detailed. Travel writing was a leading commercial genre form women at the time, and it is plain that she had every intention of seeing her experience into print, for all her declaration that nothing she did was good enough" (160–61).

[4] Jewsbury, p. 207. All further references to this poem are in the text.
[5] See Curran for his early study of the "cult of domesticity."
[6] "At Karnai, a port near Bombay," Clarke continues, "[t]here is a tale that she found an Indian child whose parents had died of cholera whom she adopted and cared for as her

Jewsbury gives voice to her anxiety most directly by exploring the psychology of the widows preparing for *sati* in "Song of the Hindu Women." She underscores the perceived stoicism of the widows through imagery of riches that pervade the poem. The narrator, one of the widows, urges another to hurry onward to their sacrifice:

> Each golden gate, and ruby key,
> And curtain of light shall ope for thee—
> Till last, and brightest of the seven,
> Where Brahma dwells shall be thy heaven! (*Phantasmagoria* 2:11–14)

Though, like Smith, Jewsbury uses the western association of the Orient with rich exoticism to portray its transcendental vision, Jewsbury reveals none of Smith's tension between this idealism and a repudiation of the imperial abuses of the colonized. This contrast between the two poets may be informed at least by the contrast in their marriages: unlike Jewsbury, who gave up a life of literature to accompany her husband to India, Smith's marriage to and early separation from William Smith, who was an EIC official and at least one catalyst to Smith's revulsion against the abuses of the Company.[7] Emma Roberts, unmarried and having accompanied her sister and brother-in-law to Benares, however, displays an alienation akin to Jewsbury's; the rich imagery describing the exotic landscape in Roberts's 1830 poem, "Song," is not enough to keep her from a desire for home: "I languish for a cottage home, / Within my native land" (39–40), in spite of her extensive writing career in India.[8]

Nondualism and the Female in Blake, Coleridge, and Percy Shelley

This book has thus far focusedon women's representations and experiences of India in the hope that underscoring their commonalities demonstrates that they

---

own—not an action calculated to endear her to the Anglo-Indians. Soon they were moved to Sholapore, where there was drought and famine, and on 8 June came an entry in her journal: an attack of 'demi-semi-cholera, only demi-semi.'... It was on the journey back to Karnai, at Poona, on 4 October 1833, that Maria Jewsbury died" (Clarke 161). Her friend, Dora Wordsworth, urged Jewsbury to reconsider the journey, since Dora felt her friend's fragile constitution would not tolerate the perils of India: "The possibility of your going to *India* never entered my head when you talked of going *abroad*—so the tidings come w/ double force" (1831, 90–91). Ironically, Dora wrote on July 19, 1832, "The Cholera is creeping round us. It is impossible to think of this disease without awe—a lady well known to dear Isabella went to bed perfectly well & was laid in her last narrow home before 12 o'clock next day" (96).

[7] See also Mary Johnson's idealized widow in her poem, "Hindu Widow on the Funeral Pile of Her Husband," in which the stoical widow is idealized, as mentioned in the introduction.

[8] Paula Feldman notes that even after her sister died in 1831, "Roberts moved to Calcutta, where she devoted herself to literature and journalism and edited a newspaper, the *Oriental Observer*" (586).

cannot be subsumed by Orientalism or the writing of their male contemporaries without distortion; the foundation of this difference has been traced through the engagement of these women with the nondualism of Vedic philosophy from which the masculinist tradition swerves due to its foundation in the dualistic philosophy of the west. The result is an alternative paradigm that is a rigorous albeit ambivalent and varied proto-feminist consciousness distinct from that attributed to Wollstonecraft and other female prose polemicists working within the gender binaries of western tradition.

This alternative paradigm can be used to address the texts of male writers that display an affinity for a female, nondual presence that challenges their place in the periodization that has been defined as canonical Romanticism. As Mellor stated in 1988, "The relationship between 'masculine' and 'feminine' Romanticism is finally not one of structural opposition but rather of intersection along a fluid continuum. Any writer, male or female, could occupy the 'masculine' or the 'feminine' ideological or subject position" (*Romanticism and Gender* 4). With the hindsight of the Asiatic Society's anxiety about their role in Anglo-India and the women writers who engaged with their translations, I would thus like to close this book by returning to the larger questions posed in the introduction regarding periodization and gender through a selection of texts by Blake, Coleridge, and Percy Shelley to demonstrate their pull towards the nondualism that Wordsworth, as the epitome of canonical Romanticism, resisted.[9]

Blake was an iconoclast whose belated canonization as a Romantic poet is ironic on many levels.[10] He most explicitly rejects Wordsworthian dualism in his marginalia to Wordsworth's preface to *The Excursion*. Where Wordsworth writes, "How exquisitely the individual Mind ... / to the external World / Is fitted" Blake interjects in his margins, "You shall not bring me down to believe such fitting & fitted I known better & Please your Lordship .... [D]oes not this Fit & is it not Fitting most Exquisitely too." Blake attacks Wordsworth's ideal of a perfect balance between mind and nature from the very premise of its dualistic assumption that the subject is separate from the phenomena she or he beholds.

Blake's complicated relationship to gender and sexuality vis-à-vis epistemology is an important facet of his cosmology that stands apart from the ideology of Romanticism, meriting reappraisal from the perspective of the women's texts of the preceding chapters. In his *Visions of the Daughters of Albion* and *Milton*, Oothoon and Ololon respectively voice some of the most rigorous anti-Enlightenment positions in Blake's poetics, demonstrating his insistence that revolution can only come about through the liberation of the female subject Oothoon as a tragically unheard voice in the earlier poem and Ololon whose redemption promises human liberation in apocalyptic terms in the latter.

Twentieth-century feminist scholars who described Blake's poetics within the Romanticism paradigm tended to reduce the feminine in his cosmology to

---

[9] See the discussion of "Tintern Abbey" in the introduction.

[10] The fact that Blake was brought into the Romantic canon belatedly is pointed out by most anthologists of literature of the period.

the misogynistic subjectivities of his male characters mistaken for authorial mouthpieces.[11] Most common among these twentieth-century indictments of Blake's representation of the female was the assumption that Blake was projecting sadistic male fantasies onto female characters such as Oothoon in *Visions of the Daughters of Albion*. Rejected by her fiancé, Theotormon, after she is raped by Bromion, Oothoon problematically offers to catch for Theotormon, "girls of mild silver, or of furious gold" and "lie beside" them and "view their wanton play" after having articulated powerful proto-feminist statements of liberation from the patriarchal virgin/whore binary (7:24–5; E. 50).

However, a handful of scholars such as Helen Bruder and James Heffernan have argued that Blake is representing a historical failure rather than participating in that failure. Bruder invokes Poovey's "Proper Lady" to claim that Oothoon is rather "sliding into the final snare, set for any woman who tries to 'cry love' at this particular historical moment" (83). It is Bruder's sense of Ooothoon's contradiction to which I would like to return from the perspective of the paradox of the dualism/nondualism binary since Oothoon's growing awareness is set against a static patriarchal structure represented by Theotormon's cave. From her self-punishment after Theotormon's rejection following her rape by Bromion, Oothoon progresses to a new vision of purity that rejects the Enlightenment subject-object duality that Theotormon's deistic god, Urizen, embodies:

> ... Arise my Theotormon I am pure,
> ... They told me that the night & day were all that I could see;
> They told me that I had five senses to inclose me up.
> And they inclos-d my infinite brain into a narrow circle. (2, 28–32; E. 47)

She gains rhetorical power when she turns from the unresponsive Theotormon to Urizen himself to reject the virgin/whore binary of patriarchal society's perspective of women. She disproves the binary by first revealing that it cannot reduce her to its rigid categories:

> And does my Theotormon seek this hypocrite modesty!
> This knowing, artful, secret, fearful, cautious, trembling hypocrite.
> Then is Oothoon a whore indeed! And all the virgin joys
> Of life are harlots: and Theotormon is a sick mans dream (6, 16–19; E. 50)

Oothoon then outright rejects it with a nondual subjectivity unparalleled in masculine depictions of the female:

> But Oothoon is not so, a virgin fill'd with virgin fancies
> Open to joy and to delight where ever beauty appears
> If in the morning sun I find it: there my eyes are fix'd
> In happy copulation; if in evening mild, wearied with work;
> Sit on a bank and draw the pleasures of this free born joy. (6, 21–7, 2; E. 50)

---

[11] See my book, *Blake's Nostos*, for a more detailed discussion of the problems with twentieth-century feminist readings of Blake.

This undifferentiated consciousness of the "free born" finds pleasure through its own subjectivity, eyes that are "fix'd / In happy copulation," sexuality released from the subject/object dualism of the western male gaze. As Heffernan states,

> Oothoon's language is not irrational or disorganized; it is rigorously controlled by her imagination, which is at once intellectual and emotional, critically acute and 'open to joy and to delight' (6.22). What makes her marginal is precisely her resistance to classification, her refusal to be polarized. Straddling the line between defiant assertion and helpless submission, Oothoon challenges all binary oppositions. (6)

Oothoon's free born joy is bound by a world that forces her into its binaries, and so the poem ends on the dissonant note of a wailing epiphany (E. 51).

Blake's *Milton* depicts the yet more intricate relationship between creativity, gender, and nondual energy repressed by the unholy trinity of Bacon, Locke, and Newton, and that, for Blake, Milton must overcome. Blake represents Milton as splintered in his fallen state, having cast out elements of himself, including not only Adam and Satan but also his female portion, Ololon, who wanders devoid of identity as a prepubescent virgin and whose own heroic journey to redemption involves casting off this objectified sense of the feminine in an embrace of the nondual:

> ... O awful Man
> Altho' our Human Power can sustain the severe contentions
> Of Friendship, our Sexual cannot....
> Hence arose all our terrors in Eternity! & now remembrance
> Returns upon us! Are we Contraries O Milton, Thou & I (41, 31–5; E. 143)

Albion can only awaken from his nightmare of human history when Milton and Ololon are reintegrated and therefore create Golgonooza, the City of Art, a place that paradoxically exists beyond the inner-outer duality. Now that the female is redeemed in this version of Blake's cosmology, Oothoon returns, "weeping oer her Human Harvest" whose apocalypse is not the end of time but the end of duality (42, 33; E. 144). The suggestion in giving Oothoon this cameo reappearance at the brink of apocalypse is that the only way she can be liberated is with the annihilation not of the world but of the illusion of duality.

Coleridge is yet more difficult than Blake to extricate from the stranglehold of Romanticist ideology because of his long-held status as a Lake poet. He too, however, warrants reexamination because of his linking of a nondual, revolutionary energy to the female. The tension in his poetry between masculinist tradition and a raw female energy that subverts it is most readily illustrated by Coleridge's 1816 poem, *Christabel*. The prudishly unreliable narrator attempts to keep propriety intact in spite of Geraldine's serpentine power over the narrative that he cannot control, as seen when Geraldine, alone with the virginal Christabel in her bedroom, disrobes and the narrator is too flustered—but apparently titillated—to describe the details: "Behold! Her bosom and half her side— / A sight to dream of, not to tell!" (246–7). The most obvious embodiment of patriarchy is Sir

Leoline and his castle; the fact that Christabel carries Geraldine over its threshold is important since it suggests that Christabel has within her the albeit repressed desire to wreak chaos of her father's proud lineage. The poem's structure itself reflects the power of the demonized and demonizing Geraldine to corrupt even narrative coherence: its parts defy linearity, with a second part that retells the first from a more controlled patriarchal perspective of the events of part 1, and most enigmatic, a brief Conclusion to Part the Second that jettisons the characters and plot and yet retains the haunting undercurrent of a perverse relationship between father and child, suggesting that the narrator himself has been ousted from the poem, the reader required to read it retrospectively through its own indeterminacy: "Perhaps 'tis pretty to force together / Thoughts so all unlike each other" (654–5). A catalogue of paradoxes, this coda to the poem dismantles the dualistic logic upon which the western tradition is founded.

Like Geraldine in *Christabel*, the explosively erotic, feminized nature of "Kubla Khan" (1797) has a will more powerful than masculine imperialism. Long known to have drawn on Orientalism, and inspired by the new awareness of the east, "Kubla Khan" gives voice to the power of a nondual, female energy that ties eros to epistemology and defies the attempts at masculine hegemony to repress it.[12] After the brief opening stanza describing Kubla's "walls and towers," a testament (pun intended) to his phallic power to restrain "fertile" nature's "folding sunny spots of greenery,"[13] nature erupts from its feminized "deep romantic chasm" that defies the "proper" docility of the female, through paradox: "A savage place! As holy and inchanted / … was haunted / By woman wailing for her demon-lover!" (12, 14, 16).[14] That this power does not merely destroy Kubla's creation but rearranges it within her own design suggests that the artist must harness this energy, "A sunny pleasure-dome with caves of ice!" (36). Coleridge connects this powerful, nondual energy with India in his notebook, where he "copied a passage from Thomas Maurice's *The History of Hindostan* (1795)…: 'In a cave in the mountains of Cashmere appears a bubble of Ice which increases in size every day till the 15th day, at which it is an ell or more in height: then as the moon decreases, the Image … does also till it vanishes'" (Halmi, et al, 183 n. 9).

That Coleridge later added the third stanza of "Kubla Khan" suggests his intention to break off the dream after this climactic moment of nondualism, instead shifting to a connection between the dream that frames the poem and the vision of the Abyssinian maid who is no mere muse but a creator of complex music that can only be conditionally accessed by the male poet: "Could I revive within me / Her

---

[12] As early as 1927, Lowes traced the poem's imagery to the description of Cashmere in the 1795 *History of Hindustan* by the Orientalist, Thomas Maurice.

[13] In *Coleridge's Poetry and Prose*. Ed. Nicholas Halmi, et al. NY: Norton, 2004. 180–83. All further references to this edition of Coleridge's poetry are in the text.

[14] Coleridge wrote, "I should much wish, like the Indian Vishnu to float about along an infinite ocean cradled in the flower of the Lotos, and wake once in a million years for a few minutes—just to know I was going to sleep a million years more" (*Collected Letters*, 1:350).

symphony and song" (42–3).[15] The artist he would be if she did not elude him is a paradoxical blend of the demonic and beatific, whose art does not emulate Kubla's but rather harnesses the power of nature as "woman wailing for her demon-lover":

> I would build that dome in air,
> That sunny dome! Those caves of ice!
> And all who heard should see them there,
> And all should cry, Beware! Beware!
> His flashing eyes, his floating hair!
> Weave a circle round him thrice,
> And close your eyes with holy dread:
> For he on honey-dew hath fed,
> And drank the milk of Paradise. (46–54)

The artist he would be if the Abyssinian maid did not elude him is a paradoxical blend of the demonic and the beatific.

Buried deep in his 1817 *Biographia Literaria* is Coleridge's brief definition of secondary imagination which has been long known to be the heart of Coleridge's poetics that he struggled against Wordsworth to articulate. I would like to extend that critical commonplace to suggest that his definition of secondary imagination grew out of his assertion of that female voice that recurs in his poetry: It "dissolves, diffuses, dissipates, in order to re-create; or where this process is rendered impossible, yet still at all events it struggles to idealize and to unify" (488). This is Geraldine's function in "Christabel," a paradox unnamable to its priggish narrator, wreaking havoc in the patriarchal abode of Sir Leoline; it is "animated nature" that "sweeps / Plastic and vast, one intellectual Breeze, / At once the Soul of each, and God of all" that he dares voice in Effusion XXXV ("The Eolian Harp") and which retreats underground when the poet is chastened with a "look of mild reproof" by his new wife (36, 39–40); finally it is that unleashed, female erotic power in nature that re-creates in its most revolutionary act of defiance against the oppressions of patriarchy.

Percy Shelley's influence by the Orientalists has been widely discussed in scholarship on the canonical poets.[16] Nigel Leask, for instance, pairs Shelley with Byron in figuring "the Other … as an (often oriental) female who turns out to be an 'epipsychidion' or wishful projection of the ego of the male protagonist" (*British Romantic Writers and the East* 6). I would like to suggest, however, that when Shelley's representation of the east is viewed through the lens of female subjectivity rather than through that of other canonical poets, one can reassess the contradictions between his feminism and the objectification of both biographical women and those in his poetry objectified as "epipsyches." The most complex rendering of Shelley's poetic connection between Indian nondualism and female subjectivity is his representation of Asia in *Prometheus Unbound*. This epic has

---

[15] See the commentary of *Coleridge's Poetry and Prose*, for the complex textual history of the poem.

[16] See the introduction for a discussion of *Alastor*.

uncanny parallels with Blake's *Milton*, splitting the traditional role of the hero between a male and female character. In Blake's case, Milton and Ololon share the hero's role of epic descent into a psychic underworld; Shelley too suggests that Prometheus is psychically chained because he has cast out love, in the form of Asia, whose name suggests the eastern nondualism she comes to represent in act 2.

Unlike Blake's Milton, who descends into Generation from a comfortable place in heaven, Prometheus must remain immobilized in act 1, chained to the rock, since for Shelley the only options in his all-male first act are either "a catastrophe so feeble as that of reconciling the Champion with the Oppressor of mankind" or for Prometheus to become another Jupiter in fighting violence with violence.[17] It is thus Asia who descends into the psychic underworld that begins "in the Indian Caucasus" and goes progressively deeper in a more paradoxical sublime than the canonical representations of the phallic sublime. The paradoxes accrue the deeper Asia goes, culminating in her paradoxically face-to-face interview with the "imageless" truth in the form of Demogorgon, from whom she wants to find out when and how Prometheus will be liberated. Demogorgon, however, takes Asia beyond the literal to a sublime where she accesses a deeper epistemology that he extracts from her through her own questions: "I spoke but as ye speak," he tells her (I.iv.12). Her questions to Demogorgon thus proceed from the naive "Who made the living world?" to progressively longer and more complex meditations on human history as cycles of struggle against patriarchal repression that, cloaked as religion, creates "famine and then toil and then disease / strife, wounds, and ghastly death unseen before" (II.iv.8, 50–51). Once Asia is liberated from patriarchal dualism, Demogorgon turns the questions back on Asia at the deepest level:

> ... the deep truth is imageless;
> For what would it avail to bid thee gaze
> On the revolving world? What to bid speak
> Fate, Time, Occasion, Chance and Change?—To these
> All things are subject but eternal Love. (116–20)

The revolution against the oppressor in the form of Jupiter can only take place when Asia is reunited with Prometheus, her own embodiment of love freeing him from repeating the cycle of violence.

In spite of the power of Asia's role in liberating humanity from patriarchy, it is nevertheless important to stress Shelley's ambivalence about such idealism, as the play's textual history reveals: The original play was in three acts, with Asia's descent followed by Demogorgon's unseating of Jupiter; Shelley himself deplored using Demogorgon as a *deus ex machina* that avoids the problem of his champion getting blood on his hands. He thus followed act 3 with *The Cenci*, a play with Beatrice, a female protagonist whose virginal appearance is at odds with the "sad reality" of her sexual and emotional victimization by her tyrannical father. In the

---

[17] Preface to *Prometheus Unbound* 206. In Reiman and Powers. All further references to this edition are in the text.

play's dedication to Leigh Hunt, Shelley decried his earlier works—the three-act *Prometheus Unbound* being the most immediate and extreme example—as "little else than visions which impersonate my own apprehensions of the beautiful and the just" (140). Shelley makes clear that Beatrice does not have the luxury of existing in an idealized world as Prometheus does. As the play proceeds with her plotting her father's murder, her trial and imprisonment, her character vacillates among moments of lucidity, heroism, tyranny echoing her father's, and derangement.

Though the play ends with Beatrice awaiting her execution, the textual history of the two plays does not end there: Shelley flees the dark tragedy with a return to *Prometheus* for a fourth act that only compounds the dramaturgical and narrative problems of the original play with Prometheus and Asia inhabiting a static utopia. This failure to realize a perfect world of nondualism suggests the reason why Blake chose to leave *Milton* on the brink of apocalypse and Coleridge to awaken from his vision before the fragments can reunify. The promise that Coleridge's poet figure can re-create the purely imaginary symphony and song of the damsel with the dulcimer is conditional, the dream itself interrupted by the visitor from Porlock.

Seen from the perspective of women writing nondualism, Blake, Coleridge, and Shelley represent the potential of a feminized nondualism to dismantle the repressive patriarchal structures of the late Enlightenment. From Oothoon's inability to transcend her sociopolitical repression in spite of the power of her vision and Ololon's liberation from the specter of virginity to Coleridge's tentative depiction of animated nature's disruption of the chaste submission his bride schools him to maintain and the mayhem that is the re-creative power of feminized nature in "Kubla Khan" to Shelley's more ambivalent depiction of Asia as the liberating force of love, their depictions of the liberation of the female in terms that link epistemology and sexuality are central to a revolution that would release the "mind-forged manacles" to the potential for a revolution of sociopolitical consequence.[18] For these late Enlightenment writers of Anglo-India, as Irigaray writes of her own grappling with binaries of east and west and of male and female, the aim is "not toward a reversal of power but a possible coexistence of perspectives, of subjectivities, of worlds, of cultures.... [P]assing beyond predominantly genealogical traditions, be they matriarchal or patriarchal ... toward the constitution of horizontal relations between the sexes (31). The male poets of the

---

[18] The connection between eastern nondualism and female sexuality is apparently still making news in the twenty-first century, as evidenced in a *New York Times* article by William J. Broad entitled "I'll Have What She's Thinking": "When I first heard of spontaneous orgasm, while researching a book on yoga, including its libidinal cousin, tantra, I figured it was more allegory than reality and in any event would prove beyond the reach of even the boldest investigators.... But sex researchers have found that the novel type of autoeroticism shows up mainly in women." Broad goes on to connect the new research to the "intermingling of sexuality and mysticism and, in particular, the teachings of tantra, which arose in medieval India as a path to spiritual ecstasy." It may be news to many in the twenty-first century, but for British writers of early Anglo-India, it was already answering their need for an alternative to the repressive limitations of the western tradition.

late Enlightenment that represent their own subjectivity as unrestricted by western binaries have a place among the matrix of women authors promising a place for the "mother of Krishna" not, however, as the Rajah, Zaarmilla, would have it in his exuberance about the Wollstonecraftian education he discovers in England, in which a woman is given a man's education and so becomes reasonable, but as Hamilton and her contemporary female authors show to be a creative assertion of nondual subjectivity.

Bibliography

Adisasmito-Smith, Steven. "Forging Bonds: Translating *The Bhagavad-Gita* in the Colonial Context." *South Asian Review*. 29.3 (2008); 13–28. Print.

———. "The Self in Translation: British Orientalists, American Transcendentalists, and Sanskrit Scriptures in English." *Yearbook of Comparative and General Literature* 47 (1999): 167–77. Print.

Anderson, Benedict. *Imagined Communities: Reflections on the Origin and Spread of Nationalism*. New York: Verso, 1983, 1991. Print.

Anon. *Hartly House Calcutta: A Novel of the Days of Warren Hastings*. Ed. Monica Clough. Winchester, Mass: Pluto Press, 1989. Print.

Anthony, Frank. *Britain's Betrayal in India: The Story of the Anglo-Indian Community*. Bombay: Allied Publishers, 1969. Print.

App, Urs. *The Birth of Orientalism*. Philadelphia: University of Pennsylvania Press, 2010. Print.

Aravamudan, Srinivas. *Enlightenment Orientalism*. Chicago: University of Chicago Press, 2012.

Armstrong, Isobel. "The Gush of the Feminine: How Can We Read Women's Poetry of the Romantic Period?" *Romantic Women Writers: Voices and Countervoices*. Ed. Paula Feldman and Theresa M. Kelley. University Press of New England, 1995. 13–32. Print.

Backscheider, Paula and Catherine Ingrassia. *British Women Poets of the Long Eighteenth Century: An Anthology*. Baltimore: Johns Hopkins University Press, 2009. Print.

Ballhatchet, Kenneth. *Race, Sex and Class under the Raj: Imperial Attitudes and Policies and Their Critics, 1793–1905*. New York: St. Martin's Press, 1980. Print.

Basham, A.L. "Sophia and the 'Bramin.'" *East India Company Studies*. Ed. Kenneth Ballhatchet and John Harrison. Hong Kong: Asian Research Service, 1986. 13–30. Print.

Bayly, C.A. *Indian Society and the Making of the British Empire*. The New Cambridge History of India. II. L. Cambridge: Cambridge University Press, 1988. Print.

Belsey, Catherine. "Constructing the Subject." *Feminist Criticism and Social Change*. Ed. J. Newton and D. Rosenfelt. London: Methuen, 1985. 45–64. Print.

Benchley, Robert. 1920 February, Vanity Fair, "The Most Popular Book of the Month: An Extremely Literary Review of the Latest Edition of the New York City Telephone Directory" New York. 69. Web. www.hathitrust.org.

Bhabha, Homi. *The Location of Culture*. New York: Routledge, 1994. Print.

Blake, William. *Visions of the Daughters of Albion. The Complete Poetry & Prose of William Blake*. Ed. David Erdman. New York: Doubleday, 1988. 45–51. Print.

Bloom, Harold. "Internalization of Quest-Romance." *Romanticism and Consciousness*. Ed. Harold Bloom. New York: Norton, 1970. 3–24. Print.

Breen, Jennifer and Mary Noble. *Romantic Literature*. NY: Bloomsbury, 2002. Print.

Brine, Kevin. Introduction. *Objects of Enquiry: The Life, Contributions, and Influences of Sir William Jones (1746–1794)*. Ed. Garland Cannon and Kevin Brine. New York: New York University Press, 1998. 1–19. Print.

Broad, William. "I'll Have What She's Thinking" *New York Times*. August 9, 2013. Web. http://www.nytimes.com/2013/09/29/sunday-review/ill-have-what-shes-thinking.html?_r=0.

Bruder, Helen. *William Blake and the Daughters of Albion*. New York: St. Martin's Press, 1997. Print.

Butler, Marilyn. *Romantics, Rebels, and Reactionaries: English Literature and its Background: 1760–1830*. New York: Oxford University Press, 1981. Print.

Byrne, Jean Marie. "Breath of Awakening: Nonduality, Breathing and Sexual Difference." *Breathing with Luce Irigaray*. Ed. Emily A. Holmes and Lenart Skof. New York: Bloomsbury, 2013. 67–82. Print.

Cannon, Garland. "Eighteenth-Century Sanskrit Studies: The British Reception of Sir William Jones's Translation of the *Sakuntala*." *South Asian Review* 6.3 (1982): 197–203. Print.

———. "Sir William Jones and British Public Opinion Toward Sanskrit Culture." *Journal of the Asiatic Society* 22.3 (1980): 1–14. Print.

———. *Sir William Jones, Orientalist*. Honolulu: University of Hawaii Press, 1952. Print.

Cannon, Garland and Kevin R. Brine, Eds. *Objects of Enquiry: The Life, Contributions, and Influences of Sir William Jones (1746–1794)*. New York: New York University Press, 1995. Print.

Cass, Jeffrey. "Homoerotics and Orientalism in William Beckford's *Vathek*. *Interrogating Orientalism: Contextual Approaches and Pedagogical Practices*. Ed. Diane Long Hoeveler and Jeffrey Cass. Columbus: Ohio State University Press. 2006. 107–20. Print.

Chakravarty, Gautam. *The Indian Mutiny and the British Imagination*. New York: Cambridge University Press, 2005. Print.

Chapple, Christopher. Forward. *The Bhagavad Gita*. Trans. Winthrop Sargeant. Albany: State University of New York Press, 1994. xiii–xxi. Print.

Chatterjee, Amal. *Representations of India, 1740–1840*. New York: St. Martin's Press, 1998. Print.

Clarke, Norma. *Ambitious Heights: Writing, Friendship, Love—The Jewsbury Sisters, Felicia Hemans, and Jane Carlyle*. New York: Routledge, 1990. Print.

Clough, Monica. "Introduction to the 1989 Edition." *Hartly House Calcutta: A Novel of the Days of Warren Hastings*. Winchester, Mass: Pluto Press, 1989. vii–xix. Print.

Coleman, Deirdre. *Romantic Colonization and British Anti-Slavery*. New York: Cambridge, 2005. Print.

Coleridge, Samuel Taylor. *Coleridge's Poetry and Prose*. Ed. Nicholas Halmi, et al. New York: Norton, 2004. Print.

———. *Collected Letters*. Vol. 1. Ed. E.L. Griggs. Print.

Cox, Jeffrey. *Slavery, Abolition and Emancipation: Writings in the British Romantic Period*. Vol. 5 (Drama). Brookfield, VT: Pickering & Chatto, 1999. Print.

Curran, Stuart, ed. *The Poems of Charlotte Smith*. Oxford: Oxford University Press, 1993. Print.

———, "The I Altered." *Romanticism and Feminism*. Ed. Anne Mellor. Bloomington: Indiana University Press, 1988. 185–207. Print.

Dakessian, Marie. "Envisioning the Indian Sati: Mariana Starke's *The Widow of Malabar* and Antoine Le Mierre's *La Veuve du Malabar*." *Comparative Literature Studies*. 36.2 (1999): 110–30. Print.

David, Alun. "Sir William Jones, Biblical Orientalism and Indian Scholarship." *Modern Asian Studies* 30.1 (1996): 173–84. Print.

Dirks Nicholas. *Castes of Mind: Colonialism and the Making of Modern India*. Princeton: Princeton University Press, 2001. Print.

Drew, John. *India and the Romantic Imagination*. Delhi: Oxford University Press, 1987. Print.

Duthrie, Peter. "Introduction." *Plays on the Passions*. By Joanna Baillie. Ed. P. Duthrie. Orchard Park, NY: Broadview: Press, 2001. Print.

Edgerton, Franklin., trans. *The Bhagavad Gita*. Part 1: *Text and Translation. Harvard Oriental Series*. Cambridge, Mass: Harvard University Press, 1952. Print.

———. *The Bhagavad Gita*. Part 2: *Interpretation and Arnold's Translation. Harvard Oriental Series*. Cambridge, Mass: Harvard University Press, 1952. Print.

Ellis, Markman. *The Politics of Sensibility: Race, Gender and Commerce in the Sentimental Novel*. Cambridge: Cambridge University Press, 1996. Print.

Elwood, Anne Katharine Curteis. *Narrative of a Journey Overland from England By the Continent of Europe, Egypt, and the Red Sea, to India*. 2 Vols. London: Henry Colburn and Richard Bentley, 1830. Print.

Embree, Ainslie. *Imagining India: Essays on Indian History*. New York: Oxford University Press, 1989. Print.

Erdman, David, ed. *The Complete Poetry and Prose of William Blake*. New York: Doubleday, 1982. Print.

Fay, Eliza. *Original Letters from India: 1779–1815*. Ed. E.M. Forster. New York: Harcourt, Brace, 1925. Print.

Feldman, Burton and Robert D. Richardson, eds. *The Works of Sir William Jones*. Vol. 2. New York: Garland Publishers, 1984. Print.

Feldman, Paula R., Ed. *British Women Poets of the Romantic Era*. Baltimore: Johns Hopkins University Press, 1997. New York: Garland, 1984. Print.

Felski, Rita. "Suspicious Minds." *Poetics Today*. 32.2 (Summer 2011): 215–34. Print.

Ferguson, Frances. *Solitude and the Sublime: Romanticism and the Aesthetics of Individuation*. New York: Routledge 1992. Print.

Ferguson, Moira. *Subject to Others: British Women Writers and Colonial Slavery, 1670–1834*. New York: Routledge, 1992. Print.

Fisher, Michael H. "Representations of India, the English East India Company, and Self by an Eighteenth-Century Indian Emigrant to Britain." *Modern Asian Studies* 32 (1998): 891–911. Print.

Franklin, Michael J. "Accessing India: Orientalism, Anti-'Indianism' and the Rhetoric of Jones and Burke." *Romanticism and Colonialism: Writing and Empire, 1780–1830*. Cambridge: Cambridge University Press, 1998. 48–66. Print.

———. Introduction to *Hartly House, Calcutta*. New Dehli: Oxford University Press, 2007. xi–lvii. Print.

———. "Radically Feminizing India: Phebe Gibbes's *Hartly House, Calcutta* (1789) and Sydney Owenson's *The Missionary: An Indian Tale* (1811). *Romantic Representations of British India*. Ed. Michael Franklin. New York: Routledge, 2006. 154–79. Print.

Freeman, Kathryn. "'Beyond the stretch of labouring thought sublime': Romanticism, Post-colonialism Theory and the Transmission of Sanskrit Texts." *Orientalism Transposed: The Impact of the Colonies on British Culture*. Ed. Julie F. Codell and Dianne Macleod. Brookfield, VT: Ashgate, 1998. 140–57. Print.

———. *Blake's Nostos: Fragmentation and Nondualism in* The Four Zoas. Albany: State University of New York Press, 1997. Print.

Fulford, Tim and Peter J. Kitson, Eds. *Romanticism and Colonialism: Writing and Empire, 1780–1830*. Cambridge: Cambridge University Press, 1998. Print.

———. "Romanticism and Colonialism: Texts, Contexts, Issues." *Romanticism and Colonialism: Writing and Empire, 1780–1830*. Cambridge: Cambridge University Press, 1998. 1–12. Print.

Ganeri, Jonardon. "The Hindu Syllogism: Nineteenth-Century Perceptions of Indian Logical Thought." *Philosophy East and West*. 46.1 (January 1996): 1–16. Print.

Gallagher, Catherine. *Nobody's Story: The Vanishing Acts of Women Writers in the Marketplace 1670–1820*. Berkeley and Los Angeles: University of California Press, 1994. Print.

Ghose, Indira. *Women Travellers in Colonial India: The Power of the Female Gaze*. New York: Oxford University Press, 1998. Print.

[Gibbes, Phebe] Goldsborne, Sophia. *Hartly House Calcutta: A Novel of the Days of Warren Hastings*. Calcutta: Thacker, Spink and Co, 1908. Print.

Gibbes, Phebe. *Hartly House Calcutta*. Ed. Michael Franklin. New Delhi: Oxford University Press, 2007. Print.

Gibson, Mary Elis. *Indian Angles: English Verse in Colonial India from Jones to Tagore*. Athens, OH: Ohio University Press, 2011. Print.

Graham, Maria Callcott. *Journal of a Residence in India*. Edinburgh: Archibald Constable and Company, 1812.

Grundy, Isobel. "'The barbarous character we give them': White Women Travellers Report on Other Races." *Studies in Eighteenth-Century Culture* 22. Ed. Patricia B. Craddock and Carla H. Hay. East Lansing, Michigan: Colleagues Press, 1992. 73–86. Print.

Halbfass, Wilhelm. *India and Europe*. Albany: SUNY Press, 1988. Print.

Halhed, Nathaniel B. *A Grammar of the Bengal Language 1778*. Menston, England: Scolar Press Ltd, 1969. Print.

Halmi, Nicholas, et al., eds. *Coleridge's Poetry and Prose*. NY: Norton, 2004. Print.

Hamilton, Elizabeth. *Translations of the Letters of a Hindoo Rajah*. Ed. Pamela Perkins and Shannon Russell. Orchard Park, New York: Broadview Press, 1999. Print.

Harlan, Lindsey. "Sati: The Story of Godavari." *Devī: Goddesses of India*. Eds. John S. Hawley and Donna M. Wulff. Berkeley: University of California Press. 1996. 227–49. Print.

Heffernan, James. "Blake's Oothoon: The Dilemmas of Marginality." *Studies in Romanticism* 30 (Spring 1991): 3–18. Print.

Hoerner, Fred. "'A Tiger in a Brake': The Stealth of Reason in the Scholarship of Sir William Jones in India." *Texas Studies in literature and Language (TSLL)* 37 (Summer 1995): 215–32. Print.

Hyam, Ronald. *Empire and Sexuality: The British Experience*. New York: Manchester University Press, 1990. Print.

Inden, Ronald. *Imagining India*. Cambridge, Mass: Basil Blackwell, 1990. Print.

Irigaray, Luce. *Between East and West: From Singularity to Community*. New York: Columbia University Press, 2002. Web.

Irwin, Robert. *For Lust of Knowing: The Orientalists and Their Enemies*. London: Allen Lane/Penguin, 2006. Print.

Jewsbury, Maria Jane. *Oceanides*. Romantic Women Poets. Ed. Andrew Ashfield. New York: Manchester University Press, 1995. 203–7. Print.

———. *Phantasmagoria; or, Sketches of Life and Literature*. Vol. 2. London: Hurst, Robinson and Co, 1825. Print.

Johnson, Mary. "Hindu Widow on the Funeral Pile of Her Husband." *Original Sonnets and Other Poems*. London: Longman, Hurst, Rees, & Orme, 1810. Print.

Jones, Anna. "Adieu to India." *Romantic Women Poets*. Ed. Andrew Ashfield. New York: Manchester University Press, 1995. 111–12. Print.

Jones, Sir William. *Poems*. Chiswick: C. Whittingham Press, 1822. Print.

———. *Sakontala; or, the Fatal Ring. The Works of Sir William Jones*. Ed. Feldman and Richardson. Vol. 1. New York: Garland Publishing, 1984. Print.

———. *Works*. London, 1807. 18 vols. Print.

Kalidasa. *Sakuntala and the Ring of Recollection*. In *The Theater of Memory*. Ed. and trans. Barbara Stoler Miller. New York: Columbia University Press, 1984. 85–176. Print.

Kaplan, Marijn S., ed. *Translations and Continuations: Riccoboni and Brooke, Graffigny and Roberts*. Brookfield, VT: Pickering & Chatto, 2011. Print.

Kearns, Cleo. *T.S. Eliot and Indic Traditions*. New York: Cambridge, 1987. Print.

Kelly, Gary. *Women, Writing, and Revolution: 1790–1827*. New York: Oxford University Press, 1993. Print.

Kelsall, Malcolm. "'Once did she hold the gorgeous East in fee': Byron's Venice and Oriental Empire." *Romanticism and Colonialism*. Ed. Tim Fulford and Peter Kitson. 243–60. Print.

Kopf, David. *British Orientalism and the Bengal Renaissance*. Berkeley: University of California Press, 1969. Print.

———. "The Historiography of British Orientalism, 1772–1992. *Objects of Enquiry: The Life, Contributions, and Influences of Sir William Jones (1746–1794)*. Ed. Garland Cannon and Kevin Brine. New York: New York University Press, 1998. 141–60. Print.

Landon, Letitia Elizabeth. "Manmadin, The Indian Cupid, Floating Down the Ganges." *The Improvisatrice and Other Poems*. 1st ed. London: Hurst, Robinson, & Co, 1824. Transcribed by Jessica Damian, Special Collections, University of Colorado at Boulder. Print.

Leask, Nigel. *British Romantic Writers and the East*. Cambridge: Cambridge University Press, 1992. Print.

———. *Curiosity and the Aesthetics of Travel Writing, 1770–1840*. Oxford: Oxford University Press, 2002. Print.

Lipking, Lawrence. "Frankenstein, the True Story; or, Rousseau Judges Jean-Jacques." NCE *Frankenstein*. Ed. J. Paul Hunter. New York: Norton, 1996, 2012. 416–34. Print.

Lonsdale, Roger. Introduction to *Vathek*, by William Beckford. Ed. Roger Lonsdale. Oxford University Press, 1983. Print.

Lowes, John Livingston. *The Road to Xanadu: A Study in the Ways of the Imagination*. Cambridge, MA: Riverside, 1964. Print.

Macaulay, Thomas. "Minute on Indian Education." *Macaulay: Prose and Poetry*. Ed. G.M. Young. Cambridge: Harvard University Press, 1967. 719–30. Print.

MacKenzie, Raymond N. *Montesquieu, Persian Letters*. Trans. Raymond N.MacKenzie. Indianapolis and Cambridge: Hackett, September. Print.

Makdisi, Saree. *Romantic Imperialism: Universal Empire and the Culture of Modernity*. Cambridge: Cambridge University Press, 1998. Print.

Malchow, H.L. *Gothic Images of Race in Nineteenth-Century Britain*. Stanford: Stanford University Press, 1996. Print.

Mani, Lata. "Contentious Traditions: The Debate on Sati in Colonial India." *Cultural Critique* 7 (Autumn 1987): 119–56. Print.

Marshall, P.J. *Problems of Empire: Britain and India 1757–1813*. New York: Barnes & Noble, 1968. Print.

Marshall, P.J. and Glyndwr Williams. *The Great Map of Mankind*. London: Dent Publishers, 1982. Print.

Maurice, Thomas. *The History of Hindostan*. 3 vols. New York: Garland, 1795–98, 1984. Print.

McClintock, Anne. *Imperial Leather: Race, Gender and Sexuality in the Colonial Context*. New York: Routledge, 1995. Print.

McGann, Jerome. "Enlightened Minds: Sir William Jones and Erasmus Darwin." *The Poetics of Sensibility: A Revolution in Literary Style*. Oxford: Clarendon Press, 1996. 127–35. Print.

———. *The Romantic Ideology: A Critical Investigation*. Chicago: University of Chicago Press, 1983. Print.

Mehta, Uday S. "Liberal Strategies of Exclusion." *Politics and Society* 18 (1990): 427–54. Print.

Mellor, Anne. "Embodied Cosmopolitanism and the British Romantic Woman Writer." *European Romantic Review* 17.3 (July 2006): 289–300. Print.

———. "Romantic Orientalism Begins at Home: Elizabeth Hamilton's *Translations of the Letters of a Hindoo Rajah.*" *Studies in Romanticism* 44 (Summer 2005): 151–64. Print.

———, ed. *Romanticism and Feminism*. Bloomington: Indiana University Press, 1988. Print.

———. *Romanticism and Gender*. New York: Routledge, 1993. Print.

Mellor, Anne and Matlak, Richard eds. *British Literature 1780–1830*. New York: Harcourt, Brace & Company, 1996. Print.

Melman, Billie. *Women's Orients: English Women and the Middle East, 1718–1918*. Ann Arbor: University of Michigan Press, 1992. Print.

Mill, James. *The History of British India*. Ed. John Clive. Chicago: University of Chicago Press, 1975 (Orig. pub. 1817). Print.

Miller, Barbara S. "Kalidasa's World and His Plays." *The Theater of Memory*. Ed. Barbara Miller. Trans. Barbara Miller. New York: Columbia University Press, 1984. 3–41. Print.

Monier-Williams, Sir M. *Sanskrit-English Dictionary*. New York: Oxford University Press, 1951. Print.

Montesquieu, Baron de (Charles de Secondat). *The Persian Letters*. Ed. and Trans. Robert Loy. New York: Meridian, 1961. Print.

Moorhouse, Geoffrey, *India Britannica*. New York: Harper & Row, 1983. Print.

Moskal, Jeanne. "English National Identity in Mariana Starke's *The Sword of Peace*. India, Abolition and the Rights of Women." *Women in British Romantic Theatre: Drama, Performance, and Society, 1790–1840*. Ed. Catherine Burroughs. Cambridge: Cambridge University Press, 2000. 102–31. Print.

Moussa-Mahmoud, Fatma. *Sir William Jones and the Romantics*. Cairo, The Anglo Egyptian Bookshop, 1962. Print.

Mukherjee, Bharati. *The Holder of the World*. New York: Fawcett Columbine, 1993. Print.

Mukherjee, S.N. *Sir William Jones: A Study in Eighteenth-Century British Attitudes to India*. Cambridge: Cambridge University Press, 1968. Print.

Mullan, John. *Sentiment and Sociability: the Language of Feeling in the Eighteenth Century*. New York: Clarendon Press, 1988. Print.

Mullholland, James. "Connecting Eighteenth-Century India: Orientalism, Della Cruscanism, and the Translocal Poetics of William and Anna Maria Jones." *Representing Place in British Literature and Culture, 1660–1830: From Local to Global*. Burlington, VT: Ashgate, 2013. 117–36. Print.

Musselwhite, David. "The Trial of Warren Hastings." *Literature, Politics and Theory*. Ed. Barker, Frances, et al. New York: Methuen, 1986. 77–103. Print.

Nanavutty, Piloo. "William Blake and Hindu Creation Myths." *The Divine Vision: Studies in the Poetry and Art of William Blake*. Ed. Vivian De Sola Pinto. New York: Haskell House, 1968: 165–82. Print.

Neff, D.S. "Hostages to Empire": The Anglo-Indian Problem in *Frankenstein, The Curse of Kehama,* and *The Missionary.*" *European Romantic Review* 8 (Fall 1997): 386–408. Print.

Newman, Gerald. *The Rise of English Nationalism: A Cultural History 1740–1830.* New York: St. Martin's Press, 1987. Print.

Niranjana, Tejaswini. *Siting Translation: History, Post-Structuralism, and the Colonial Context.* Berkeley: University of California Press, 1992. Print.

Nussbaum, Felicity. *Torrid Zones: Maternity, Sexuality, and Empire in Eighteenth-Century English Narratives.* Baltimore: Johns Hopkins University Press, 1995. Print.

———. "Women and race: 'a difference of complexion.' *Women and Literature in Britain: 1700–1800.* Ed. Vivien Jones. New York: Cambridge University Press, 2000. 69–88. Print.

O'Brien, Conor Cruise. Introduction. *Reflections on the Revolution in France.* Ed. Conor Cruise O'Brien. New York: Penguin, 1968. 9–76. Print.

O'Quinn, Daniel. "Torrents, Flames and the Education of Desire: Battling Hindu Superstition on the London Stage." *Romantic Representations of British India.* Ed. Michael Franklin. New York: Routledge, 2006. 65–83. Print.

Owenson, Sydney [Lady Morgan]. *The Missionary.* Ed. Julia Wright. New York: Broadview Press, 2002. Print.

Oxford English Dictionary. Web.

Pachori, Satya S. "Shelley's 'Hymn to Intellectual Beauty' and Sir William Jones," *The Comparatist* 11 (1987): 54–63. Print.

Paine, Jeffery. *Father India: How Encounters with an Ancient Culture Transformed the Modern West.* New York: HarperCollins, 1998. Print.

Pandit, Lalita. "Orientalism and Anxiety of Influence: Seeking *Sakuntala* in Goethe's *Faust.*" *Journal of Commonwealth and Postcolonial Studies (JCPSt)* 1.1–2 (spring/fall 2004): 114–42. Print.

Perkins, David. General introduction to *English Romantic Writers* Ed. David Perkins. New York: Harcourt Brace, 1995. 1–28. Print.

Perkins, Pamela and Shannon Russell. Introduction. *Translations of the Letters of a Hindoo Rajah.* Ed. Pamela Perkins and Shannon Russell. Orchard Park, New York: Broadview Press, 1999. 7–48. Print.

Pocock, J.G.A., ed. *Reflections on the Revolution in France.* Edmund Burke. Indianapolis, Indiana: Hackett, 1987.

Poovey, Mary. *The Proper Lady and the Female Writer.* Chicago: University of Chicago Press, 1984. Print.

Postans [Young], Marianne. *Cutch; or, Random Sketches, [taken during a residence in one of the northern provinces of Western India; interspersed with Legends and traditions].* London: Smith, Elder and Co, 1839. Print.

———. *Western India in 1838.* 2 Vols. London: Saunders & Otley, 1839. Print.

Pratt, Mary Louise. *Imperial Eyes: Travel Writing and Transculturation.* New York: Routledge, 1992. Print.

Prasad, Madhava. "The 'Other' Worldliness of Postcolonial Discourse: A Critique." *Critical Quarterly* 34.3 (Autumn 92): 74–89. Print.

Priestley, Joseph. *A Comparison of the Institutions of Moses with Those of the Hindoo and Other Antient Nations.* Northumberland: Andrew Kennedy, 1799. Print.

Quillinan, Dorothy. *Letters of Dora Wordsworth.* Ed. Howard Vincent. Chicago: Packard and Co, 1944. Print.

Rajan, Balachandra. "Feminizing the Feminine: Early Women Writers on India." *Romanticism, Race, and Imperial Culture: 1780–1834.* Ed. Alan Richardson and Sonia Hofkosh. Bloomington: Indiana University Press, 1996. 149–72. Print.

———. *Under Western Eyes: India from Milton to Macaulay.* Durham, NC: Duke University Press, 1999. Print.

Reiman, Donald H. and Neil Fraistat, eds. *Shelley's Poetry and Prose.* New York: Norton, 2002.

Reynolds, Nicole. "Phebe Gibbes, Edmund Burke, and the Trials of Empire." *Eighteenth-Century Fiction* 20.2 (Winter 2007–2008). 151–76. Print.

Richardson, Alan. "Romanticism and the Colonization of the Feminine." *Romanticism and Feminism.* Ed. Anne Mellor. Bloomington: Indiana University Press, 1988. 13–25. Print.

Richardson, Alan, and Sonia Hofkosh, eds. *Romanticism, Race, and Imperial Culture: 1780–1834.* Bloomington: Indiana University Press, 1996. Print.

Ricoeur, Paul. *Freud and Philosophy: An Essay on Interpretation.* New Haven, CT: Yale University Press, 1970. Print.

Roberts, Emma. *Scenes and Characteristics of Hindostan with Sketches of Anglo-Indian Society.* 3 Vols. London: William H. Allen, 1835. Print.

———. "Song." *British Women Poets of the Romantic Era.* Ed. Paula R. Feldman. Baltimore: Johns Hopkins University Press, 1997. 588. Print.

Rocher, Rosane. "British Orientalism in the Eighteenth Century: The Dialectics of Knowledge and Government." *Orientalism and the Postcolonial Predicament: Perspectives on South Asia.* Ed. Carol A. Breckenridge and Peter van der Veer. Philadelphia: University of Pennsylvania Press, 1993. 215–49. Print.

———. "Weaving Knowledge: Sir William Jones and Indian Pandits." *Objects of Inquiry: The Life, Contributions, and Influences of Sir Willaim Jones (1746–1794).* Ed. Garland Cannon and Kevin Brine. New York: New York University Press, 1995. 51–79. Print.

Rosenthal, Matthias. "Apocalypse, Technology, Translation." *Poetry, Poetics, Translation.* Ed. Mahlendorf, Ursula and Laurence Rickels. Wurzbburg: Konigshausen & Neumann, 1994. 199–205. Print.

Ross, Marlon. "Romantic Quest and Conquest: Troping Masculine Power in the Crisis of Poetic Identity." *Romanticism and Feminism.* Ed. Anne Mellor. Bloomington: Indiana University Press, 1988. 26–51. Print.

Rudd, Andrew. *Sympathy and India in British Literature, 1770–1830.* Basingstoke: Palgrave MacMillan, 2011.

Sabin, Margery. *Dissenters and Mavericks: Writings About India in English.* New York: Oxford University Press, 2002. Print.

Said, Edward. *Culture and Imperialism.* New York: Knopf, 1993. Print.

———. *Orientalism.* New York: Random House, 1978. Print.

Sargeant, Winthrop, trans. *The Bhagavad Gita.* Albany: State University of New York Press, 1994. Print.

Schwab, Raymond. *The Oriental Renaissance.* New York: Columbia University Press, 1984. Print.

Sertoli, Giuseppi, "Edmund Burke." *The Johns Hopkins Guide to Literary Theory and Criticism.* Ed. Groden, Michael and Martin Kreiswirth. Baltimore: Johns Hopkins University Press, 1994. 122–5. Print.

Sharpe, Jenny. *Allegories of Empire.* Minneapolis: University of Minnesota Press, 1993. Print.

Shelley, Mary. *Frankenstein.* NCE 2nd ed. Ed. J. Paul Hunter. New York: Norton, 1996, 2012. Print.

Shelley, Percy. *Shelley's Poetry and Prose.* Ed. Reiman, Donald and S. Powers. New York: Norton, 1977. Print.

Singh, Charu Sheel. "Bhagavadgita, Typology and William Blake." *Influence of Bhagavadgita on Literature Written in English.* Ed. T.R. Sharma. Shastri Nagar, Meerut: Shalabh Prakashan, 1988. 23–36. Print.

Singh, Jyotsna G. *Colonial Narratives: Cultural Dialogues: Discoveries of India in the Language of Colonialism.* New York: Routledge, 1996. Print.

Smith, Charlotte. *The Poems of Charlotte Smith.* Ed. Stuart Curran. Oxford: Oxford University Press, 1993. 217–47. Print.

Southey, Robert. "The Curse of Kehama." *Poems of Robert Southey.* Ed. Maurice H. Fitzgerald. New York: Oxford University Press, 1909. Print.

———. Review. "Periodical Accounts relative to the Baptist Missionary Society." *Quarterly Review* 1 (1809): 193-226. Print.

———. Review. *Periodical Accounts relative to the Baptist Missionary Society, for propagating the Gospel among the Heathen. Annual Review and History of Literature* 1 (1803): 207–18. Print.

———. *Thalaba the Destroyer. Poems of Robert Southey.* Ed. Maurice H. Fitzgerald. New York: Oxford University Press, 1909. Print.

Spear, T.G.P. *The Nabobs: a Study of the Social Life of the English in Eighteenth Century India.* London: Curzon Press, 1932, 1980. Print.

Spivak, Gayatri. "Can the Subaltern Speak?" *Marxism and the Interpretation of Culture.* Ed. Cary Nelson and Lawrence Grossberg. London: Macmillan, 1988. Print.

Spurr, David. *The Rhetoric of Empire: Colonial Discourse in Journalism, Travel Writing, and Imperial Administration.* Durham: Duke University Press, 1993. Print.

Starke, Mariana. *The Sword of Peace; or, Voyage of Love* (1789). *Slavery, Abolition and Emancipation: Writings in the British Romantic Period.* Vol. 5, *Drama.* Ed. Jeffrey Cox. Brookfield, VT: Pickering & Chatto, 1999. 129–34. Print.

———. *The Widow of Malabar: A Tragedy in Three Acts.* [1791]. New York: Readex Microprint, 1953. Print.

Stevenson, Lionel. *The Wild Irish Girl: the Life of Sydney Owenson, Lady Morgan.* New York: Russell & Russell, 1936, 1969. Print.

Stokes, Eric. *The English Utilitarians and India*. Oxford: Clarendon Press, 1959. Print.
Suleri, Sara. *The Rhetoric of English India*. Chicago: University of Chicago Press, 1992. Print.
Sunstein, Emily W. *Mary Shelley: Romance and Reality*. Boston: Little, Brown, 1989. Print.
Teltscher, Kate. *India Inscribed: European and British Writing on India 1600–1800*. New York: Oxford University Press, 1995. Print.
Thapar, Romila. *Sakuntala: Texts, Readings, Histories*. London: Anthem Press, 1999. Print.
Todd, Janet. *Sensibility: An Introduction*. New York: Methuen, 1986. Print.
Trivedi, Harish. *Colonial Transactions: English Literature and India*. New York: Manchester, 1995. Print.
van Buitenen, J.A.B. Introduction to *The* Bhagavadgita *in the* Mahabharata*: Text and Translation*. Vol. 1. Chicago: University of Chicago Press, 1981. 1–29. Print.
———. *The* Bhagavadgita *in the* Mahabharata*: Text and Translation*. Chicago: University of Chicago Press, 1981. Print.
Viswanathan, Gauri. *Masks of Conquest: Literary Study and British Rule in India*. New York: Columbia University Press, 1989. Print.
Wallace, Miriam, ed. *Enlightening Romanticism, Romancing the Enlightenment*. Burlington, VT: Ashgate, 2009. Print.
Wallace, Tara. "Reading the Metropole: Elizabeth Hamilton's *Translations of the Letters of a Hindoo Rajah*. *Enlightening Romanticism, Romancing the Enlightenment*. Ed. Miriam Wallace. Burlington, VT: Ashgate, 2009. 131–41. Print.
Wheeler, Kathleen. "'Kubla Khan' and Eighteenth Century Aesthetic Theories." *The Wordsworth Circle* 22.1 (Winter 1991): 15–24. Print.
Wilkins, Sir Charles, trans. *Fables and Proverbs from the Sanskrit*. 3rd ed. New York: Routledge and Sons, 1888. Print.
———, trans. *The Bhagavat-Geeta, or Dialogues of Kreeshna and Arjoon*. London, 1785. Print.
Wollstonecraft, Mary. *Vindication of the Rights of Woman*. New York: Norton, Ed. Deidre Shauna Lynch. 3rd Edition. New York: Norton, 2009.
Wordsworth, Dora. *Letters*. Ed. Howard Vincent. Chicago: Packard, 1944. Web. http://babel.hathitrust.org/cgi/pt?id=mdp.39015030151198;view=1up;seq=106.
Wordsworth, William. *Selected Poems and Prefaces*. Ed. Jack Stillinger. Boston: Houghton Mifflin, 1965. Print.
Wright, Julia. Introduction to *The Missionary*, by Sydney Owenson. New York: Broadview Press, 2002. Print.
Wu, Duncan. *Romantic Women Poets: An Anthology*. Malden, MA: Blackwell, 1997. Print.
Zaehner, R.C., trans. *The Bhagavad-Gita*. In *Hindu Scriptures*. Ed. R.C. Zaehner. New York: Dutton, 1966. 247–325. Print.

Index

"Adieu to India" (Anna Jones) 16–17
advaita (non-dualism) 9, 25, 65n5
Anderson, Benedict 32, 72n14
Anglicism 14–15, 35, 65, 74, 122
Anglo-India (India under British rule) 103–17, 119–32
Anglo-Indians (sub-caste) 32–4, 72, 102, 105, 124n6; *see also* mixed caste
Arjuna 28–43; 85–7; *see also* Krishna; *Bhagavad Gita, The*
Armstrong, Isobel 4, 8, 15, 46, 78, 89, 120
Asiatic Society of Bengal 1, 5–7, 13, 16–17, 21–6, 45; *see also* Orientalism
  and *Hartly House, Calcutta* (Gibbes) 64–5
  and *Missionary, The* (Owenson) 81

Beachy Head (Smith) 17, 120–22; *see* Smith, Charlotte
Behn, Aphra
  and Mariana Starke 103
  Oroonoko and Phebe Gibbes 68
Bengal
  Bengali 35
  and East India Company 21, 26–7, 33, 35; *see also* Hastings; Asiatic Society of Bengal
  and *Hartly House, Calcutta* (Gibbes) 64–7
Bhabha, Homi 6, 80; *see also* postcolonialism
Bhagavad Gita, The 6n12, 8, 13, 17–18, 22, 25–9, 31, 33–7, 39–43, 56, 63, 75, 85–7; *see also* nondualism; translation; Sanskrit; Wilkins, Charles
bhakti 83–5, 91–109; *see also Missionary, The* (Owenson)
binaries (*see* dualism)
Blake, William 5n10, 7, 8n20, 12n24, 13n26, 16n3, 20, 124–5
  Milton 127
  Visions of the Daughters of Albion 126–7, 130–31

Bloom, Harold 2, 97
Brahma 17, 25, 34n31
  in *Missionary, The* (Owenson) 85–90
  in *Widow of Malabar, The* (Starke) 112
  in *Oceanides, The* (Jewsbury) 124
Burke, Edmund 30, 35, 53, 80n23, 95n2
  definition of the sublime 7–8, 120
  prosecution of Hastings 26, 45n3, 54, 58, 64

Cannon, Garland 2n4, 23, 25n8
canon, the 25n8, 47; *see also* gender; masculinity; non-canonical women writers 2, 20
  and Romanticism 2–5, 12, 15, 19–20, 22n4, 63–4, 66n7, 77, 97–8, 107n12, 125, 129–30
caste, caste system
  half-caste; *see* Anglo-Indians; mixed caste; *varna-sankar*
  in *Hartly House, Calcutta* (Gibbes) 72–3
  in *Missionary, The* (Owenson) 87–8, 91, 111
  and translation 27, 29, 33–5
  in *Translations of the Letters of a Hindoo Rajah* (Hamilton) 48, 52
Catholicism, British attitudes towards presence in India 32, 72n14
Christianity; *see also* conversion; deism; evangelism; Judeo-Christian tradition
  in *Hartly House, Calcutta* (Gibbes) 75, 78n20, 80, 83–4, 86, 88–9, 91–3
  in *Missionary, The* (Owenson) 49–52, 55, 57, 61
  and Orientalist translation 23, 28–31, 34–7, 40–41, 49
  in *Translations of the Letters of a Hindoo Rajah* (Hamilton) 50, 52, 55, 57, 61
  in *Widow of Malabar, The* (Starke) 113–17

Colebrooke, Henry Thomas 6, 26
Coleridge, Samuel Taylor 5n10, 12n24,
    13n26, 16n31, 20, 66n6, 77n17,
    124–5, 131
    Biographia Literaria 128
    Christabel 127–8
    "Kubla Khan" 128–31
conversion 31, 37; *see also* evangelism
    in *Missionary, The* (Owenson) 82–4,
        87, 90–92
    in *Widow of Malabar, The* (Starke) 111,
        115–16
Curran, Stuart 3, 50, 61n22, 77n17, 119,
    120n2, 121, 123n5

deism (deist, deistic)
    and creation 22–3
        in *Translations of the Letters of a*
            Hindoo Rajah (Hamilton) 45,
            54, 58, 60, 78–81
        in *Missionary, The* (Owenson) 79, 83,
            87, 89
    and Orientalism 8, 29, 79, 83, 87, 89
        compared to evangelical deism
            22n2, 23, 28
        deistic monotheism and Vedic
            nondualism 36–9, 43, 81
    and Smith, Charlotte 20, 119–22
    and *Visions of the Daughters of Albion*
        (Blake) 126
dharma
    and law 18, 29
        in *Bhavagad Gita, The* 33–6, 42
        in *Missionary, The* (Owenson) 87
domesticity 4
    and Jewsbury, Maria Jane 123
    and *Sword of Peace, The* (Starke) 101
    and *Translations of the Letters of a*
        Hindoo Rajah (Hamilton) 49
    and Wollstonecraft 67
dualism 4–5, 16, 21
    and nondualism 4–5, 21–2, 43, 126
        among canonical writers 8
            Christabel (Coleridge) 128
            Milton (Blake) 127
            Prometheus Unbound (Shelley)
                130
            Visions of the Daughters of
                Albion (Blake) 126–7

and Orientalist renderings of *advaita*
    9, 24
    Bhagavad Gita, The (trans.
        Wilkins) 29n15, 38, 40, 43
    Sakuntala (Kalidasa, trans. Jones)
        24–6
and the Romantic sublime 7–13
    Wordsworth, William 125
and women writers 20, 119
    Beachy Head (Smith) 120, 125
    Hartly House, Calcutta (Gibbes)
        64–5, 75, 78–9
    Missionary, The (Owenson) 82, 98,
        100–101
    Sword of Peace, The (Starke) 107
    Translations of the Letters of a
        Hindoo Rajah (Hamilton) 56,
        59n19, 60
    Widow of Malabar, The (Starke)
        108n15, 110, 114

east, the 1n2, 7, 122
    east/west binary 9n20
        in *Hartly House, Calcutta* (Gibbes)
            65, 75
        and Irigaray 131
        in *Missionary, The* (Owenson) 7–9,
            81n24, 89
        in *Translations of the Letters of*
            a Hindoo Rajah (Hamilton)
            48–9, 51–2, 56, 59
        in *Widow of Malabar, The* (Starke)
    eastern nondualism 4–6, 9n20,
        22–3, 26, 43, 119–20, 130; *see also*
        Vedas
    representation by canonical Romantic
        poets 11–12, 128–9
    eastern sublime 120–22
East India Company 6, 21, 26–7, 32, 36,
    45n2, 46
    in *Hartly House, Calcutta* (Gibbes) 64,
        66–7, 69, 71–2
    in *Sword of Peace, The* (Starke) 97–9
    in *Widow of Malabar, The* (Starke) 116
Enlightenment, the 21, 131–2
    Blake as anti-Enlightenment 125–6,
        131
    and deism 119
    and Orientalism 37, 39–40

late Enlightenment epistemology 1–2, 34
   and Anglo-India 4–5, 9; and Orientalism 21, 25–9, 31
   and nondualism 8
   sublime 13
   and women writers 4
      in *Missionary, The* (Owenson) 77–84, 89, 98
      in Smith, Charlotte 120, 122
      in *Translations of the Letters of a Hindoo Rajah* (Hamilton) 49, 54, 57–60
      in *Widow of Malabar, The* (Starke) 109, 111
eroticism; *see also bhakti*; gender
   in Coleridge's poetry 128–9
   and epistemology
      in *Hartly House, Calcutta* (Gibbes) 70
      in *Missionary, The* (Owenson) 83–6, 109
      in *Widow of Malabar, The* (Starke) 111

Fay, Eliza 32n19, 63, 78
   on *sati* 14–15
female; *see also* dualism; eroticism; gender; India; Orientalism; Romanticism; sensibility authorship; subjectivity
   and Gibbes, Phebe 63, 66, 73–4, 77–9
   and Hamilton, Elizabeth 18–20, 46–53, 59–61
   and Owenson, Sidney 90
   and Starke, Mariana 95–103, 105, 107–12, 116
   female sexuality 7, 131n18
   female sublime 13, 20
   Orientalists on female principle in *Vedas* 8, 24
   representation by male poets 5n10, 10, 12, 124–5, 127–30, 132
   and women writers 3–5, 14–17, 119, 121, 132
feminism 16n31, 48, 60, 129
   French feminism 4, 20
Franklin, Michael 8, 19, 63–5, 67, 71–4
French Revolution 30–31

gender
   and authorship 3,13, 20–21, 47n6, 71, 77, 79–80, 85,112
   binaries 4–6, 12–13, 78, 100–102, 120; *see also* dualism
   and empire 82, 103–4, 108
   and male writers 12n24, 125, 127
   and Orientalism 8, 13, 16, 18
   and subjectivity 23, 43, 77, 109, 125
   and the sublime 8n17, 107n12; *see also* Burke; female sublime
Gibbes, Phebe 63–4
   and *Hartly House, Calcutta* 2, 13, 18–19, 61, 63–76
Goldborne, Sophia (protagonist, *Hartly House, Calcutta*) 19, 63, 111
Graffigny, de, Madame 47
Graham, Maria Callcott 30n15, 32, 110n18

Haitian uprising 21, 32, 72
Halbfass, Wilhelm 21, 22n2, 28, 35
Hamilton, Charles 18, 45n1, 56n15
Hamilton, Elizabeth 13, 16, 119n1, 132; *see also* Orientalism; translation; *Translations of the Letters of a Hindoo Rajah*
   and authorship in *Translations of the Letters of a Hindoo Rajah* 18, 45–61, 63, 93, 110
Hartley, David 65–6
Hartly House, Calcutta; *see* Gibbes, Phebe
Hastings, Warren
   and the Asiatic Society of Bengal 8,13, 21, 26–7, 36–7
   as governor-general of Bengal 35
   trial of 8, 13, 27, 30; *see also* Burke, Edmund
   response to by women writers
      Gibbes 64–5, 74–7
      Hamilton 13, 45–6, 49, 53–5, 57–8, 61
      Starke 100
Hinduism 56, 65
   and Christianity in *Missionary, The* (Owenson) 81n24, 82, 84, 90–91
   and nondualism 21, 22, 25, 31, 49
Hyam, Ronald 32n20, 32n21, 32n22, 33n23
"Hymn to Narayana" (Jones) 22n4, 23

India; *see also* Anglo-India; caste; female; Sanskrit; *sati*; Vedas
- British representations of 2, 6–7, 21
- and gender 14–15, 22
- in *Hartly House, Calcutta* (Gibbes) 63–76
- of an Indian sublime 8–9, 25, 119–22, 128, 130–31
- in *Missionary, The* (Owenson) 76–80, 82-92
- social structure; *see* caste (system)
- in *Sword of Peace, The* (Starke) 98–105
- in *Translations of the Letters of a Hindoo Rajah* (Hamilton) 45–58
- in *Widow of Malabar, The* (Starke) 108–16
- and colonialism 21; *see also* East India Company
- Indian perceptions of British 34
- and Orientalism 12, 15, 18, 23–43; *see also* Asiatic Society of Bengal; Sanskrit; translation
- travel between England and India 16–17, 20, 122–4; *see also* Fay, Eliza; Graham, Maria

intersubjectivity 2, 34, 43; *see also* dualism; gender; Romanticism; subjectivity
- in *Missionary, The* (Owenson) 76–7, 82, 89
Irigaray, Luce 4, 131

Jewsbury, Maria Jane 20,122–4; *see also Oceanides, The*; "Song of the Hindu Women"
Jones, Anna 16–17, 19, 119, 122; *see also* "Adieu to India"
Jones, William 6–8, 11, 19, 22–5, 27–8, 35–6, 81–3, 85; *see also* Asiatic Society of Bengal; "Hymn to Narayana"; *Sakuntala*; Sanskrit
Judeo-Christian monotheism 9n20, 36–40

Kalidasa; 24–5; *see also* Jones, William; *Sakuntala*; Sanskrit
karma 29, 40–43; *see also Bhagavad Gita, The*; Sanskrit; Wilkins, Charles

Landon, Letitia Elizabeth 28n11; *see also* "Manmadin, The Indian Cupid, floating Down the Ganges"
law 15, 29–30, 34–6, 43; *see also dharma*; *karma*; Jones, William; *Manusmrti*; *sati*
- and *Hartly House, Calcutta* (Gibbes) 72
- and *Missionary, The* (Owenson) 70
- and *Translations of the Letters of a Hindoo Rajah* (Hamilton) 57, 59
- and "The swallow [*sic*]" (Smith, Charlotte) 122
- and *Widow of Malabar, The* (Starke) 109, 111–12, 115
Leask, Nigel 7n14, 11n23, 15n29, 19n37, 79n22, 81n24, 83n26, 129
Luxima 19, 23n6, 77–93, 109, 112, 115–16; *see also bhakti*; *Brahma*; Hinduism; *Missionary, The* (Owenson); Owenson, Sidney; *Prophetess, The* (Owenson); subjectivity

Macaulay, Thomas 6, 13, 26, 65; *see also* Anglicism
"Manmadin, The Indian Cupid, floating Down the Ganges" (Landon) 28n11
Manusmrti 36; *see also Bhagavad Gita, The*; Jones, William; law
masculinity 2, 4–8, 12–13, 16, 18, 20–22, 43, 119n1, 125; *see also* canon, the; dualism; gender; Orientalism; Romanticism
- and *Christabel* (Coleridge) 127
- and *Hartly House, Calcutta* (Gibbes) 64, 67n10, 73, 76–7, 79, 82
- and "Kubla Khan" (Coleridge) 128
- and *Missionary, The* (Owenson) 77, 82, 93
- and *Sword of Peace, The* (Starke) 98, 100–102
- and *Translations of the Letters of a Hindoo Rajah* (Hamilton) 46–51, 55, 60–61
- and *Visions of the Daughters of Albion* (Blake) 126
- and *Widow of Malabar, The* (Starke) 108
McGann, Jerome 3, 23n6, 98n5

Mellor, Ann 4–5, 13n26, 43, 47, 50n10, 51n12, 60n21, 98n5, 108–9, 115–16, 125
meta-textuality
 in *Hartly House, Calcutta* (Gibbes) 73, 75
 in *Missionary, The* (Owenson) 19
 in *Translations of the Letters of a Hindoo Rajah* (Hamilton) 18
meta-theatricality (*also* meta-drama) 20; *see also* Starke, Mariana
 in *Sword of Peace, The* (Starke) 97, 107
 in *Widow of Malabar, The* (Starke) 108, 110–11, 113–15
Miller, Barbara Stoller 24, 28–9, 33, 35n25, 41
miscegenation 18, 20, 32–3, 61, 63, 68, 72–3; *see also* Anglo-Indians; *Bhagavad Gita, The*; caste; mixed caste; race; *varna sankar*
Missionary, The (Owenson) 7n14, 12n25, 19, 63, 76–80, 85–6, 89, 93, 109, 116; *see also* Luxima; Owenson, Sidney; sentimental novel, the; subjectivity
mixed caste 18, 33
 social structure; *see* caste (system) 4, 72; *see also* Anglo-Indians; *Bhagavad Gita, The*; caste; miscegenation; race; *varna sankar*
monotheism 36–81; *see also* deism; nondualism; polytheism; Vedic philosophy
Montesquieu 47, 61

Neff, D.S. 30n17, 33n23, 34, 79
Niranjana, Tejaswini 27, 28n12, 36n28
nondualism 4–5, 7–10, 12, 16–17, 19–26, 29, 36–40, 43, 46, 63–6, 80–82, 89, 112, 119, 122, 124–6, 128–31; *see also* deism; dualism; gender; India; monotheism; Romanticism; Vedic philosophy
noncanonical writers 2–5, 20; *see also* canon; gender; Romanticism

objectification 3–4, 8, 13n26, 21, 25, 28, 43, 46n5, 53, 56, 63–5, 71, 83, 85, 92, 98–100, 103, 105, 110–11, 120, 126–7, 129; *see also* dualism; gender; Romanticism; subjectivity; sublime, the

Oceanides, The (Jewsbury) 122–3
"On the Literature of the Hindus" (Jones) 81; *see also* Asiatic Society of Bengal; Hinduism; nondualism; Orientalism; translation
Orientalism 1–2, 5–7, 12–13, 15, 17–18, 21–2, 25–8, 31n18, 36, 43, 45–8, 56–8, 61, 63–5, 70, 76–7, 82, 122, 125, 128; *see also* Anglo-India; Asiatic Society of Bengal; Hamilton, Elizabeth; Hastings, Warren; Jones, William; postcolonialism; Said, Edward; Wilkins, Charles
Outcast 72, 79, 87–8, 93, 112; *see also* caste; Luxima; *Missionary, The* (Owenson)
Owenson, Sidney [Lady Morgan] 7, 12n25, 16n32, 18–19, 23, 61, 63, 76–87, 89–93, 109, 115–16; *see also* *Missionary, The*

polytheism 22, 24, 28, 37, 83; *see also* deism; Hinduism; monotheism; nondualism
Postans Young, Marianne 15
postcolonialism 2–3, 5–6, 13, 15–16, 21–2, 25–8, 35, 43; *see also* Bhabha, Homi; Said, Edward
publication 2–3, 26, 43, 46n5, 63, 65n4; *see also* Asiatic Society of Bengal; gender

race 6, 14, 20, 32–3, 43, 60, 63–4, 68, 70, 72n12, 87–8, 104–5; *see also* Anglo-Indians; *Bhagavad Gita, The*; caste; miscegenation; mixed caste; *varna sankar*
reason 20, 27, 31–2, 39–40, 42, 49–51, 59–60, 66, 72, 78–84, 89–90, 93, 109, 111–12, 114, 116, 131–2; *see also* deism; dualism; Enlightenment, the; Romanticism; sensibility; Wollstonecraft, Mary
Romanticism 2–5, 7, 9, 12–13, 15, 19–22, 25, 43, 50n10, 63–4, 66, 77–83, 88, 93, 97–9, 101, 107, 119–21, 125, 127; *see also* canon, the; gender; India; Enlightenment, the; sensibility; sentimental novel, the

sacrifice 28–9, 37, 39–41, 52, 63, 73, 80, 82, 85, 90–92, 101, 112, 115, 124; *see also* Bhagavad Gita, The; Luxima; *sati*; translation; Wilkins, Charles; *yajna*

Sakuntala (Kalidasa) 23–4; *see also* Jones, William; Kalidasa; Sanskrit; translation

Sanskrit 1, 5–9, 11, 13–14, 16–18, 21–7, 29, 31, 33–43, 46, 49, 55, 62, 65, 82, 122; *see also* Asiatic Society of Bengal; *Bhagavad Gita, The*; Jones, William; Orientalism; translation; Wilkins, Charles

sati 2, 4, 13–15, 18–20; *see also* Anglicism; gender; law
  and *Hartly House, Calcutta* (Gibbes) 71, 73–5
  in Jewsbury's poetry 122, 124
  and *Missionary, The* (Owenson) 90–91 (and the *auto da fe*)
  and *Translations of the Letters of a Hindoo Rajah* (Hamilton) 48–52
  and *Widow of Malabar, The* (Starke) 108–12, 114–15

sensibility 3–4, 15, 20, 28n11, 46n4, 119, 121
  in *Hartly House, Calcutta* (Gibbes) 73–4, 76
  in *Missionary, The* (Owenson) 78–80, 82–4, 86, 88–90, 93
  in *Sword of Peace, The* (Starke) 102
  in *Translations of the Letters of a Hindoo Rajah* (Hamilton) 50, 61
  in *Widow of Malabar, The* (Starke) 104–7, 112

sentimental novel, the; *see also Missionary, The* (Owenson); Owenson, Sidney

Shakespeare, William
  and *Hartly House, Calcutta* (Gibbes) 65
  Othello 68–71, 76
  Jones on Kalidasa as the Indian Shakespeare 23, 25n8

Shelley, Mary 3, 9
  and *Frankenstein* 9, 12
    in *Translations of the Letters of a Hindoo Rajah* (Hamilton) 57, 59–60

Shelley, Percy Bysshe 5n10, 9, 12, 13n26, 16n31, 20, 22n4, 124–5, 129
  and *Alastor* 10–11
  and "Hymn to Intellectual Beauty" (influence by Jones's "Hymn to Narayana") 22n4
  and *Missionary, The* (Owenson) influence by 83n26
  and *Prometheus Unbound* 130–31

Siva 24

Sivavedanta (trans. Jones) 81

Smith, Charlotte 3, 20, 60n21, 119, 124; *see also* deism; Romanticism; sensibility; subjectivity
  Beachy Head (Smith) 17, 120–21
  "The swallow [sic]" 121–2

Smith, Nathaniel 26–7, 36–7; *see also* East India Company; Hastings, Warren; Orientalism

"Song of the Hindu Women" (Jewsbury) 14, 124

Southey, Robert 30–32, 34

Spivak, Gayatri 13–14; *see also* gender; postcolonialism; *sati*

Starke, Mariana 93, 95–6
  and dramaturgy 20
  and *The Sword of Peace* 74n16, 95–107
  and *Widow of Malabar, The* 23n4, 108–17
  sati in 13, 15n30

subjectivity 2–5, 10–12, 14–20, 23, 34, 43, 63, 67, 120–21, 126–7, 129, 132; *see also* dualism; gender; intersubjectivity; nondualism; objectification; Orientalism; Romanticism
  in *Missionary, The* (Owenson) 76–8, 80–82, 84–5, 87, 89–93
  in *Translations of the Letters of a Hindoo Rajah* (Hamilton) 45, 56, 61
  in *Widow of Malabar, The* (Starke) 108, 115–16

sublime, the 1, 7–10, 12–13, 17, 20–21, 23, 25–6, 107n12, 120, 130; *see also* Burke, Edmund; dualism; gender; India; Orientalism; Romanticism; translation
  in *Missionary, The* (Owenson) 82–3, 87

in *Translations of the Letters of a Hindoo Rajah* (Hamilton) 56–7
Sword of Peace, The (Starke); *see* Starke, Mariana

translation 1–2, 5–6, 8, 11, 13–14, 16–19, 22–9, 33–41, 43, 119, 122, 125; *see also* Asiatic Society of Bengal; Jones, William; Orientalism; Sanskrit; Wilkins, Charles
  in *Hartly House, Calcutta* (Gibbes) 72
  in *Missionary, The* (Owenson) 8, 15, 85–7
  in *Translations of the Letters of a Hindoo Rajah* (Hamilton) 47n7, 49–52, 54–6, 61
  in *Widow of Malabar, The* (Starke) 108, 110n18
Translations of the Letters of a Hindoo Rajah (Hamilton) 18, 45; *see also* Hamilton, Charles; Hamilton, Elizabeth; India; Orientalism; Sanskrit; translation

Vedas, vedic philosophy 1–2, 4–5, 11n23, 13, 16–18, 21–3, 25–8, 36–41, 46n5, 56, 64–6, 70, 72, 74, 81–3, 112, 119, 122, 125; *see also* Asiatic Society of Bengal; Hinduism; nondualism; Orientalism; Sanskrit; translation

west, the (western epistemology, philosophy, tradition) 1, 5–9, 13, 16–18, 20–29, 31, 35–7, 39–40, 43, 119, 124, 127–8, 131–2; *see also* dualism; Enlightenment, the; Orientalism
  in *Beachy Head* (Smith) 120–21
  in *Hartly House, Calcutta* (Gibbes) 64–5, 75
  in *Missionary, The* (Owenson)78–80, 84, 88–9, 92
  in *Oceanides, The* (Jewsbury) 124
  in *Widow of Malabar, The* (Starke) 97
  in *Translations of the Letters of a Hindoo Rajah* (Hamilton) 48–52, 56, 59, 60–61
  in *Widow of Malabar, The* (Starke) 108, 111
Widow of Malabar, The (Starke); *see* Starke, Mariana
Wilkins, Charles 6n12, 8, 13, 18, 22, 25–9, 31, 33–43, 55–6, 63, 72, 85–6; *see also* Asiatic Society of Bengal; *Bhagavad Gita, The*; Christianity; Enlightenment, the; deism; dualism; Orientalism; Sanskrit; sublime, the; translation
Wollstonecraft, Mary 3, 20, 125; *see also* dualism; reason; sensibility
  and Gibbes, Phebe 65
  and Hamilton, Elizabeth 47–50, 52–3, 59–60, 132
  and Starke, Mariana 97–8, 103n9
Wordsworth, William 7, 9, 11–13, 121, 124, 129; *see also* dualism; Romanticism; sublime, the
  and *Hartly House, Calcutta* (Gibbes) 66
  and *Missionary, The* (Owenson) 77n17, 79
Tintern Abbey 9–10, 107

yajna 40–41; *see also* Asiatic Society of Bengal; *Bhagavad Gita, The*; Orientalism; Sanskrit; translation; Wilkins, Charles
yoga 29, 41, 87, 131n18; *see also* *Bhagavad Gita, The*; nondualism; Hinduism; Vedic philosophy